THE NEARNESS OF YOU

THE NEARNESS OF YOU

Students & Teachers Writing On-line

Edited by
Christopher Edgar and
Susan Nelson Wood

Teachers & Writers Collaborative
New York

The Nearness of You: Students & Teachers Writing On-line

Library of Congress Cataloging-in-Publication Data

> The nearness of you : students & teachers writing on-line / edited by
>   Christopher Edgar & Susan Nelson Wood. — 1st ed.
>   p.   cm.
>   Includes bibliographical references.
>   ISBN 0-915924-47-1 (pbk. : alk.paper)
>   1. English language—Rhetoric—Study and teaching—Data
> processing. 2. Academic writing—Study and teaching—Data
> processing. 3. English language—Computer-assisted instruction.
> 4. Online data processings—Study and teaching. 5. Authorship–
> –Collaboration—Data processing. I. Edgar, Christopher, 1961–
> II. Wood, Susan Nelson. 1954–
> PE1404.W7288 1996
> 808'.042'0285—dc20   96-7637
>   CIP

Acknowledgments

Much of the work described in this book was made possible by grants from The Bingham Trust (to the Kentucky Telecommunications Writing Project) and the DeWitt Wallace-Reader's Digest Fund (to the Bread Loaf Rural Teacher Network).

Teachers & Writers programs are made possible, in part, through support from the National Endowment for the Arts. Teachers & Writers Collaborative receives support for its programs from the New York State Council on the Arts and the New York City Department of Cultural Affairs.

T&W also thanks the following foundations and corporations: American Stock Exchange, Anonymous Donor, Apple Computers, Bertelsmann USA, The Bingham Trust, Bronx City Council, The Bydale Foundation, Chemical Bank, Consolidated Edison, Charles E. Culpeper Foundation, Aaron Diamond Foundation, Heckscher Foundation for Children, Morgan Stanley Foundation, M&O Foundation, Network for Social Change, New York Times Company Foundation, NYNEX Corporation, Prudential Foundation, Queens City Council, Rockwell Group, Helena Rubinstein Foundation, The Scherman Foundation, Schieffelin & Somerset Co., Variety-The Children's Charity, and the Lila Wallace-Reader's Digest Fund.

Teachers & Writers Collaborative
5 Union Square West
New York, N.Y. 10003-3306

Cover and page design: Christopher Edgar
Printed by Philmark Lithographics, New York, N.Y.

TABLE OF CONTENTS

It's not the pale moon that excites me,
that thrills and delights me,
oh, no
it's just the nearness of you.

Excerpt from "The Nearness of You"
Words by Ned Washington
Music by Hoagy Carmichael
(1937)

Editors' Preface

When we first sent out a call for submissions for this book, we felt the need to answer the skeptics who doubt that technology really can be a positive force in education. The fact was, however, that the two of us were rather skeptical ourselves. We did not want to reiterate the claims certain policymakers have made—that if schools buy computers and make the students "computer-literate," educational standards will instantly be met and surpassed. But we also knew that a number of adventurous teachers had turned the technology issue on its head, so to speak; that they had taken the more basic network technologies and used them in their own projects, finding new audiences for their students and developing small, vital on-line communities, and in the process changing the dynamics of their classrooms. Put another way, some of the far-reaching claims made by technology advocates were coming true—technology *was* bringing students and teachers together, eradicating distance, helping students learn more effectively.

But this was happening due to the intelligence and effort of the students and teachers who had the courage to dive in, and the wisdom to see that the quality of the work was the important thing, not the hardware and software. We believe the essays here form ample evidence of what can happen when the right conditions—and values—are in place. It was our belief in the "human side" of technology that brought the book its whimsical title, from an old romantic Hoagy Carmichael tune about people coming closer together.

Another of our aims was to create a book that would not be out of date before it came back from the printer. Hardware, software, and the Internet change by the minute. So we tried to create a guide that would show teachers how to integrate technology and the curriculum, not just plug in a modem and use communications software. The vast majority of projects described in *The Nearness of You* are excellent models for teachers and students, which will survive the tests of time and changes in technology.

Finally, we would like to acknowledge our gratitude to The Bingham Trust for supporting the publication of this book, and to The Bingham Trust and the DeWitt Wallace-Reader's Digest for their generous support of much of the work described herein. We would also like to acknowledge our debt to all the students and teachers who continue to prove the skeptics wrong.

—*Christopher Edgar and Susan Nelson Wood*

Introduction

By Dixie Goswami and Rocky Gooch

The Nearness of You: Students & Teachers Writing On-line reviews where teachers stand in relation to technology and innovative ways to teach writing, especially imaginative writing. The contributors' experiences and perspectives are quite different, ranging in levels from elementary through college, from the use of small-scale networks to the Internet. While the authors locate changes in the broad context of new technologies in education, they also locate them in personal views, scenarios of classrooms and events, and documentations of work with children, young people, and their colleagues. This introduction attempts to show how the ideas in these narratives and essays relate to each other and form the intellectual framework of the book.

From the Computer Lab to the Internet

Bill Bernhardt's "Less Is More" is a detailed account of how he managed a writing class with five students per computer workstation and in the process discovered that they accomplished more than students at individual workstations. His practical suggestions about everything from the range of writing that flows from these particular arrangements to tips about selecting software are especially useful. Karen Ferrell's "Writing Roulette" shows how members of the New Jersey Writing Project in Texas took a familiar strategy for collaborative writing and adapted it first for local use in classrooms equipped with several computers and computer labs, and later to Internet exchanges. Ferrell recommends looking carefully at best practices as a way for writing teachers to experiment with technology. Phyllis Geren's "Global Connections on the World Wide Web" explains what is possible on the Web and how surfing, searching, and publishing are learning tools that complement libraries and promote authentic research and writing. Greg Siering argues that MUDs (or "Multi-User Dimensions") embody a powerful communication model that combines the "productive union of work and play." Tharon Howard's essay "Mapping the Minefield of Electronic Ethics" invites us to go beyond easy claims that writing on-line will help democratize schooling and encourage egalitarian discourse, to examine the hard realities of "teaching ethically defensible netiquette to our students."

"From the Computer Lab to the Internet" is a fairly neutral title for five essays that present challenging ideas with many implications. According to these contributors, teaching with technology requires us to become active learners ourselves as we rethink theory and practice, acquire new skills, adapt to new roles and relationships, and invent alternative kinds of professional development. "From the Computer Lab to the Internet" is not about commercial packages and computer-assisted instruction: these contributors are imagining teachers who plan, make decisions, struggle, search for resources and information, experiment, and evaluate. They're imagining teachers who are aware of the social and political issues that cluster around the use of technology. This opening section introduces a developmental pattern revisited elsewhere in the book: teachers on-line expand their audiences (and genres and purposes) for writing at the same time that students expand their audiences from their own classrooms and schools to include readers from around the world.

Students and Teachers

Beverly Paeth's "Writing Conferences and My Chapter 1 Students" describes how her classroom changed over several years and the role that the Kentucky Telecommunications Writing Project (KTWP) played in the process. Nancy Stout Bell writes about her eighth grade student, Julie "Maverick" Kasper, and the impact of Julie's on-line fiction writing on her classmates and students at other KTWP sites. In "Going On-line," Bette Ford reflects on key experiences that have shaped her use of electronic networks as a teacher and as a teacher-researcher. Linda Hardin's "Just Cruising" tells of three networking activities that she and her rural South Carolina seventh grade students did over the course of a year: e-mail, computer conferencing, and accessing information from remote sources.

Taken together, these essays argue that technology can be a powerful catalyst for changing—and improving—the teaching of writing. These accomplished teachers note that teaching with technology allows them to spend more time with individual students; present more complex material to them; let students make more choices about their own reading and writing; and bring more voices, genres, and reasons to write into their classrooms. With these essays we begin to have some answers to the question of incentives: what motivates teachers to persist with the challenging task of incorporating new technology into their writing classrooms? What can policymakers and professional development programs learn from these stories? How can individual teachers critique, apply, and adapt particular principles and practices?

Writers On-line

Robin Lambert's essay about a one-year experiment undertaken as a project of the Kentucky Telecommunications Writing Project serves as a guide to readers interested in on-line partnerships among students, teachers, and writers. Lambert writes about practical lessons learned from the Kentucky Authors Project; when she discusses the advantages of telecommunications, she makes it clear that the project's main goals were to connect students and authors in ways that would result in much informal discourse and that would lead each student to produce a polished piece of writing for her or his portfolio—not computer literacy. Beverly Paeth's "Dear Jenny" is a companion piece to "The Kentucky Authors Project," telling about what happened when eight young women from her junior high classes in Kentucky worked for several months with Jenny Davis, a writer and teacher from Lexington. Time, choice, and response were the essential features of this residency, according to the young writers, Jenny Davis, and Paeth herself. Paeth's essay is useful both as an insider's guide to a small-scale electronic residency and as a model of a project that generates many questions for research, practitioner-initiated and otherwise. We also get to hear from Jenny Davis herself, in "Being 'Dear Jenny.'"

"An Odd Pleasure," by Trevor Owen, describes Canada's Writers in Electronic Residence (WIER) program. Owen states that WIER's primary purpose has had "little to do with the technology that sustains it . . . [but has] always been "to link students and teachers with Canada's authors in an exchange of original writing and commentary . . . WIER embodies a pedagogy that emphasizes the use of technology as a catalyst for learning rather than a 'tool' of production." The notion of an interactive pedagogy that privileges the making of meaning and frames the use of technology in classrooms and networks is central to many of the projects described in *The Nearness of You*. The distinction that Owen makes between "information technology" and "interaction technology" and his opposition of "electronic networking" and "computer conferencing" clarify the processes and understandings that teachers describe elsewhere in this book. Claire Bateman, a poet and teacher who participated in a computer conference on poetry, writes about fearing at first that the computer was too much of the world of science for her, but later finding the on-line world actually to be "quite magical, like a coral reef that grows by self-accretion."

On-line Writing Projects

R. W. Burniske's "Great Expectations: Electronic Novellas in the Making" is an example of a "new literacy" project, as it is defined by John Willinsky in *The New Literacy: Redefining Reading and Writing in Schools*. According to Willinsky, "The New Literacy is not seen as an isolated set of skills. Rather, it goes well beyond this to recognize literacy as a 'form of life' that connects community and school, history and biography." In his fascinating account of a telecommunications project at the International School of Kuala Lumpur, Burniske shows how he and his twelfth grade students read *Great Expectations* aloud in installments, just as Dickens's original readers had done; wrote electronic novellas; read (and responded to) responses to their novellas from tenth graders; reflected on their reading and writing processes; and created electronic portfolios that students took with them, as works-in-progress, from school to university. The project was entirely local, with the primary goal of using technology to build a classroom community of readers and writers.

The Elementary Books Project described in Janice Stuhlmann's essay "Calling All Characters!" is a cross-age, cross-school project, planned and realized by April Lloyd (third grade) and Jeradi Hochella (ninth grade remedial reading), teachers whose schools are within forty miles of each other. Stuhlmann focuses on changes engendered by the project: the structure of the classrooms shifted from competitive to cooperative and from teacher-centered to student-centered; students felt more successful and accomplished; teachers had more time for individualized instruction; the curriculum became richer and more diverse; teachers and students had more fun. The technical and logistical difficulties are part of this story, but observing students move from relative silence as readers and writers to expressing their ideas freely and at length provided Lloyd and Hochella with strong motivation to continue their collaboration.

"Designs of the Mind and Heart: Creating an Anthology of Writing On-line" by Scott Christian, a middle school teacher in Alaska who is a member of a national rural network, describes the process by which he and his students became publishers and editors of an anthology that included sixty-three writers from twenty-four classrooms across the country. The student editors solicited manuscripts and corresponded with authors via e-mail. Anyone who has edited a book—or a single article— will appreciate the debates that are part of the editorial process, the stress of dealing with on-time schedules and technical glitches, and the terrific relief and joy of publication day. Christian suggests that on-line projects need to be documented, studied, and questioned if we are to learn from them and if we are to build the case for a new vision of literacy, and recommends that students serve as co-researchers. Christian's own growth as a part of this "immersion" experiment is an important subtext here, as it is in other essays in this section of *The Nearness of You*.

Kurt Caswell (English teacher in Hokkaido, Japan) and Doug Wood (middle school teacher in South Carolina) spent a good part of one summer figuring out how to put a year-long on-line exchange at the center of their very different instructional programs. The dialogue presented in "Making Connections" gives a sense of the intense flow of electronic conversations that took place for nine months between Caswell and Wood and the parallel messages that their students exchanged as they studied calligraphy, Japanese and English, local history, culture, and geography. The year-long exchange culminated in a trip to Japan by Wood's South Carolina students. Caswell and Wood admit that they didn't know what they were letting themselves in for: they have some practical advice for teachers who might be interested in trying similar projects. This essay emphasizes the opportunities that writing on-line can provide for teachers and students to look critically at what they are doing—to become researchers. In this case, transcripts of all exchanges were available to Caswell and Wood, who could check their impressions against the reality of the transcript; look for patterns, topics, and questions; figure out what it meant; and write about it. The image of teachers such as Caswell and Wood, who are free to design, carry out, and assess risky, "maverick" projects, is fairly typical of the other teachers in this book.

A raptor project may seem a strange place to focus on issues of race and culture, but that's exactly what Vicki Hunt does in her essay about an on-line conference that involved herself (an American Studies teacher in Peoria, Arizona), her colleague Dwight Rawlings (ESL Biology teacher), and Phil Sittnick (Language Arts teacher, Laguna Middle School, New Mexico). While "The Raptor Project" is about the integrated curriculum that grew out of this exchange and, in particular, the writing students did on-line, an equally significant thread is the teaching and learning that the teachers did among themselves. All the contributors to this book are engaged in what we could call the "New Professional Development," which is decentralized, collaborative, teacher-centered, inclusive of students, grounded in practice, and always being questioned, rethought, and revised. There's much talk among policymakers and teacher educators about the gap between the technology and teachers' knowledge: the contributors here make a strong case for networks (local and otherwise, but mostly small-scale) that provide teachers with a place to experiment, critique, and use what Trevor Owen calls "Interaction Technology."

Telecommunications and Reform

Most of the contributors to *The Nearness of You* have written about their experience as members of small networks or as individual teachers using computer conferencing and other technology. Carol Stumbo describes the effects of the Kentucky Education Reform Act (KERA) and the Kentucky Educational Technology System (KETS): how the technology is changing relationships among individuals, agencies, and districts, "flattening traditional hierarchies." Stumbo is keenly interested in changing meaning and values: "Everyone involved is on a first-name basis and connected by the work. Knowledge seems as important as position." Shifting from the top-down aspect of KETS and reform in Kentucky, Stumbo describes her personal experience with telecommunications, how her work as a classroom teacher with a small, grassroots network a decade ago prepared her in some ways for her present work for the Kentucky Department of Education. Stumbo argues that telecommunications has, in fact, changed values, practices, and relationships at the Department. She also understands that changing the way we as teachers see ourselves and our students is the "real state that we must change."

Emmy Krempasky's "Hurricane KERA" is a companion piece to Carol Stumbo's "Changing a State": Stumbo writes about how Krempasky's experience in the Kentucky Telecommunications Writing Project (KTWP) helped Stumbo understand what leaders such as herself were failing to do as they engaged teachers in reform. Krempasky writes about how KTWP helped her survive as she plunged into the "hurricane" of KERA activities and how involving her fourth grade students helped them respond to one of the KERA mandates: "students must learn to write and write to learn." As do several other contributors, Krempasky insists that computer conferencing was a catalyst for creating a community of readers and writers that helped both her as a teacher and her students as learners. She concludes with her belief that teacher research and reflection must be at the heart of successful reform efforts. Together, Stumbo and Krempasky's essays invite us to study the understandings that develop over time as these widely separated educators write on-line.

Susan Nelson Wood's "Electronic Networks: Students and Teachers Creating a Common Place" reflects a recurring theme of this book: rather than waiting for staff development, for in-service workshops, for commercial programs and memberships, teachers and students can create their own networks. Wood argues that teachers are well served by looking at their own best practices and the theories and research that underlie them, and by using the technology as a catalyst to enrich and inform their own curricula. Wood examines several "homegrown, grassroots" networks, with the aim of showing how they differ from commercial and state-sponsored ones: she advocates networks that allow for professional collegiality, "small spaces and human places" that foster the uncommon types of teachers who must be at the heart of meaningful change.

In "Computer Conferencing and the Changing Nature of School-work," Chris Benson offers a number of instances that illustrate the changes that interaction technology is bringing about: profound changes in our concepts about schoolwork and the products of schoolwork. Benson describes how the social nature of computer conferencing raises questions about grades, about the nature of collaboration, and about cross-age and cross-disciplinary conferences, and in turn fosters new, collaborative ways of learning.

The contributors to *The Nearness of You* challenge conventional forms of classroom life and conceptions of literacy itself. They invite us to speculate about what we and our students need to know and to be able to do to function independently and critically in classrooms where technology is a catalyst for the making of meaning and community. They suggest that centralized, standardized models and traditional forms of professional development aren't appropriate for the creative, collaborative, dynamic educational practices that can flow from computer conferencing and interaction technology. They demonstrate that interaction technology and small-scale networks change relationships and increase teachers' and students' control over texts: they do not claim that technology solves the inequities that dominate our society. Rather, they are keenly aware of troubling issues, including copyright and intellectual property violations; privacy of on-line writing; censorship versus free access to information; training and support; the lack of time—and the lack of incentives provided by school systems for experimenting with, documenting, and questioning the use of new technologies. They understand that deciding to spend money for equipment, technical support, and training means that the money won't be available for other necessities.

One of the features that makes *The Nearness of You* such a useful book is the authors' focus on what actually happens in schools, class-rooms, and networks—even in state departments of education. The engaging style of their essays and narratives is entirely appropriate for the topics and processes they explore. Finally, these authors help us envisage schools where instead of strengthening current mechanistic policies and programs, technology promotes cultural and social change while changing the ways reading and writing are taught.

Bill Bernhardt

Less Is More

Collaborative Writing in the Computer Lab

I FIRST DISCOVERED how using computers could benefit my own writing in the early 1980s. Although I knew nothing about computer science and had to rely, at first, on more knowledgeable friends to walk me through the most fundamental practical procedures, I could see that this technology offered me an easier way to write. Not only could I compose with greater confidence and facility than on a typewriter, but I could edit and proofread faster and easier (cutting and pasting whole sections was almost as effortless as changing a single letter). I was getting a lot more done in less time and with less effort.

I was eager to share this experience with my students, especially as I could see that it really wasn't necessary to know much "about" computers in order to use them as instruments for writing. However, at the time, teachers in only a few departments had access to our computer labs (mostly people teaching typing—it wasn't even called "keyboarding" yet—and certain science courses). English was definitely not considered an appropriate subject to be allotted lab time. Luckily, a kind colleague who was teaching a very small advanced science class in a large, nearly empty lab invited me to bring in my basic writing class and fill up the empty seats, with the result that I spent a semester circulating quietly among my students' twenty stations while my colleague's booming voice echoed from the front of the room.

A short time later, funds materialized for the creation of a "Writing Lab," and I found myself in a spacious, air-conditioned room with thirty computers and about half that many printers. The students in both my remedial and "regular" classes were delighted at the opportunity to enter the computer age, and attendance was always better on the days we were scheduled to meet in the lab. I also found confirmation of my belief that students could master certain basic skills by doing and exploring, rather than by listening and following directions.

Still later, I tried to share my enthusiasm for writing with computers with other teachers. In conducting workshops for teachers in the U.S., Brazil, China and Japan, I often heard the protest, "But at my school we have at least thirty-five students in a class and the lab only has twelve stations!" or "What am I going to do, we only have four computers."

It was only when I faced a summer class of forty-five students and a lab with twenty-nine stations (with fewer actually working on any particular day) that I felt sufficiently challenged to create exercises and activities for two to five students per computer. To my surprise, utilizing a reduced number of stations resulted in greater progress in both writing and word-processing ability than in any previous class. Further experimentation over several semesters with other composition and basic writing classes confirmed that, indeed, "less is more."

Preparing to Enter the Lab for the First Time

On the basis of previous experience, I assume that every class has students with a wide range of computer experience, from absolute beginner to expert user, and—perhaps more important—a similarly wide range of emotions, from confidence to terror. At the same time, I haven't found it useful to ask students about their experience and attitudes. More often than not, the guy who claims he knows all about the hardware and software we are using is the person who causes the other students to lose their files, and the girl who claims to be computerphobic becomes totally proficient in record time. So instead, I simply announce that we are going to be working in a computer lab on a regular basis and that no prior experience is expected or assumed.

For the first visit, I assign groups of two to four students per station. In making up the groups, I try to make sure that each group is mixed in terms of gender and ethnicity (if possible), because, in my college, students will otherwise tend to stick with students exactly like themselves. I've found that students perform less well than when jolted out of their accustomed groupings.

I should mention that our labs really aren't set up for more than one person at each station. In most cases, they are in factory-style rows on small tables resembling the desks I remember from my first grade classroom. Still, we manage to squeeze as many as forty-five people into a lab created for thirty. Students complain about the crowding, but generally not for very long. In any case, from the teacher's perspective the small size is a plus because I have only fifteen to twenty stations to oversee instead of thirty or forty.

Prior to this initial visit to the lab, I generally have the technical support staff boot up all the stations in advance (and open word-processing files created in advance) so that what the students see when they first sit down is a screen ready for writing. (Sometimes I have to do it myself.) I want them to be able to write first and learn how to do housekeeping chores later. *At the beginning, the technology should be invisible.* As recently as two or three years ago, certain preliminary preparations were essential in order for this first visit to proceed smoothly. In this way, I could be sure that each disk we used on the first day was properly formatted and in working order. But with the networked computers and Windows or Macintosh software in many labs and classrooms today, complicated preparations aren't necessary. It's even possible to walk the students through the process of booting up and opening a file in three to five minutes.

Whether there are several students for each computer station or one per station, I want to make sure that the major emphasis on the first day is on writing. I've noticed that there is a difference in the way that most people interact with the computer when they are members of a group. Anxiety (where it is exists) is reduced. People are more playful and exploratory, better able to live with the uncertainty of entering and engaging a new environment, able to recover more quickly from the consequences both of their own mistakes and equipment failures.

Starting with a "Prompted Dialogue" between Bobby, Bobbie, and Bobbi (and possibly Bobbye)

As soon as the students are seated around the computers, I ask one student from each group to take the keyboard and type the following:

BOBBY: How could you say that?

Then I ask him or her to pass the keyboard to another person in the group, who types

BOBBIE:

and then adds a sentence responding to Bobby. Subsequently, a third speaker—Bobbi—enters the conversation, if there are three people in the group, and so forth.

During the next ten minutes or so, the members of the group pass the keyboard back and forth among themselves as they continue the conversation. I circulate among the groups, encouraging them to make their exchanges as long as possible and insisting that there be at least five statements by each participant.

Even though the students have only been writing for a short time, and some may be eager to continue the conversation, I interrupt them as soon as most of the groups have exchanged five statements so that they can reflect on their experience while it is still fresh, and can see the extent to which this initial experience confirmed and/or conflicted with their preconceptions about writing with a computer. In most instances, students are surprised not only by the ease with which they are filling up the screen, but also by their own ability to draw forth so many words from a single question. ESL students are particularly struck by the fact that so little can trigger so much. This is the important thing in my opinion: that the technology is enabling rather than controlling.

Of course, some students do experience difficulty with the mechanics of using the keyboard. They may feel anxious because of all the things they don't yet know how to do—such as how to turn the machine on, load the program, etc. Some are so perfectionist that they erase more than they compose. Or they may discover (or already know) some of the word-processing program's features on their own and start using the spell-check or playing with fonts and sizes rather than composing. But this happens less than when the students are working individually. Most of the groups complete the assigned task and produce a longer and more literate product than first-time users working alone.

From Dialogue to Narrative

I want the students to be aware, from the very first day, of the fluidity of computer-generated text. Students are always surprised—some amazed—at the extent and ease with which they can modify their text on the screen with a minimum of retyping. This, rather than anything else they have previously been told, is what convinces most of them that a computer is more than a glorified typewriter. But if it's easy for them to express their admiration for the machine, it's far more difficult to get them to acknowledge the extent to which these new capabilities reflect their own powers of imagery, inner speech, and intuition. I suggest that they now use the arrow keys (or mouse) to scroll up to the beginning of their document, where they will begin a series of alterations resulting in the transformation of the dialogue into a narrative. For example, they can insert information about the identities of Bobby and Bobbie at the beginning of their text, along with description of each character's gender, age, appearance, etc., or add sentences around the dialogue to provide a larger narrative context.

In providing the students with these instructions, my guiding principle is: "The less said by the teacher the better." I want the students to use the resources of the group to work things out for themselves, to the greatest extent possible. I start out by giving directions that are deliberately vague; in most cases it isn't necessary for me to explain what I "want" in detail because one or another in each group will prompt the others. Someone will say, "Look, we haven't put down the shoes that Bobby's wearing; we could write that." I am supplying them with a structure, but they are coming up with all the details.

This process of embellishing the narrative moves more slowly than composing the dialogue, in part because it requires more discussion and collaboration between the writers in the group. At the end of the first lab session, most groups leave the room still lacking a conclusion for their story. Many of the stories also lack clarity and coherence. I have to ensure that each group's work is saved for further development and revision. Fortunately, this is a lot easier to do with ten to fifteen groups than it would be with thirty to thirty-five students each working alone.

In carrying the project forward to its completion—the printing out of an edited and proofread "Bobby and Bobbie"—each group needs to focus on issues of narrative consistency, coherence, clarity of language, and so on. To accomplish this, one person, or a succession of individuals, can take charge at the keyboard, although everyone shares responsibility for shaping and clarifying the narrative. Inevitably, there is considerable discussion (and experimentation) about how to make the word-processing program do what the group wants it to do (and how to prevent it from doing what the students don't want it to do). As they argue about different ways of moving around in a document (cursor keys versus mouse), formatting paragraphs (tabs versus tapping on the space bar), and moving text (cut and paste versus deleting and re-typing), their command of the program grows.

For the most part, each group seems to discover their own solutions to most problems, both literary and technical. It often happens that an entire class can survive and even prosper for an entire semester without any computer or word-processing instruction per se. But there are usually one or two groups who require some hand-holding by the instructor or the student aide (usually a computer science major) assigned to the lab. We try to respond to their queries by showing them what to do with a minimum of explanations.

One of the most intriguing aspects of this exercise is how students' genders, ages, races, and ethnicities play a role in determining the finished product. For example, when a young man who had recently arrived from the former Soviet Union was teamed up with an African American student his same age, the two produced a polite but wary exchange between two men who accidentally rubbed up against each other on a Brooklyn street corner. Groups with mixed ages tend to present family arguments crackling with dramatic tension.

Moving toward Publication

The students are always eager to print their pieces. If I gave them unrestricted access to the printer, they would probably print out their pieces at least three times and then make multiple copies for me and each member of the group. To keep them from rushing to the printer every few minutes (and to save our forests from extinction), I forbid printing until each group's "Bobby and Bobbie" has passed my on-screen inspection for typos and other easily corrected errors.

When a particular group falls behind the others, I may allow them to print proofs they can study and correct in preparation for the next class. However, as much as possible I try to encourage on-screen editing and proofreading in the interest of greater efficiency and less waste of paper, and for another reason as well: I've noticed that students who want to "take it home to revise later" instead of working it out here and now are often people who tend to substitute busywork for creative work—just the way some writers will "edit" a manuscript by copying the identical words over again on a fresh piece of paper without making any real changes.

A class of twenty-five to thirty students, divided into groups of three or four each, will produce anywhere from six to eight "Bobby and Bobbie" manuscripts. It is possible (and I have done this) to collect them all into a class "book" for subsequent reading, review, and discussion. Of course, when all of the pieces are collected into a single volume, the job of printing, collating, and stapling is major (especially if I, the teacher, end up doing it), and massive amounts of paper are required to provide each student with his or her own copy. I prefer to create three or four separate "books," each consisting of two or three pieces that have been given a final going over by a student "editorial committee." This committee decides on the order of contents and the volume's design. Because the books can be read in a relatively short period of time, only a couple of copies are necessary in order to circulate them among all the students.

From Narrative to Essay

In some classes, it is enough to create "books" consisting of the students' "Bobby" pieces. If possible, however, I like to take another step and have the students collaboratively compose an introduction or preface for each of their books. This constitutes a critical move in the course, because it involves discovering and practicing conventions of discourse that students find more challenging than storytelling.

As each group discusses its "book"—what title to select, how to introduce its contents to other readers, etc.—the students become involved in a complex discussion. Obviously, the introduction has to have a voice, but what voice is most appropriate? How long does the introduction need to be? Can all of the contents be described together or must categories be created? Is it sufficient to describe what the book contains, or is it also necessary to tell how it came to be written? In some instances, I won't offer any guidance because I am convinced the group can resolve all of these questions on its own. In other cases, I establish certain ground rules, such as: your introduction must be at least two pages long, it must be written in third person, present tense.

When the students compose introductions collaboratively, the process moves slowly (and noisily), but the results are often impressive. They tend to speak concretely, referring to examples and illustrations from the texts they've just written. The voice they adopt thus carries a considerable measure of authority, and ranges over the entire contents of the book with apparent ease. They employ strategies such as "comparison and contrast" and "cause and effect" without any explicit instruction on my part. They create a structure for themselves, following conventions they know or inventing new ones out of common sense.

Once books have been "published," they can be treated as "literature." That is, they can be reviewed, criticized, appreciated, and compared with each other or with other texts in magazines, textbooks, or library books. Individual reviews (in essay form) of class books are an obvious next step.

The Teacher's Role

When students work in groups, they tend to find the answers to many of their questions by themselves. There are always going to be some students who have more technical experience than others, or who have a gift for figuring things out by trial and error, and can share what they know with others. Gradually, however, they all become more proficient in handling disks and files, setting margins, coping with unintentional deletions and changes that can't be undone, loading paper into a printer after someone else has caused it to jam, and so forth.

Further, when the students confer among themselves their common sense will lead them to solutions to many of the immediate problems that come up in composing and editing, such as how to start and stop, when examples need to be added and when they can be dispensed with, if it makes sense in a particular document to mix present and past tenses . . . the list of what they can figure out on their own is quite extensive.

Still, there are some things that students cannot—will not—do by themselves. More than anything else, they need a teacher to make them reflect, to pose questions that help students become aware of how much they have to say, that they have the linguistic resources for expressing themselves, and that the results are of their own making. If we fail to do this, students may go away with the mistaken idea that it is the computer that is making them into writers rather than what they themselves are doing, both individually and collectively, to make it happen.

Working with fewer computers has taught me several lessons. First, I've learned that collaborative work can often be more efficient and productive than individual work because "two heads are better than one." Second, I've learned that each student learns the most by involving himself or herself in the composing process, not only by the minutes spent actually striking keys and entering text. But the most important lesson for me is that it doesn't matter if I can't provide a computer for each person and it doesn't matter if I can't get around the room fast enough to tell everyone just what to do and how to do it. What is important is that less giving and helping by the teacher makes it possible for the learners to do more with themselves and each other.

After Word Processing, What? Using Off-the-Shelf Software

For me, word processing remains *the* indispensable software for all writing classrooms. For a long time, in fact, I wasn't aware of any other kinds of programs, except for the dreary drill-and-practice (workbook-on-a-screen) junk that administrators were always trying to sell to us (justly suspicious) teachers. There are a lot of things you can do with *any* word-processing program, such as having the students create specialized files for freewriting, daily journals, drafts, etc. I like to create "lesson files" with prompts, lists of questions, creative writing assignments, etc., and copy them onto each student's disk. In contrast to a paper-and-pencil worksheet, the space between prompts in a lesson file can always expand or contract to fit an individual student's work. Or the students have the option of erasing the prompts and questions entirely from the final product. And all this without any recopying!

When the computers are networked, a whole new range of possible collaborative writing exercises comes into being. I am still exploring these with my students. During the past year, for example, "groupware" features have been added to some of our word-processing programs. Students sitting at different stations can now collaborate on a single document, while at the same time carrying on a conversation about what they're doing, in a separate "window" on the screen. It's a wonderful idea, but not without its problems, especially when the students start carrying on x-rated conversations instead of completing their document.

Because I had young children of my own growing up as members of the first computer generation, I started noticing the kinds of software that were being marketed for kids to use at home. This alerted me to the fact that there were programs available which extended the creative possibilities beyond what word processing offered, and at an affordable price: stripped-down versions of "professional" software for computer-aided design (CAD); desktop publishing (DTP) programs, which can convert word-processed documents into quarto-sized books printed on both sides; accounting spreadsheets and computerized slides and transparencies (presentation software); and simulation software (such as the fabulously successful Simcity). There is also an intriguing type of software (for which there is, unfortunately, no catch-all term) that combines text and images. In fact, it is impossible to list all the new types of software and how they can be used in the classroom because they are appearing all the time. The prices are initially high (as with all software products), but rapidly come down. All of these programs are extremely easy to install and use; on the basis of my own experience I can say, "So easy even a parent or teacher can use them."

Of all these "off-the-shelf" software packages, I find that the programs that allow the user to manipulate both text and pictures are the most interesting and versatile (notably, Storybook Weaver from MECC Software). Like the emerging (and much more expensive) multimedia technology, they permit the teacher to work with students at the intersection of visual and textual perception and conceptualization.

Characteristically, such programs divide the screen into two areas, a "picture window" and a "writing window." Unlike "draw-and-paint" programs, which present a considerable challenge to anyone's motor coordination, the images here are easily accessed from menus of clip art (arranged in categories such as "scenery," "people," etc.) and then combined into "pictures" by a simple click, drag, and drop. Furthermore, it is easy for the user to toggle back and forth between creating text and pictures, and to compose "books" with a sequential story or theme. Given the flexibility of the images and the ease with which they can be manipulated—layering over one another, re-sizing them, flipping them, recoloring them, etc.—it is possible to create a visual counterpart to fit virtually any set of words on any subject. Stories or poems can be created and then illustrated, or the pictures can trigger the words.

Surprisingly, I've found that not many of my students do very good work when they are permitted total freedom with these programs. They tend to keep "surfing" from one set of images to another, on a single page, without going on. I had the same trouble when I tried it myself: with hundreds of ready-made images to choose from, it's easy to get overwhelmed. It's much easier when the task is limited in some way. For example, when I give the students a verbal prompt of two or three words to copy into the writing window at the start, and tell them to expand it into an illustrated story, they manage very well, both individually and in small groups. I've also had good results when everybody works from a visual prompt given by one of the students.

Story-making and illustrating are clearly what the originators of these programs had in mind when they invented them. However, as a teacher who works with ESL students and native speakers with grammar and usage problems, I have also found that these programs can be used in another, even more powerful, way. I dictate a statement to the students, such as, "Some books are on a chair next to the bikes on the young woman's left," for them to put into the writing window. Then I ask them, working individually or collaboratively, to create a picture that adequately and *precisely and correctly* mirrors the statement. A sentence like the one above seems pretty simple, but it poses some of the greatest difficulties in English from the point of view of an ESL student, because of its use of prepositions and articles. I've heard students discussing how many chairs and women can be included without violating the meaning of the words, and about how many books are "some."

To take a totally different example, I sometimes use the program's ability to enlarge and shrink images to create a picture of several members of the same family, who differ in height. This can provide the basis for a series of written statements using comparatives and superlatives, such as, "The young man in the middle is taller than. . . . The one at the end is the tallest." Further, a sequence of related pictures (that appear on the screen as a succession of "pages") can be employed to focus on tense. What appeared on a previous page, and is now no longer visible on the screen, is clearly in the "past"; whereas a person moving across the screen before our eyes is "present." In all of these activities, imagery is used to trigger and support language awareness: language is used to reflect situations that are understood visually.

Another feature of programs such as Storybook Weaver is the range of images they provide, and their flexibility in manipulating those images—for instance, the ability to change skin color. When I was using the software in Brazil, a sentence about a beach evoked palm trees and dark-skinned swimmers in the picture window, whereas the same sentence triggered very different images from a group of teachers in New Jersey. This feature is important, I think, because it encourages students to draw on their own mental images.

Guidelines for Choosing Software

What I look for
Above all, I'm looking for software that engages my creativity as a teacher and seems likely to mobilize the creativity and intelligence of my students. I want it to be software that makes me and my students want to grab the mouse, put our fingers on the keyboard, and start working with an absolute minimum of explanations—whether on-screen or in a printed manual.

I want to make sure that it will help us do something that we can't as easily do with chalk and talk, pencil and paper, or some simpler and less expensive technology.

I want it to be cheap ($50 or less for a single copy, a few hundred dollars or less for a site license or network version), easily accessible from reputable vendors (with full technical support), and easy to install. I don't want to waste my weekend trying to make it work, or run up my long distance phone bill calling a help line that puts me on hold forever.

As a teacher in a system where getting software purchases approved is a nightmare, I'm drawn to programs when I can afford to buy a single copy myself, and that are flexible enough so I can try using a single copy in class. (Then, if it's really great, I can persuade the powers that be to buy more copies.)

As a teacher who uses collaborative learning in all my classes, and sometimes has classes that are too large for every student to have his or her own individual station, I'm particularly drawn to programs that lend themselves to group work.

Where I look to find it
I have found, as a rule of thumb, that software that is available from only a single vendor (who may also be its publisher) is less likely to live up to

promises, is less easy to install, and is generally less satisfactory than others that are more widely available. (I've learned to be particularly wary of the type of software that turns up in the "bargain pages" of catalogues or the "bargain bin" at my local software retailer.)

There are a lot of software catalogues that one can get in the mail, usually for free. I find that the ones targeted to the educational market aren't necessarily the best, because too often they feature either very expensive programs or dreary drill-and-practice software. I suggest casting one's net as widely as possible, so that it takes in specialized as well as general-interest markets. Many of the best programs have been designed for those most difficult customers to satisfy—young children.

Questions I ask myself in making selections

The single most important question is: "Do I want to work with this program myself?" If I think it's stupid or dull, chances are that the students will feel the same way.

Is there anything about the program that will be unacceptable to my students? I've had to reject some otherwise quite impressive programs because they were too "cute" or condescending.

How hard is it to start using? If I can plunge in and learn by trial-and-error, that's one thing. But if I have to spend a lot of time reading manuals beforehand, it's probably not good for students (who may be less patient than I am).

How versatile is it? Can it be used for more than one purpose and in more than one situation? For example, can a program that enables students to design and print their own business cards also do illustrations and posters?

Can the software be used by students working in small groups? Some programs are very hard to use in groups, if only because the print is too small unless you are right in front of the screen. There may also be something in the concept that limits or even precludes sharing. For example, programs for making family trees and personal timelines can be used by only one person at a time.

Can I use it when making presentations in class? Assuming that you don't have a projection device for your in-class computer, it's important to notice whether the text and/or images are clear enough to be seen from a distance.

How many copies do I really need to do what I want to do? Is it available in a school version, lab pack or network version? It's easy to assume that you have to have a copy of the software for every station, but that often involves unnecessary expense. Five stations could be dedicated to a particular software if you buy a "lab pack," and then used in rotation while the rest are using the word-processing software your school has a site license for.

Will it work with the level of technology at my site? Do we have enough memory to run it, and is it compatible with our current system software? This is a critical question, and one that will be easier to check if you order by phone from a catalogue than if you shop in a store. I've found that salespeople in stores are not always reliable on technical questions. In any case, most software publishers have a dedicated phone line for answering technical questions.

Going beyond the Stand-alone Computer and the Local Network
I have been working in labs with networked computers for several years but, for the most part, our major use of networking has been to share word-processing software and printers—and occasionally to exploit the possibilities of "shareware." It wasn't until the past year that I was able to start using computers for writing projects that reached beyond a single room.

Communicating back and forth with my students via e-mail has been a lot of fun for me and it was certainly exciting for them to be able to write informal letters to each other and to friends elsewhere in the U.S. and abroad, letters they could send postage-free. But aside from the low cost and speed of the messages, I can't say I feel it's really different from any other form of letter writing. Furthermore, the problems I encountered setting up e-mail accounts for my students were numerous, as were additional worries associated with setting them loose on the Internet. (Some did in fact get into some of the x-rated domains of that vast universe.)

For me, a much more rewarding enterprise is an on-going project I'm participating in that connects middle and high school students from Staten Island with students in Santos and São Paulo, Brazil. The purpose of this project is to create a "virtual time capsule" (incorporating text, images, and sound) on the Internet's World Wide Web that reflects the "hemispheric youth culture" of students from both countries.

In the first stages of the project, the students in Staten Island and Brazil sent each other e-mail messages (on a certain, prearranged day) in which they introduced themselves according to a common format: twenty-five personal statements beginning with the words "I am. . . ." (Some of the students wrote their pieces out in advance so that they could be quickly typed in and sent.) This required only a couple of computers at each end; the pieces were then printed out and xeroxed for all of the participants.

Later on, the students asked each other questions based on the initial statements and began trading suggestions for what they felt should be in the "time capsule." During the past few months (while both groups of students have been on vacation), "experts" at both ends have set up rudimentary "home pages" on the Web so that when the students return to school in August (Brazil) or September (Staten Island) there will be something for them to work with. In fact, we (the teachers and computer nerds working on the project) have deliberately made the prototypes as simple as we could, so the students will assume an active role. We're hoping that the students in both Staten Island and Brazil will use multimedia and hypertext to create unusual and dynamic Web sites.

I want to emphasize that at this stage what we are doing really only takes two computers, one at each end. However, if we choose to make our "pages" available, they can be accessed by *any* computer in the world that is connected to the Internet and has our World Wide Web addresses. We know we'll encounter some technical limitations that will make it impossible for the students to fulfill all of their ambitions, but nonetheless I think the experience as a whole will be a valuable one for them.

(This article was originally presented in a somewhat different form at the MacBeth National Conferences on Computers in the Liberal Arts, Bethany, West Virginia, 1993–1995.)

Karen Ferrell

Writing Roulette

STUDENTS TYPE feverishly at their computers. A timer chimes. Some students desperately add just one more word. They know what is coming. The teacher announces simply, "Change." Chairs scrape across the floor. A few students giggle in anticipation. Others look longingly back at the computer and story they left behind. "Begin," the teacher commands. Silence reigns only for a minute, then a hailstorm of typing fills the room.

Writing Roulette, developed by the New Jersey Writing Project in Texas Institute, is an exercise in which students freewrite collaborative narratives on computers, in the computer lab or classroom. It adapts easily for use with any word-processing program. The exercise requires almost no preparation on the teacher's part—good news for the already inundated teacher.

To begin, copy a set of writing prompts onto index cards. You need one set of cards for each group of students (four students to a group). Each set of cards contains the same writing prompt. Divide students into their writing teams by color-coding the cards, or by matching stickers or shapes onto a set of cards. Provide exciting statements designed to catapult the imagination into action. For example:

"I couldn't believe it, but there it lay at my feet."

"I told her not to look in the room. Now it was too late."

"All the kids on the block wondered why a purple light glowed every night inside Mr. Cratchety's ramshackle hut."

"I wonder if anyone knows why the (bluebonnet) is our state flower? Legend has it that. . . ."

"Who can forget the day that our pets ran the city?"

Visual prompts, such as scenic postcards or portraits of people, stir creativity and are especially good for elementary level students. An excellent source is *The Mysteries of Harris Burdick* by Chris Van Allsburg, a book of captioned pictures.

Next, randomly distribute one index card to each student, dividing the class into groups of four by card color. Every member of the same group should thus have the same prompt. If groups don't come out evenly, the teacher can participate to complete a group—or you can opt to have one or more groups of three.

Position group members next to each other. Optimally, each student should have his or her own computer station. If there are not enough computers, include a few "stations" where students compose on paper, but make sure every student gets the opportunity to use a computer at least once during the process.

Take the precaution of adding a minimum number of restrictions to the students' creative license. Use names of fictional people only. Avoid incorporating members of the class into the storyline to intercept any chance of hurt feelings. Include only schoolworthy subject matter—no excessive violence, blood, guts, profanity, etc.

Give students a moment to settle in and to transfer the prompt from their card to the screen (or paper).

Now the fun begins. Set the timer for four minutes. At a signal, students type. Their mission—to create an introduction, establish characters and setting, and generate a conflict in the time allotted.

After four minutes, the timer sounds. Students stop, in mid-thought, mid-word, mid-sentence, or mid-paragraph. No time for regrets, corrections, or proofreading.

Then students move to the next station, rotating within their groups, keeping to the same prompt but switching stories. Reset the timer for five minutes this time, to compensate for the time it takes students to read the stories inherited from their predecessors. Their mission—to build characterization, enhance the plot, deepen the conflict, maintain the story structure, and, above all, to have fun getting the main characters into all sorts of trouble. After all, *this* student doesn't have to resolve *this* conflict. Someone else does.

The timer sounds. The students rotate again. Reset the timer for six minutes. Students concentrate on further story development, adding their own ideas while staying within the storyline already established.

The timer sounds once more. Students rotate for the fourth and last time. Briefly remind students of their final mission—to create a satisfactory conclusion for the story in front of them. Depending on the success of the story's previous three authors, this usually proves quite a challenge. Allow seven minutes for completion, and then have the students save and print the final stories.

Share the results. Form a reading circle or invite students to read to the class from an "author's chair." Have students evaluate a particular group's success at making a piece sound like the efforts of only one author. See if they can guess where one author stopped and another began, based on the story's structure and on their knowledge of the authors' personalities. Ask the "first section" authors to reflect on their original intentions for the stories, and to discuss how they were changed in the final product. Read several stories originating from the same prompt, and then compare them.

One seventh grade team produced the following story (unrevised) from the prompt "It all began when someone left the window open. . . ." (A line space indicates where one author ended and another began.)

> Now our house is gone. You see, a hurricane came yesterday. Our whole family went to stay at Grandma's house because we heard it was coming. Leaving your window open during a hurricane. The wind got in our house and now it's gone.
>
> But when we came home to our long gone house we started to clear things out of the way and see if we could find anything but unfortunately the hurricane took everything. It's just like the hurricane came and took our whole house, like he picked it up gently and carried it away.
>
> It is a nightmare, nothing familiar for me to hold or comfort. I have to face this one on my own.
>
> We had called the police and tried to find it but so far nothing. My family and I were really nervous, until a policeman started coming toward us. He asked if we were the ones who lost the house we said yes. He told us that he had some good news. He said that he found our house, we were so happy because he said it was in Hawaii and we had always wanted to live there.

From "One morning on a glittering sunrise . . ." a fourth grade team wrote (I've corrected the spelling):

> I saw a spark of light it was blue it rose quickly in the air then took formation of a small wishing child. Then it said wish on me 5 wishes to you who sees the sunrise.
>
> The child said I want to make a wish so he wished for a bright sun in the morning. The next morning it was the brightest sun in the world.
>
> The next day then Andrew went to school and Andrew's friend the sun was not there. Andrew was very lonely after school. Andrew's mom tried to
>
> bring the sunlight back but she could not. So she went to ask the wise dog man.

This entire process *can* be accomplished with only paper and pencil, but using the computer provides numerous advantages. Typed text is simpler to decipher than four handwriting styles—particularly when students are reading to the class. Determining where one author began and another ended remains a mystery if a team succeeds: typed stories eliminate handwriting as a potential clue. If authors or groups want to polish this prewriting into a finished piece, the text is already typed and saved.

Here are a few tips and possible variations:

• Have all groups work from the same prompt, for later comparison of results.

• If you have only one computer in your classroom, rotate students through the computer, starting a new story and prompt after every fourth child.

• Vary the time allotted for each rotation depending on the age, grade level, and skill of the students involved. Fourth graders need more time to type than do high schoolers.

• Partner students with children their own age from other classes in your school.

• Use telecommunications to do a large-scale version of Writing Roulette. Get on the Internet and initiate a three-way e-mail exchange with classes in other districts, states, or countries. Post an invitation to your favorite newsgroup and find two or three teachers with whom your classes can exchange stories. Provide a specific timeline for completion of each phase of the activity. Include four weeks for students (and teachers) to practice sending, receiving, uploading, downloading, and printing electronic mail before the project begins. Break down the rest of the activity into two-week segments for each part of the story: beginning, middle, more middle, and end. (You can have each student write a story to exchange—which involves more students, time, effort, and e-mailing—or have each class collaborate as one author. Either way, make sure the partner classes understand exactly what you expect, otherwise you may end up contributing to thirty stories instead of one.) Upon completion of the project, ask teachers and students to evaluate the project and make suggestions for improvement.

This freewriting exercise encourages students to get their thoughts down on paper. They learn story structure and the purpose of each of its components—beginnings, middles, ends, conflict, characterization, sequencing, setting, and elaboration. And don't forget the computer skills they gain—creating a document, keyboarding, editing, saving, and printing. Students enjoy doing almost anything associated with computers, and writing can be one of those things. Although typos and "invented" spelling abound, so do the children's unhampered imaginations.

Writing Roulette remains a favorite activity for both my students and me. The fast pace, frequent movement, excitement, and surprise keep everyone actively engaged in creating and writing. Its adaptability to a variety of classroom environments allows teachers to utilize it despite equipment or facility restraints.

"It's a marvelous way to combine writing and technology," said Linda Schuff, Northwest ISD Middle School teacher and NJWPT trainer. "It makes the computer seem more friendly because Writing Roulette is fun to do."

"This is the only lesson I've ever taught where the students applauded when I finished," confirmed LaWanda Bailey, Northwest ISD's Writing Specialist. "They're learning a whole slate of skills, but all they think they're doing is having fun."

The computer as a tool provides a variety of rich writing experiences for students. Play, experiment, experience, and adapt. After all, isn't that what we expect from our students? Can we model anything less?

Bibliography

Carroll, Joyce Armstrong and Edward E. Wilson. *Acts of Teaching: How to Teach Writing*. Englewood, Colorado: Teacher Ideas Press, 1993.

Van Allsburg, Chris. *The Mysteries of Harris Burdick*. Boston: Houghton Mifflin Co., 1984.

Phyllis Geren

Global Connections on the World Wide Web

What is the World Wide Web Anyway?
From a computer in a Honolulu classroom, primary students (grades K–2) check e-mail, conduct Internet searches, and collaborate in downloading up-to-date graphical information young children can "read." Members of a whole language classroom, these children have teachers who have dared to be learners too, and together they are discovering a wealth of resources on the World Wide Web.

The technology nudging us all toward a "new literacy" may *seem* convoluted and highly technical, a sticky web designed to entrap novices, but the opposite is true. Simply think of the World Wide Web as a new-fangled library. When Benjamin Franklin started the first library in this country, he envisioned a service all could use. In a way, the World Wide Web is like Franklin's Free Library, which is a huge building housing a myriad of resources and still operating today in Philadelphia. Anyone can use it if they know how to get there. To help you find your way to the World Wide Web, we attempt here to explain the Web, how teachers and students might use it in classrooms, and how "surfing," searching, and publishing can be learning tools.

One Thing Leads to Another: from E-mail to the World Wide Web
Back in the late 1960s, amidst Cold War concerns, the United States Department of Defense perceived a need to create a fail-safe backup communication system. Instead of phones connected to phones, they wanted terminals connected to their mainframe computers to "talk" to each other. Computers linked to other computers allowed person-to-person messages to be sent and data exchanged. Military researchers communicated with each other using the first (and still most popular) on-line service, electronic mail. The researchers also transferred and received data across this network. Their communications network, ARPANET, became the start of the Internet, as universities, other governmental agencies, and organizations around the world eventually

networked their computers, and linked those networks with other networks, thus creating one vast network of networks. Because of the "grass-roots" nature of its development, nobody is really in charge of the Internet, making it democratic, almost anarchistic. Various national and local agencies, as well as volunteers, maintain the Internet—for example, the National Science Foundation.

Until recently, the Internet's services have all been text-based—the only things seen on the screen were words. Data was accessed and transmitted in several ways: electronic mail, file transfer protocol, gopher, and telnet.

Electronic mail or e-mail: Messages sent person-to-person or person-to-group via computer. E-mail messages are most often sent through—and stored in—computers called servers.

File transfer protocol (FTP): Allows the transmission of files back and forth across computer networks. In the process, Computer A tries to get a file (download) located on Computer B, or Computer A sends a file to Computer B (upload).

Gopher: One computer holds information and another computer accesses that information, which is organized in files located in directories and subdirectories.

Telnet: Computer A contacts and connects with Computer B. Once connected, Computer A operates as if it were a terminal or workstation on Computer B's network. For example, from a computer at home we can call the public library to access its electronic card catalogue, and what we see on a remote computer screen is exactly what a patron would see on a terminal in the actual library.

These services—e-mail, FTP, gopher, and telnet—are all text-based. After years of such text-based resources, we now have the capability to experience multi-media content (graphics, animation, sound) as well. In 1989, the World Wide Web evolved at the Swiss particle physics lab CERN in Geneva. Instead of directories and subdirectories located on a single computer, the World Wide Web uses what is called a hypertext system. Instead of having to log on and log off using different software to access different services on the Internet, World Wide Web browser software allows us to connect to resources anywhere in the world. Because each site on the Web has a unique address (called a URL, for Universal Resource Locator), once you've visited one Web site, you can easily access other sites by tabbing to hyperlinks on the current screen or simply typing the address of a site you want to visit. Often sites on the Web have hyperlinks to related sites. Access was infinitely more complicated in a text-based system.

The development that really popularized the World Wide Web was the invention of Mosaic software at the University of Illinois at Champaign-Urbana in 1993. Mosaic is a type of software called a Web browser, that resides on an individual computer and works with a mouse. With a point and a click, you can direct the browser to connect to global information resources. Another exciting feature of the browser software is that it allows you to access multimedia files. You can also download software programs and files from the Internet to your own home or school computer.

What Do You Need to Get on the Web?
In order to access the World Wide Web, you need three things: hardware resources, the appropriate software, and a connection to the Internet.

1. In terms of hardware—or the actual computer—the makes can vary, but at the very least you need an IBM-compatible computer that uses Windows or an Apple Macintosh, and a modem with a baud rate of at least 14.4 bits per second, or a dedicated line for Internet access requiring no modem, usually offered only through universities and large organizations. A color monitor is not essential but highly desirable, as Web sites have color graphics (which will, of course, appear in black and white on a black-and-white monitor), and the faster the computer, the better.

2. You will need the appropriate browser software, so your computer can make sense of information being transmitted to it. Currently, the trend is to bundle all this software together; the current versions of Netscape, for example, come as a complete package requiring no other software for e-mail, FTP, gopher, telnet, and Web browsing.

3. Finally, to access the World Wide Web you have to be connected to the Internet. You can do this one of three ways: through commercial on-line service networks like Microsoft Network System, Compuserve, or America Online, which charge an hourly fee; through Internet access providers that charge a flat monthly fee; or through organizations such as universities, which provide access to faculty, students, and sometimes other teachers.

Surfing the Web is Like Browsing in a Library
The first time you walk through the doors of a library, you probably look around, get a sense of where everything is located, and then start hunting

for exactly what you want. On the World Wide Web, you start by doing the same thing. Taking time to just get familiar with the look of the Web is an important first step. The documents you are viewing are called home pages. In Web terminology, browsing or "surfing" means simply calling up home pages on your screen, looking them over, and then, with your mouse, pointing and clicking on hyperlinks to check out related pages and sites. In this way, you quickly get a feel for what kind of information is available.

Through the Web, you can access not only World Wide Web sites, but also many of the other Internet services. The form of the URL address is very important; it must be entered exactly, with no spaces, and it sometimes provides information about the Web site it denotes. For example, a simple address might be http://www.apple.com. The first portion of a URL identifies the type of Internet service—in this case, "http" (hypertext transfer protocol) signifies that this site is a World Wide Web resource. The rest of the address identifies the computer that holds the file and the company or organization that publishes the home page ("apple"). The last three letters indicate the general "domain" the site belongs to ("com" indicates a commercial/business venture). Typically, "edu" means a university, "gov" governmental agency, and "mil" military. Sometimes the address reflects the geographical location: "il.us" represents Illinois in the United States, "my" Malaysia.

Finding addresses to use as starting points is easier than you might think. They can be found in books and magazines, and from people who recommend sites. Visiting one page can link you to a host of others, often in other countries. These hypertext links are colored and underlined on the home page, and all you have to do is point and click, point and click. When you arrive at a new site, its address (URL) automatically appears at the top of your screen. Surfing around, you end up going, almost without realizing it, from one site, to a second, to a third. You might go from a resource in Australia to one in Florida, then to Asia or Europe, just by clicking. You can then go back the way you came using the "Back" button, keep surfing, or quit.

You can tell by the URL what home page you are accessing. One of the nice features of the browser software is that you can create an address book of resources (Web sites) to return to. For example, if you're surfing around and you come to http://www.pathfinder.com, a home page of Time Warner Communications, you can look up information on their publications. If you find this information valuable, you create a bookmark, or hot list, making a permanent record of the address. You can organize these bookmarks by topics and save them as files, which you can then share with friends and colleagues.

Doing Research on the Web

Searching for information on the Web can be likened to the story of the five blind men touching the elephant. All anyone can see at any one time is only a single piece of the Internet, and the information resources out on the Internet are dynamic and changing. What was there yesterday might not be there today. People are constantly deleting files or adding new files, making it impossible to do a comprehensive search of the Internet.

Henry Wadsworth Longfellow praised libraries for holding "the ruins of an antique world and the glories of a modern one." In terms of education, the Web is an excellent resource for having students do research, right from the classroom. But be forewarned, certain topics are very well represented and other topics are very minimally represented. Because the Internet has no "head librarian," it's really up to the organization that publishes the home pages to determine what topics or fields will be represented. In the U.S., because of the role of the National Science Foundation in the development of the Internet, you can find lots of information relevant to science, technology, space travel, astronomy— perhaps more than you can handle.

Different organizations, however, have designed software to assist with locating information on a particular topic. Two kinds of tools can help you search the World Wide Web. The first is the "subject-structured catalogue," a catalogue with an alphabetical list of main topics. You choose a topic from the main topic menu, and then move to other screens with more specific topic headings. Moving from screen to screen, you search the subject catalogue until you find the information resources, with addresses and content descriptions, that meet your needs. Yahoo (http://www.yahoo.com), first developed at Stanford, is one of the most popular subject-oriented catalogues.

Keyword "search engines" are a second tool for searching the Web. These allow you to search using keywords and boolean logic, and can be accessed by clicking on the Netsearch button in Netscape. When you use one of these search tools, such as Lycos, Infoseek, or Excite, you will see a little horizontal rectangle on your screen. You click in it and type in the subject or name you are interested in. The search engine locates resources containing your keyword in databases of WWW sites and/or documents. It then goes through that database and gives you a list of sites that include your keyword, providing you with the names, addresses, and, in some cases, the passage of text where the keyword appears. What you then see on your screen are links to those resources—all you have to do is point and click. The browser will connect to that site and you'll see whether you've found what you wanted. Of course, search engines are not "context-sensitive," so sometimes you get information that has nothing to do with what you're looking for.

Different search engines require different search techniques. Each engine has general ways of searching that often include a set of hints to help you formulate your specific search terms. Often what you'll be using is a melding of that subject catalogue approach with a keyword search approach—as in Yahoo, for instance.

As a teacher, searching the Web for resources can be very useful. For example, if you have a subject you want students to know about, you can first peruse the Internet yourself. You can use one of the search engines, put in your keyword, look at the different information resources, create a bookmark of the resources you deem appropriate, and save that bookmark file. This makes it easy for your students to find that site, when they're studying endangered species, the rainforest, or whatever. As your students get more accustomed to doing research on the Web on their own—which they will, quite quickly—you can just let them loose. At the end of this piece, I give a list of Web sites.

Another way to use the Internet for research in the classroom is through "Expert" projects—for example, "Stumpers" or "Ask a Scientist." In "Ask a Scientist," students can e-mail their questions to a large group of volunteer scientists who are happy to answer children's questions. The children e-mail a question and tell what they've done to solve it themselves. The scientists then respond.

Publishing on the Web (Creating Your Own Web Pages)

Throughout this book are examples of classrooms where teachers and students use e-mail and electronic conferencing to connect and do collaborative projects—between different schools, states, and countries. While somewhat more complex than electronic mail, the World Wide Web similarly offers many opportunities. You can do e-mail through the Web, but you don't need the Web to do e-mail. As well as surfing or searching for information, you can also publish on the Web. This happens when you become the creator of your own information resources—the proprietor of your own home page. This requires a little more technical capability. In order for you and your students to publish on the Web (and many teachers and students are doing this), you'll need to learn the basics of

HTML (hypertext markup language), the scripting language of the World Wide Web—find someone willing to convert your files to HTML or use one of the newer add-ons to word-processing programs (e.g., ClarisWorks or Microsoft Word) that convert your word processing documents for you. HTML is not a very complex language, really just a matter of adding "tags" to indicate the format of the pages at the site, as well as links to other places in the site and outside resources. Graphics also have to be "anchored" in the text by HTML code. Happily, there is software to help you design Web pages that is easy to use. Some is in the public domain, and programs from commercial manufacturers are relatively inexpensive.

In addition, you need a server to "mount" your Web site—in other words to store the HTML files you create at a given URL so that other teachers, students, and interested individuals can visit it. Many states are establishing state networks, and state boards of education are setting up computers designated as WWW servers. At the local level, many school districts have their own servers. Failing this, you can have a private concern perform this service for a fee.

Publishing on the Web is a higher-level issue, requiring an understanding of HTML and setting up a computer to be a WWW server, but many teachers and students have mounted their own pages. It's being done and is not a highly expensive process. It's a great way for students to get their work into the public eye—an audience of some thirty to forty million worldwide. Web 66 (http://web66.coled.umn.edu) gives a listing of Web sites created by teachers and students. Check it out to see what schools throughout the U.S. are doing.

*   *   *   *   *

The World Wide Web is a great tool for locating information about particular topics, but in no way does it replace books or libraries. Rather, it is an excellent addition to those resources. Only a fraction of the existing reservoir of information has made its way onto the Web. But by the same token, the Web is a great place to research current events and topics. For example, if a child wanted to research telecommunications, the library would have very little information, and most of it outdated. You could find loads of information on the Web. When the Kobe earthquake occurred in Japan, within six to eight hours a Web site was up, publishing information on what was going on there, the extent of the disaster, and so on. More and more magazines and newspapers—domestic and foreign— are publishing on the Web, updating their pages daily. This explosion in

Web sites is partly due to the fact that it's a more efficient—and inexpensive—process to publish information on the Web than to write, publish, and distribute through stores.

Researching, locating information resources, is very much what the Web is about, but with a number of caveats. Students have to be taught information literacy skills. Children and adults need to know how to gauge the accuracy of the information that they find. This is an important issue for schools and classrooms. We know we shouldn't judge a book by its cover, but in truth a book's cover does give us some hints about what's in there. Looking at a book—considering its cover, seeing who the publisher is, feeling the quality of the paper—really does give us some information about its contents. The Web is very democratic, in a number of ways. Some Web sites have more eyecatching graphics, but on the whole the pages look more or less alike. On the World Wide Web, you have no way of distinguishing the work of an expert in a given field from that of a crank who knows nothing. You need to develop powers of discernment. (The Colorado Department of Education publishes a set of model guidelines; see the Web address below.)

New skills are required as you use the Web. Students need to learn search and retrieval, how to evaluate the information accessed, how to synthesize information, and how to cite electronic resources. Because a lot of what is seen on the Internet is visual, visual literacy skills, such as gathering information from graphics or reading charts and graphs, are especially important. Ethical issues, copyright issues, and security issues all need to be addressed when you open a classroom to the world (see Tharon W. Howard's essay in this book). The Internet reflects the good, the bad, and the ugly of society. Schools and teachers are beginning to address these issues.

Web Sites of Interest to Teachers

Colorado Dept. of Education Model Information Literacy Guidelines
(http://www.cde.state.co.us/infolitg.htm

Teachers & Writers Collaborative
http://www.twc.org

Institute for Learning Technologies
http://ilt.columbia.edu

The Elements of Style, William Strunk
http://www.columbia.edu/acis/bartleby/strunk/

The Children Page
http://www.pd.astro.it/local-cgi-bin/kids.cgi/forms/

Kids, Fun, Games, Toys, Friends
http://kids.com/

The Philadelphia Writing Project
http://www.gse.upenn.edu/philwp/philwp.html

Teacher Talk
http://www.mightymedia.com/talk/working.htm

Heinemann Today
http://www.heinemann.co.uk/heinemann/htoday/htoday.html

Global Schoolhouse Project
http://kl2.cnidr.org/gsh/gshwelcome.html

Greg Siering

MUDs in Education

Learning through Communication and Construction

IN RECENT YEARS, the explosive growth of the Internet has changed the way we perceive computer technology, moving us from viewing computers as dehumanizing and isolating machines towards seeing them as a means of interacting with friends and colleagues around the world. Modems are now standard equipment on many personal computers, e-mail and World Wide Web addresses appear regularly on business cards and advertisements, and companies providing Internet access can be found in most sizable American cities. We have become—and are still becoming—a culture where computer technology is moving from being a relatively simple tool to being a medium not just for isolated computing but for complex on-line human interaction. For example, when I began my college career about ten years ago, I used my first computer primarily as a word processor and video game; the only social aspect about that old machine was the crowd it gathered when some friends in the dorm and I played the computer version of "Jeopardy." Now my computer is more a communications medium than a computing tool; I spend far more time on my modem than I do my telephone, and rarely does a day go by that I am out of touch with friends across the country. In fact, writing this very essay is one of the few solitary activities I've used my computer for—but then again, I am hardly an isolated writer in a techno-garret, since most of my contact with the editors of this volume has been via e-mail.

This shift toward using computers as a medium for human interaction is also evident in education: we are now seeing less emphasis on keyboard skills and drills with pre-packaged software and more on on-line communication and collaboration. And with the expansion of the Internet, this new on-line interaction frequently takes place beyond the walls of one school or the boundaries of one district, potentially making the world our classroom and changing how we view learning. One Internet tool that is of great potential value to educators is the MUD, a type of on-line conferencing that allows people around the world to talk and interact on-line in real time, all from the comfort of their personal computers. In this essay, I'd like to explore a few ways MUDs can enhance the way we interact and learn on-line.

Just what does the acronym MUD stand for, you might ask. What are they, really? MUDs, or "Multi-User Dimensions" (or "Multi-User Dungeons") are programs that run on computers somewhere out on the Internet. By using the Internet utility called Telnet, users can hook their computers directly into the computer hosting the MUD. The key to MUDs, however, is that many users can connect to the MUD-host at the same time, so they are interacting with each other, not just the program running on the host computer. In fact, MUDs originally grew out of computer adventure games where several players could cooperate in slaying dragons and collecting treasure (hence their original name of "multi-user dungeons"). The rooms were dungeons and castle hallways, and the objects were weapons, treasures, and beasts. While such thematic, game-oriented MUDs still exist, many are now being created for educational (and other social) purposes, often utilizing variations of MUD programming with the exotic names MOOs, MUSHes, and MUSEs.[1] A growing number of MUD designers and educators are building MUDs specifically for students, creating virtual worlds with particular themes and atmospheres conducive to learning.

Let me depict a MUD at its most basic level. Imagine yourself carrying on a dialogue with other people via your computer. Using a few simple keystroke commands, you can "speak" to others in the MUD. Your words appear simultaneously on all participants' computer screens in a format that looks very much like a constantly scrolling transcript of a conversation:

> Chris says, "So, Greg, how is that chapter about MUDs coming along?"
> Greg shrugs, "Not bad. I need to make some time to work on a revision, though."
> Chris thinks Greg plays too much golf when he should be working.
> Greg says, "Well, once winter gets here I'll get more work done. It's hard to sit inside and work on a pretty fall afternoon."
> Chris laughs and reminds Greg what kind of "doctor" he is studying to be.

As this example shows, the text identifies MUDders' on-line names and their words or actions. In essence, we can carry on typed conversations through the MUD, spicing up the dialogue with gestures and asides to add depth to the communication. MUDs offer much more than simple on-line chat, however; they also simulate physical contexts for these conversations, by providing different environments or "rooms." Just like in many computer and video games, MUD users can move their on-line characters from room to room, conversing with others they find along the way. In MUDs, however, the "visuals" are entirely text-based. Here, for example, is the description of a room used for Netoric's Tuesday Cafe, an on-line project I'm involved in:[2]

Tuesday Cafe
A cheerful but quiet and peaceful cafe overlooking the lobby of the Netoric Headquarters. Sunlight pours through the skylights, and out the windows you see a well-kept English garden. The smells of fresh coffee and tea drift toward you as you join your colleagues for some shop talk. Lots of comfortable chairs and tables are scattered about, and when more of your colleagues arrive, you simply push more tables together. Each Tuesday at 8:00 P.M. Eastern, the computers and writing crowd gather here to discuss—what else?—issues related to the use of computers in the teaching of writing. To see the topic for a particular Tuesday night, enter LIST TOPICS.

Tari Fanderclai, a colleague of mine in the Netoric Project, wrote this creative room description with a specific purpose in mind: to help set a comfortable atmosphere for collegial on-line discussions about teaching with technology. When we gather in this on-line room, we hold conversations that look like the transcript above, with the words of a dozen or so people going by as quickly as real-life coffee shop chat. In addition to adding atmosphere, the "room" allows us to hold a conversation distinct from those going on in other rooms. In the example above, there is an exit from the Cafe called "down" that leads to another room called Netoric Headquarters, where a totally separate discussion may be taking place; you can go from one to the other just by typing the command "down." In fact, for some Netoric events, we actually break into small group discussions, each located in a different room, and then come back into one MUD room for a final large group discussion.

What makes MUDs most fascinating, though, is that rooms can hold "objects" as well as people. Like MUD rooms, the objects in a MUD are described in text. They can, however, be used in ways similar to their real-life counterparts; using a few simple commands, you can "look" at an object to see its description, pick it up and put it down, and activate special commands to make it work like the real thing. For example, there is a "sign" in the Tuesday Cafe described above that can be read just like a real-life sign; by entering the command "read how," you get a list of instructions. These instructions describe how to use another object in the room, a "slide projector" named Introjector. This object can be used to display pre-recorded text to everyone in the MUD room, just like a real-life slide projector; when I show one of these "slides," its text appears on everyone's screen, right along with the text of our conversation. The Introjector is a handy tool for giving instructions and an introduction to the week's discussion topic—far more convenient than typing in all the information on the spot. There are many other common MUD objects that can also prove useful, such as bulletin boards on which comments can be posted and read, robots that can respond when they hear key words, and maps that give visual representations of the MUD—the possibilities are bounded only by the imagination. So the objects in a MUD aren't just for decoration; rather, they can be programmed to be used like their metaphorical cousins in real life, and are designed to enhance interaction in the text-based virtual world of MUDs.

Now that I've given a whirlwind tour of MUDding, let's move on to how specifically MUDs can fit in with education.

Why Use MUDs in Education?

MUDs are often described as something other than "real life," yet they tend to reflect basic elements of our everyday lives, particularly the productive union of work and play. Think of the most productive and enjoyable workshops and conferences you've been to, and you are likely to admit that the mixture of work and play was integral to the learning experience. We also know that our students learn far more when they are engaged in some productive yet enjoyable activity. MUDs are marvelous places to take advantage of this creative combination of work and play, whether it be among colleagues or within classes. Participants in the Tuesday Cafe discussions exchange valuable insights and ideas each week partly because our time together provides a relaxing and entertaining break from our more "serious" academic lives. While this claim for MUDs may seem idyllic, I'll ask that you play what Peter Elbow calls the "believing game" and accept this premise for the moment, while we explore these new environments as sites for education and learning.

To explain further the educational benefits of MUDs, I would like to offer two models of MUD pedagogy: the communication model and the construction model. These models are not mutually exclusive—or conflicting—by any means, but they do provide a useful introductory framework.

The Communication Model

In the communication model, MUDs are primarily tools for conversation, often between geographically distant persons. While students may create their own rooms and objects in the MUD, this is secondary to the conversations taking place in those rooms. These conversations may involve students within the same class, group partners in distant classes, or even guest speakers or interviewees. Whoever the participants and whatever the purposes, however, what really matters is the actual on-line communication.

Students within a single class can use a MUD as a means of holding computer-based class discussions, similar to those held by classes using locally networked programs such as Daedalus InterChange.[3] Instead of having a face-to-face conversation, students do their "talking" on-line, adding their comments to a constantly scrolling dialogue. While this might seem only to complicate matters—particularly in elementary and middle schools where computer and keyboarding skills are less developed—it can actually extend traditional classroom conversations in a number of ways. First, the ability to capture logs (transcripts) of MUD conversations provides participants with an exact record of their discussions. Logs are extremely valuable when MUD sessions are used for brainstorming or similar fast-paced activities: participants can make full use of the speed and spontaneity of MUD discussions, knowing what they say can be carefully reviewed and reflected upon later. Second, students do not have to compete for the chance to be heard; everyone can "speak" at once on-line.[4] While assertive or extroverted students tend to dominate traditional classroom discussions, even the shyest of students can add to MUD conversations in his or her own way and at his or her own pace. While many class discussions shift topics before every student has his or her say, MUD-based conversations offer participants the opportunity to add to their ideas when they are ready. Contemplative thinkers and shy students who don't leap right into the fray can still comment on a topic even after others have moved on in another direction. The results of these "multi-vocal conversations" can be confusing at times, but are often far more diverse and rich than traditional ones.

Finally, like other forms of computer-mediated communication, MUDs provide a type of "psychological filter" for participants, giving them enough distance from their audiences and words to overcome some of the limitations and inhibitions inherent in face-to-face dialogue. Since MUD participants can name and describe themselves on-line any way they wish—even creating fictional characters—they can take on identities or characteristics that allow them to participate more comfortably. Race, sex, appearance, and physical handicaps need not play a dominant role. There is a better opportunity for students to create impressions based on words and ideas rather than on their physical appearance, as happens in many classrooms and situations. For example, I have a few female friends who have taken on male personas in MUDs in order to be taken more seriously in the male-dominated world of computer programmers. Certainly, MUDs do not offer a utopian classroom—some physical or gender characteristics and their accompanying biases do make their way into MUD conversations as well—but the "psychological filter" MUDs provide is a significant help to many students.

As I hint at above, the on-line discussion in MUDs often moves beyond the MUD itself, with these on-line chats acting as just one element in a larger interaction. Commonly, the discussion branches off into individual e-mail exchanges. Students—particularly those at distant sites—can exchange stories, papers, or notes via e-mail before coming together at pre-arranged times to discuss them in the MUD. The integration of e-mail into such a plan is vital, since MUD conversations do not favor the use of large blocks of text; the best use of on-line time and resources in MUDs comes through interaction and conversation. With younger students, teachers may need to play a central role in the e-mail exchange, but with older students, the exchanges can be "student-directed," with a number of groups working independently.

Perhaps the greatest strength of the communication model of MUD pedagogy, however, is that it allows students to work with people around the country and the world, enriching the electronic classroom with a variety of voices, cultures, and specialists. Students from urban and rural high schools can share different perspectives, as can college students from the Midwest and West Coast, or teachers from the United States and Great Britain. At the time of this writing, there are dozens of teachers who use MUDs for group writing collaborations between high school and college classes in various states, and between distant college composition classes. Teachers in these projects report that the writers interact—in writing—with a relatively unknown audience beyond their local context, which not only enriches the conversations with multiple perspectives, but also requires more attention to a variety of issues related to audience. Since in MUDs or through e-mail, everything must be explained in writing, tone, clarity, word choice, and development all assume even more importance.

Other teachers have used MUDs to bring in "guest experts" for their students to interview. As one such "expert," I found the experience fascinating. I sat at my office computer at Ball State University, in Muncie, Indiana, while being interviewed by Tari Fanderclai's class of writing students from the University of Louisville in Kentucky. While my hands were aching from trying to answer a deluge of questions, I was excited by the depth and breadth of the conversation; more students in the class were able to ask a greater variety of questions than they could in a real-life interview. As long as I kept typing responses, the interview could go in several directions at once, and I never had to cut off important follow-up questions. The teacher had prepared her students well for the interview, and the class took full advantage of the opportunity, even capturing the whole conversation in a transcript for later review. It was the flexibility and versatility of MUDs that made such an interview possible; it could probably never happen any other way.

MUDs and e-mail are even being used in a handful of college writing centers to offer on-line tutoring to both local and off-site students.[5] Students e-mail their papers to the tutors and then meet on-line to discuss revision possibilities. This use of MUDs not only makes tutoring available to off-campus students, but it encourages emphasis on texts, since the tutoring occurs only in writing. These uses of MUDs for on-line communication and learning are expanding rapidly, and new techniques and approaches are continually evolving as more teachers explore this learning environment.

The Construction Model

The second educational use of MUDs, the "construction model," relies on having students invent and build their own "MUD worlds" as an integral part of some larger project. This can range from the construction and description of simple rooms to the programming of interactive objects, and can be completed with fairly simple MUD commands. An excellent example of a MUD-based project following the construction model was done by Leslie Harris's students at Susquehanna University. After reading Dante's *Inferno,* students constructed an interactive model of some of the levels of hell Dante wrote about. Visitors can walk between the various MUD rooms that are described as the different levels, read explanatory notes about them, and even initiate dialogues between pre-programmed representations of Dante, Virgil, and several denizens of hell. This project, currently housed at Diversity University MOO,[6] represents the creative power of MUD-based learning: the students obviously had fun constructing their virtual *Inferno,* and at the same time the process helped them deepen their understandings and interpretations of the book.

Not all construction projects have to be so complex. Even simple room-building can mobilize students' creative energies on various levels and encourage investment in their work and education. Students who construct their own spaces within MUDs, whether as models like the *Inferno* project or simply as their own places to hold conversations, build more than MUD rooms: they build the pride and comfortability so important to learning. For example, several of Michael Salvo's basic writing students constructed a Dream House on DaedalusMOO, partially as a way of combating their homesickness for New York City as they moved into the more rural SUNY-Binghamton campus. According to Salvo, the students put a good deal of thought into their construction, as well as a good deal of themselves. Now the students do not simply have a place to go for on-line conferencing, but they have *their own place* to go, making them more comfortable in their discussions. So while Salvo's use of a MUD may be primarily for communication, he and his students have also found the benefits of construction in a MUD.

Another good example of the creative power of MUDs comes from the MariMUSE Project, a program sponsored by Phoenix College in Arizona. During several three-week camps, students from nearby Longview Elementary School were bussed to a computer lab at the college for daily three-hour sessions. (Longview now has access to MariMUSE through its own computers at the school.) There they used MariMUSE—the college's MUD—to interact with each other and their adult helpers both from the college and elsewhere around the world. In addition to on-line discussions, students built models in the MUSE to represent the projects they were working on. For example, a group of students studying about rain forests created a virtual one on MariMUSE. The result was a "rain forest" MUD room with references to the many resident animals and plants. While much simpler than the rooms in the *Inferno* project (these younger students were simply not capable of the more advanced programming used by the college students), the MariMUSE students worked very hard on the project, and were actively engaged in learning about both the rain forest and computers.

Amy Bruckman, a leader in the design and use of professional and educational MUDs, visited the MariMUSE campus. The young students' difficulties with programming influenced her to begin constructing MOOSE Crossing, a MUD utilizing a simplified set of child-friendly programming commands. Bruckman's goal is to allow teachers and students to "see through" the technology to a certain extent; she contends that encouraging students to program in MUDs not only supports active learning in a general sense, but also provides the context and opportunities for children to learn more about computer science and technology.[7]

Difficulties in MUD-Based Education

In the above sections, I have explored several benefits of using MUDs in education, but no examination would be complete without also discussing MUDs' limitations and possible drawbacks. I freely admit that most MUDs are not magical or utopian places. The most notable difficulty teachers experience with MUDs is the new and different classroom dynamic the virtual environment creates. Many teachers describe on-line classwork as too chaotic, with students joking around or talking about off-task topics. A teacher cannot guide or control students the same way in a MUD he or she can in the traditional classroom, and at times this lack of control can certainly be unnerving. But at the same time MUDs encourage active learning; having students log in and then sit quietly would be somewhat self-defeating. Instead, teachers must come to accept a certain loss of traditional authority when bringing a class into a MUD, and then learn to manage classroom learning and interaction more through goal-setting than through concrete rules and set procedures. We can carefully define goals, tasks, and deadlines before students enter the MUD, and then play more of a "helper" role on-line as students work toward those goals in their own creative ways, finding their own order amidst apparent chaos. Granted, such student-directed learning is difficult to manage at times, but so are most student-centered pedagogies within our top-down educational system. More than anything else, MUD-based education requires time for careful preparation and planning, as does any new approach to teaching.

Part of the planning required for teaching in a MUD involves training students to access and use the virtual environment. This task may seem daunting at first, particularly if class plans involve the building—and programming—of MUD rooms and objects. The MUD's on-line help is eventually useful, but it often takes new users a while before such help screens are accessible and understandable. "Cheat sheets" of basic MUD commands can help students pick up MUDding quickly, as can plenty of individual help, from both people in the computer lab and those already in the MUD. In addition to learning commands, new users generally need time to adjust to MUD conversations; making the most of free-for-all discussion is an acquired skill. As with most elements of MUDding, however, these skills will come quickly with practice and support—and some patience and enthusiasm on the part of the teacher. Teachers exposing students to MUDs might consider getting help from experienced assistants for the first few visits: other teachers who use MUDs, volunteers from local colleges, and former MUD students. Recruiting such guides, however, does not absolve us teachers from acquiring extensive experience in MUDs ourselves. Any tasks we ask of the students should already be somewhat familiar to us. Then a support system of more experienced MUDders can help with any technical problems that may arise. Again, preparation and practice are the keys to successful use of MUDs in education, as are patience and an excitement about the potential of on-line work.

More Information on MUDding
The hardest part of writing this essay has been trying to add a sense of shelf life to such a dynamic new topic. I first logged into a MUD in the winter of 1993, and in the few years since then I've seen explosive growth in the professional and educational use of the medium. This field is so new and dynamic that a essay like this can serve only as an introductory guide and a framework for further explorations. If you are interested in using MUDs in your own teaching or professional work, I encourage you to read more on the topic and to contact those teachers who have already taught successfully in an on-line environment. Many of the resources listed below will provide information about finding MUDs and using them in your work. Technical questions about actually connecting to a MUD, however, are best answered at the local level; contact your local computer services personnel for assistance on those matters.

Because of the newness of the field, much of the current information about educational MUDs has not yet made its way to traditional print media, appearing instead at conferences and on the Internet. Rather than list several Internet addresses that will probably change over time, I encourage you to try several keyword searches of the World Wide Web: *MUD and education*; *MOO*; *OWL*; *MariMUSE*; *Diversity University*; *Netoric*; and *ACW*.[8] This last resource might be the most valuable: The Alliance for Computers and Writing (ACW) provides a clearinghouse for information about teaching with technology, including the educational uses of MUDs. The ACW World Wide Web site may be a key place to start your exploration of the exciting educational possibilities of MUDs.

Notes
1. MOO stands for MUD—Object-Oriented, MUSH for Multi-User Shared Hallucination, and MUSE for Multi-User Simulated Environment. While these MUD variations differ in their underlying programs and some surface commands, moving between them is relatively easy.

2. The Netoric Project offers various ways of learning more about the use of MUDs in education. Founded in 1993 to offer a series of MUD-based discussions and workshops on the use of computer technology in writing instruction, the Netoric Project is a valuable resource for meeting and working with teachers who already use MUDs in their own teaching and professional work. For information about the Netoric Project, do a keyword search of the World Wide Web for *Netoric.*

3. Daedalus InterChange is a locally networked program that allows for on-line chatting like that in MUDs, but only the conversation, not the rooms or objects. The English department at the University of Florida has developed its own MUD called "MOOville" for local use in writing classes. While many high schools and universities have purchased programs such as Daedalus InterChange, this department had the resources and personnel to create its own MUD for such uses.

4. Many MUDs can be programmed to control the dynamics of a conversation through the use of "moderating programs." In MUD rooms with such programming, participants must wait for a turn to speak or must be called on by a moderator. While such programs have their uses, they often seem contrary to the interactive nature of MUDs. In other words, if one wants the teacher-controlled dynamics of the traditional classroom, going to a MUD for that type of conversation is often self-defeating.

5. Of particular note here are such programs at the University of Arkansas at Little Rock, the University of Missouri at Columbia, the University of Michigan, and Purdue University. Such programs are often called OWLs, or On-line Writing Labs. A search of the World Wide Web for *OWL* should return information on such resources.

6. Diversity University MOO (DU) is a large educational MUD patterned after a college campus. DU is host to classes from a variety of disciplines, most of them on the college level. Many instructors on DU are active in assisting teachers new to MUDs in learning to use this medium in their courses. To obtain information about DU, do a keyword search of the World Wide Web for *Diversity University.*

7. A number of Bruckman's papers about MUDs, including the text of her dissertation proposal concerning MOOSE Crossing, are available on the Internet. For current locations of these documents, and for current information on MOOSE Crossing, do a keyword search of the World Wide Web for *Bruckman.*

8. Keyword searches of the World Wide Web are easy and effective ways of finding resources such as these. For an introduction to the World Wide Web, see Phyllis Geren's essay in this volume.

Bibliography

Barker, Thomas, and Fred Kemp. "Network Theory: A Postmodern Pedagogy for the Writing Classroom." *Computers and Community: Teaching Composition in the Twenty-First Century.* Ed. Carolyn Handa. Portsmouth, N.H.: Boynton/Cook, 1990.

Tharon W. Howard

Mapping the Minefield of Electronic Ethics

LIKE MANY EDUCATORS today, when I began using telecommunications in my writing classes back in 1988, I was initially attracted to the Internet by the claims that putting my students "on the Net" would democratize my classroom and significantly enhance the kind of student-centered pedagogies I thought I wanted to encourage. Citing Selfe and Meyers, Susan Romano has also observed that writing teachers are often drawn to the Net because of three pervasive claims that much of the early literature made about networked classrooms:

> 1) that computer-based exchanges may encourage egalitarian patterns of involvement; 2) that computer-based conferences may support alternate power structures by erasing socio-economic cues; and 3) that the anonymity provided by pseudonymous written exchanges further encourages egalitarian discourse patterns.[1]

Indeed, the openness of the Net and the impossibility of ever centralizing its "many-to-many conferencing systems" seemed to me at the time to encourage a polyphony so centripetal that it could never be dominated by any single group. "At last," I thought to myself, "here's an opportunity to empower my students with techno-literacy on an electronic publishing system that has built into its very architecture an anti-censorship and liberatory politics that even Thomas Paine would have found admirable."[2]

I didn't realize that teaching on-line would, in fact, frequently force me to play the very gatekeeper role I sought to avoid by taking my students into electronic environments in the first place. Like the growing number of teachers I see every day becoming "road kill" on the "Information Superhighway," I found myself under-prepared for the moral, legal, and ethical problems that I've encountered in my various roles as a teacher, network administrator, listowner, and webmaster. Even though I've never taken a computer science course, teaching on-line has meant that I've had to learn to wear all these different hats and, more specifically, it has meant dealing with issues connected to (and incidents of):

- hate messages and "flaming"
- libel
- sexual harassment
- erotic and pornographic materials on the Net
- copyright and intellectual property infringement
- "cyber-rape"
- electronic surveillance of students
- commercial uses of state-supported computing resources

Yet, despite the unpleasantness and anxiety these incidents created for me, I do not wish to discourage anyone from taking their students on-line. I continue to advocate the use of networked instructional technologies in writing classrooms. I know of no superior method of teaching students that writing is a meaningful and public act of communication that has communal consequence both for writers and readers. Teaching on the Net means helping students see that knowledge isn't just a collection of pre-existing facts but rather the product of collaborative learning, and that writing is fundamental to the process. So rather than discouraging other educators, I hope to encourage the use of networked classrooms by helping teachers avoid the ad hoc and often painful approach I had to take to arrive at administrative policies and curricular designs that will protect my school, my colleagues, and my students from becoming "road kill" on the Net. Or to switch metaphors, my goal is to provide teachers with a map that will help them negotiate the minefield of electronic ethics by outlining potential problems to avoid and by describing some of the specific "bombs" my students and I have exploded when we blindly stomped through cyberspace.

Netiquette

Of all the different types of problems teachers may encounter when they take their students into wide-area networking systems (or "WANS"), perhaps the most frequently encountered and persistent problems result from students violating network etiquette ("netiquette"). Although people who've never experienced WANS, such as the Internet, commonly believe that e-mail messages are merely the same sorts of letters you might send to a friend via the postal service, public e-mail messages in an on-line conference actually represent an altogether different genre, with different standards of propriety.

E-mail messages exchanged between friends on an electronic discussion group or conference differ radically from letters between traditional pen-pals, and these differences are largely due to differences between the media. For example, e-mail messages are usually read from a screen which displays one-third the text found on a 8 1/2" x 11" page, and often "e-readers" can't scroll back and forth between passages the way someone reading a letter can flip back to a previous page. As a result, the convention for e-mail messages is that they are much shorter, much more direct, and limited to one or two topics. Indeed, many networkers consider it rude to send long e-mail messages. Also, since electronic networks allow people to send a message and receive replies within seconds, e-mail messages are more oral in tone and register than are traditional letters—which partly explains why networkers describe public exchanges on-line as having a "conversation" in a "conference." However, perhaps the most significant differences between e-mail and "snail mail" are due to the fact that, despite all the tremendous computing power of WANS, a writer can do more with page design, formatting, and visual appeal on an typewriter than on most WAN e-mail systems. To overcome this limitation, networkers have developed some fairly elaborate conventions, conventions which over the years have become codified into "netiquette."

Most "netiquette" issues that students encounter on-line have little to do with ethics. I've had a number of students, for example, receive severe rebukes from people on a conference because the students posted messages in capital letters. In netiquette terms, an entire message in uppercase is considered "SHOUTING" and is guaranteed to generate a stream of angry responses. This isn't really an ethical issue, though it might be argued that teachers who fail to teach students some basic netiquette before allowing them on the Net are actually harming their students by leaving them vulnerable to the often vociferous and cruel messages networkers send in response to perceived netiquette violations. There are, however, several netiquette conventions that unfortunately are closely connected with ethical behavior.

"Flaming" & Hate Messages

"Flaming" is a term networkers use to describe the practice of sending an acrimonious and scathing attack to a specific individual, and a "flame war" is the public back-and-forth exchange of flames. Generally speaking, flaming is the electronic equivalent of taking a punch at someone, and it usually entails *ad hominems* that are frequently profane. Unfortunately, flaming is one behavior that students are probably going to encounter. In fact, since a high percentage of flames result from some minor netiquette infraction like SHOUTING, students are particularly vulnerable if they are electronic writers.

Students may also encounter hate messages. The Internet has an international population of over thirty million people, and any group that size is bound to have some individuals given to racial prejudices or social bigotry. It's unlikely that a teacher can prevent students from reading hate messages if the students are actively searching the Net on their own. Fortunately, my students rarely report encountering hate messages on the Net since I keep them busy working in discussion groups that either I have created and control or which I know from experience to be relatively free of hate messages. Nevertheless, about the best a teacher can hope for is to alert students to the dangers of hate messages and flame wars; in fact, good teachers can actually use flaming as an opportunity to teach students about audience awareness and the difference between critiquing ideas and attacking people.

Still, though flaming and hate messages are disruptive and ugly, most educators and network administrators regard them as relatively minor problems, and—as long as the teacher or administrator has a formal, stated policy—they can usually be handled pretty much like any other classroom disciplinary problem. However, teachers and administrators should be aware that flaming can escalate into something far more serious when it moves into the realm of libel.

Libel

Libel, as any lawyer can testify, is extremely difficult to define legally and prove, and it's even more difficult to differentiate between flaming and libel than it is between a flame war and a passionately argued debate. What's more, the question of who may be held legally responsible for libelous e-mail messages is complicated by the fact that electronic publishing media don't fit into current legal categories regarding libel. In practice on the Net, the main distinction between flaming and libel seems to be that a flame is an angry, peevish response to a previous message that is addressed directly to its author, and has about as much effect as a child's temper tantrum. Libel, on the other hand, is a calculated attempt to damage someone's reputation. It's unlikely, however, that this distinction would hold up in a court of law, and it may be that the only way to differentiate between the two is whether or not the person being flamed decides to sue. However, I've experienced several situations in which students have taken advantage of their access to the Net in order to publish libelous messages, and an examination of these might help clarify why this is an area educators must address.

In these situations, the students sending the messages felt that they had been wronged by their schools' faculty and administration. The initial problem was that the students had been evaluated, were judged to be below standard, and experienced negative consequences. The students, frustrated by their inability to get school administrators to reverse the decisions, lashed out at the faculty and administration by making their cases public on the Net. They sent e-mail messages to the professional e-mail conferences where the messages would do the most serious damage possible, naming specific individuals and accusing them of unprofessional, unethical, illegal, or immoral behavior.

For the slandered faculty and administrators, it may seem that the course of action to take is obvious—simply to deny the student access to the Internet through the institution's system. However, in two of these situations, the students weren't sending the mail from the institutions' systems; they had already found access methods through alternative channels. Furthermore, eliminating a student's access privileges is a fairly extreme measure. In many of the courses I teach, for example, taking away a student's access would be equivalent to preventing that student from participating in the course, so that either I would have to fail the student or go to the trouble of developing an entirely new, independent study for that student. In some cases, denying a student access might actually be equivalent to expulsion since, in computer science and engineering programs, for example, it's simply impossible to complete the program without computing resources. Clearly, therefore, denying students access to computers is a drastic solution, and one that will often produce infuriated parents and may even get the institution involved in costly litigation.

Given that it's not always possible or desirable to remove a student from the local computing system, an alternative might be to contact the people who maintain the discussion group (or "list," as such groups are called) in question and request that they bar the student from sending additional messages. Like other teachers on the Net, I often serve as a "listowner" (the person responsible for maintaining an electronic discussion group). One of the lists I created and maintained on my school's computer was populated by several hundred composition teachers and graduate students in rhetoric, and it was to this list that two students, on different occasions, began sending slanderous messages about their faculty and schools.

Again, the seemingly obvious solution of barring the students from the list was far from simple since I had no formal policy for such situations. If I removed the students from the list as requested, then I might be violating the students' rights and open myself and my school to litigation. In fact, the *Chronicle of Higher Education* reported that, on the SWIP-L or "Society for Women in Philosophy List," one SWIP-L member threatened to sue the listowner and the university that supports the list if he was removed, arguing that there was nothing in the list's policies that prohibited his participation in that public forum.[3]

Since both the individuals had a history of litigious behavior, and since it seemed unethical to silence voices of dissent simply because people didn't want to hear what they had to say, removing them from the list didn't seem like a good option. On the other hand, not taking such action seemed equally problematic, since it wasn't—and still isn't—clear whether or not listowners can be held legally accountable for libelous messages published on their lists. Lance Rose, a legal expert on network issues, has suggested that just as newspaper editors may be held accountable for articles in their papers, under some circumstances listowners may be likewise liable for the messages distributed on their lists.[4] In fact, for example, the commercial service CompuServe was sued in 1991 for libelous messages distributed on public areas in its system.[5] Also, in addition to the legal issues involved, not taking some action meant ignoring whatever moral and ethical responsibilities I, as a teaching professional, might have had to the colleagues being attacked. In short, I was caught between the horns of a cruel dilemma which, no matter what actions I did or did not take, could have put both myself and my school at risk. As a result of these experiences, for each new list or conference that I've created I now post formal policies that make perfectly clear that violation may lead to expulsion from the list.

Sexual Harassment

Most teachers teach their students to avoid sexist language in their writing, and have effective techniques for dealing with students who sexually harass other students. I've rarely had to deal with students who used their network access to sexually harass someone else, and when I have, the administration's existing policies work well. More perplexing difficulties are those situations in which students are harassed by someone outside of local sites.

I had one student who constantly received sexually explicit and harassing messages because of her e-mail address. Like many other systems on the Net, our site automatically assigns people user ids for their personal e-mail accounts by using a combination of an individual's first and last name. In this case, the computer generated "LOVEALL" for this unfortunate and unsuspecting young woman. Initially, she didn't have any trouble; her outgoing e-mail messages were mainly to in-class discussions at our site, but as she gained confidence and began participating in network-wide computer conferences, she began receiving an increasing number of unsolicited personal e-mail messages from individuals as far away as Australia, Nova Scotia, and Japan. In many of these messages, she was often only asked about such things as her major, her interests, her age, and, in fact, until she began to recognize that she was "being hit on," she actually tried to engage in conversations with many of the people who contacted her. Once she realized what was happening, however, the situation made her very uncomfortable. In this case, the simple solution was to change her user id to something less suggestive, and since then, I've been careful to monitor my students' user ids for potentially risqué connotations. More importantly, however, this experience reinforced the importance of alerting students to how they can become victims of their own innocence and blind trust in others.

In another case, I had a student complain when she began receiving messages asking questions about what positions she preferred during sexual intercourse and was told about the sexual fantasies of the author of the message. We could determine no reason why she had been targeted, except that she remembered sending messages to discussion groups which may have revealed that she was female. And in another case, a student of mine was embarrassed when an ex-suitor sent an e-mail message to a list received by all her peers. In his message, he recommended that all the male students take notice of her since she was "such a hot babe."

In cases like these, there are five courses of action. The first and most obvious is to send a message directly to the offender threatening legal action if the abuse doesn't stop, warning that federal statutes make obscene and harassing communication subject to criminal prosecution. A second course of action is to send a message to the "postmaster" at the user's local site. There's an old convention on the Net that allows networkers to contact network administrators for a particular site by addressing an e-mail message to POSTMASTER@NODE.DOMAIN. So if you were receiving abusive mail from some user whose e-mail address ended (heaven forbid!) in CLEMSON.EDU, then you could send a message to POSTMASTER@CLEMSON.EDU, and your message would probably reach a network administrator who could address the problem. Unfortunately, not all sites on the Net have administrators who are aware of network conventions, so if the POSTMASTER (or sometimes POST-MAN) trick doesn't work, a third tactic is to look up the address for the site at a NIC or "Network Information Center." Many sites are registered with NICs. If your site supports it, you can connect to a NIC, search the database for the site address you want, and usually get the e-mail address for the system administrator at that site. (The exact way you go about connecting to a NIC varies from site to site, so the first time you try it, you'll probably need to contact your local system administrator for assistance.) If this doesn't work, a fourth alternative is to look up the site in Tracy LaQuey's (1990) book *The User's Directory of Computer Networks*. This is usually one of my last options since any book on networks is going to be dated before it's printed. Still, LaQuey's book is as close to a "telephone directory" of administrators at sites around the Internet as anything I've seen. Finally, as a last resort you can contact your local system administrator and ask him or her to resolve the problem. I dislike this approach because my students want as few outsiders involved in the situation as possible; however, you may find yourself with no other option.

There is one last point about tracking down the authors of abusive messages: you should know that, often times, you just plain can't. For one thing, an offender can simply claim that someone must have used his or her account. Also, even if you could identify the person responsible, they may be in a country where the laws and attitudes regarding such issues may differ dramatically. Finally, there are several "anonymous remailers" available that make it virtually impossible to trace a message back to its origins.[6] As the term suggests, "anonymous remailers" are systems which take the original message, strip out addressing and routing information in the header, and then remail it with pseudonyms in place of the original names and addresses. The most famous and popular of the anonymous remailers are the Finnish ANON.PENET.FI and Berkeley's SODA.CSUA.BERKELEY.EDU, and if you receive abusive messages which have been redistributed from these addresses, there's almost nothing you can do to trace a message back to its author. About the best you can do is to get your students' addresses changed.

Erotic and Pornographic Materials

Sexually explicit, erotic, and pornographic materials can indeed be found on the Net. Someone with unlimited access to the Internet and a knowledge of tools such as UUDECODE, BINHEX, and ftp can obtain images of nude bodies as easily as from the top racks of magazines at a convenience store. The problem is, of course, when students get copies of *Playgirl* or *Penthouse* from the convenience store, it's the store's problem; when they get images off the Net, they're usually doing it on the school's computer network which, like it or not, makes it our problem. In fact, our congressional leaders, ignorant about the ways WANS operate yet determined to make a political statement by wiping out network "filth," have progressively made schools legally more and more responsible for pornographic materials which may pass through their systems. Ironically, the "Exon Amendment" or the Communications Decency Act of 1995—supposed to make the Net safer for students—may actually make the Net so costly and dangerous for schools that students and educators will not be able to get connected to the Net in the first place.

What makes pornography on the Net so difficult to control is that there is no single, centralized system behind the Net, and in fact, what I've been calling "the Net" really doesn't even exist. Terms like "the Net," the "matrix,"[7] or the "Information Superhighway" are only convenient metaphors which are used to describe an amorphous and dynamic connectivity between thousands of small subnetworks that are usually themselves composed of even smaller subnetworks. These various subnets maintain their own historical, administrative, and economic identities. The Internet, for example, operates in an entirely different fashion than does the USENET. Yet, because the two "speak a common language," they may be linked so transparently that many Internet users have never heard of the USENET, in spite of the fact that they may connect to it every day to read "newsgroups" like misc.headlines or the famous alt.sex.

The reason for this seemingly chaotic architecture is due, at least in part, to the fact that progenitors of the current Internet (DARPANET and ARPANET) originally used for Department of Defense research were developed in the 1960s and 70s, and were designed to survive a thermonuclear attack.[8] Thus, instead of having a single centralized command and control center that could be knocked out by a single warhead, the network was designed around diverse and distributed "routers," individual computers which sat at various points on the network and, in a sense, "learned" how best to route information around the system because they "told each other" about the network conditions around them. Thus huge holes might be blown in the network, but the routers would "know about them" and simply go around the holes. It also turns out that what works with thermonuclear devices works just as well with at-tempts to censor pornography; the Net's architecture just flows around the censorship.

If you're an authoritarian-minded senator bent on eradicating "inde-cency," the Net is going to drive you crazy. You might be able to write a little legislative "bomb" that will take out pieces of the Net under your direct control, but the rest of the Net will simply go around your little bomb and keep delivering files to the networkers who request them. Since you can't control the Net itself, you could try to maintain control by terrorizing the system administrators who oversee user access to the Net. And unfortunately for educators, this seems to be precisely the direction in which both Congress and the Justice Department are heading.

At the time this piece was written, Congress was in the process of considering the Communications Decency Act, better known as the "Exon Amendment." An early draft of the legislation provides that anyone who "makes, transmits, or otherwise makes available any comment, request, suggestion, proposal, image, or other communication which is obscene, lewd, lascivious, filthy, or indecent," and anyone who "knowingly per-mits any telecommunications facility under his [sic] control to be used" in such a manner "shall be fined not more than $100,000 or imprisoned not more than two years, or both." The proposed amendment goes on to say that network service providers ("carriers") may avoid prosecution under this proposed legislation if a "carrier demonstrates" that action "was taken in good faith to restrict access" which would prevent such activity (47 U.S.C. 223 as amended by S. 314).

The logic here is simple: since the government can't effectively con-trol the Net or its users, it will pressure system administrators into be-coming e-mail spies and network police. In other words, as a system administrator, in order to avoid prosecution I have to make a "good faith effort" to ensure that "indecent" content neither enters nor leaves my system. This would mean that I'll have to take time away from the classes I teach, my research, and my on-line duties. It would also mean addi-tional funding for the additional time and trouble involved. The addi-tional costs involved, the potential threat of criminal prosecution, and the privacy and free speech concerns raised by this federally mandated police action will, no doubt, deter a number of schools from getting con-nected to the Internet. It's already difficult enough to convince school administrators that the costs of connecting students to the Net are justifi-able. This will only make our jobs that much harder. For those schools that are already connected, or which will be able to get connected, here are some "hot spots" that young students ought to avoid.

USENET Newsgroups to Avoid

As mentioned earlier, the USENET (or merely "news," as it is often called) is a volunteer network accessible through the Internet. But instead of e-mail messages, USENET users submit "articles." Rather than being delivered to an individual's account directly, USENET articles are "posted" to a pre-existing "newsgroup," i.e., a place where articles dealing with roughly the same topic are collected together. Users browse the articles collected in a newsgroup. Since USENET's newsgroups aren't sent directly to individual users, but are stored in a central location on a system, it's easy for an administrator to control which newsgroups are accessible at a local level.

Many newsgroups are extremely useful to students and can truly enrich the writing classroom. I have, for example, had students read articles from a newsgroup called misc.headlines that describes newsworthy current events from all over the world. In order to help students understand biases in the media, for example, I asked students to compare the way the Panama invasion was reported on American television with the way it was described in other countries by using misc.headlines. As a result, students learned a great deal about the role nationality plays in interpreting the world around us.

But just as the international forum of USENET produces some useful newsgroups, it also produces sexually explicit and pornographic material. Groups like soc.couples, soc.singles, alt.sex, alt.sex.bondage, alt.sex.bestiality, and a whole host of other alt.sex groups specializing in various fetishes, contain highly explicit discussions. Also, X-rated images and video clips are available in groups like alt.binaries.pictures.erotica and alt.binaries.multimedia.erotica. Accessing these images and videos is difficult because it often requires an understanding of various image formats, shell scripts, and file conversions; however, once students locate the help files that describe how to display these images, they will be able to view uncensored images of sodomy, sado-masochism, child porn, and so on. Obviously, if you decide to have your students explore USENET, some care must be taken to ensure that these newsgroups are not stored on a school's local system.

World Wide Web Sites to Avoid

The "World Wide Web," "WWW," or simply "the Web," as it is sometimes called, is an electronic publishing system on the Internet that allows
networkers to view text in different fonts, images, audio clips, and video
clips. (For an introduction to the Web, see Phyllis Geren's essay in this
book.) The simplicity of the Web finally gives educators a resource that
breaks down the walls of their classrooms and puts their students in touch
with information resources around the world. However, simplicity and
access once again have a price, for just as students may access great libraries and museums through the Web, they may also access sites some
may find more controversial. In addition to reputable publishing houses,
Playboy and *Penthouse* have established an early presence on the Web,
and (at least at the time this article was written) both *Playboy* and *Penthouse* allow anyone accessing their Web pages to view nude photographs.
So unlike the local convenience store, students don't even have to sneak
past a sales clerk to gain access to these publications. They only need to
know the correct addresses (URLs), and those are easily discovered.

Unfortunately, shutting off access to a particular site isn't nearly so
easy as preventing a particular USENET newsgroup from being delivered
to your local system. In fact, in several of the schools I've visited, network
administrators simply deny their users Web access because the administrators don't know how to prevent students from accessing sexually explicit sites. This cut-off-your-nose-to-spite-your-face approach seems
rather crude. A far more elegant (though time-consuming) approach is:
1) to identify sites with potentially offensive material; 2) to determine if
the material is unacceptable for users at your site (clearly, the most difficult part of the process); and 3) to "deliberately break your network" so
users can't reach that particular site.[9] Basically, the way a network administrator can "break the network" is by editing a file known as the
"routing table." On a network, when Computer A wants to "talk" to
Computer B, the first thing it has to do is to look up the address for
Computer B in the network's routing table—roughly analogous to looking up a number in a telephone book. If someone has tampered with your
phonebook and changed the phone number for the specific person you
wanted to call, then you're obviously not going to get through to that
person. The same pertains for computers on a network. If the network
address for, say, *Playboy* were changed in the routing table to a non-existent network address, then every time a user on the network tried to connect to *Playboy*, the request for a connection would be routed nowhere.

However, as Mike Marshall, one of the longtime system administrators at my site, has warned me, this technique of sabotaging your own network is pretty dramatic and may produce unexpected consequences—for instance, losing access to the information on First Amendment rights on the Net which is stored at the *Playboy* address.

IRC Channels

The final, major area where my students have complained about encountering sexually explicit materials on the Net are various Internet services that allow networkers to participate in real-time, synchronous communications. Of these, perhaps the most difficult to control is IRC or "Internet Relay Chat."

Often called the "CB radio of the Internet," IRC allows networkers to connect to "channels" where they can exchange short, usually one-line comments with others simultaneously connected to the same channel. Text any one person transmits to the channel appears almost immediately on the screens of everyone else, and since messages are exchanged in real time, the results of an IRC dialogue end up looking something like a transcript of a CB radio conversation. Unlike CB radio, however, there are no limits on the range of the transmission or the number of channels available. IRC users "talk" in real time to people all over the world, and any user can create a channel on any topic of interest to him or her. It's this constant opening and closing of channels that makes it so easy for students (or anyone else for that matter) to stumble into sexually explicit conversations and that also makes IRC so difficult for system administrators to control. The transitory nature of IRC channels makes it impossible for teachers and/or system administrators to prevent students from encountering potentially offensive material. Yet, the outraged parents and potential legal consequences that may result from not taking any action are quite ugly. Educators are left with a choice between shutting down all IRC access or ignoring the potential consequences. Indeed, it takes an administration with a strong commitment to First Amendment rights to keep a school from deciding to prohibit all IRC connections.

Intellectual Property

Networks are of course designed to share rather than to protect information; the whole point of a network is to make data accessible to anyone who wants it, regardless of whether or not that person ought to have access to it. As a result, network technologies tend to work against existing laws written for a society that depended on print as the primary medium for exchanging intellectual property.[10] Consequently, until our legal system catches up with new networking technologies, students and educators must realize that it's easy to violate intellectual property laws. Three areas where I've seen my students and colleagues encounter the most difficulty are "cyber-rape," Web graphics, and "wareZ ftp sites."

Cyber-Rape

"Cyber-Rape" initially referred to the practice of reproducing someone's private, intimate communications in another medium or forum. A cyber-rapist would engage an individual in an intimate conversation, keep an electronic log of the conversation, and then reproduce it on a professional, public e-mail discussion group where it would embarrass the victim and/or seriously harm his or her professional status. Initially, the term cyber-rape was only applied to sexually revealing conversations, but over time it has come to be used for almost any situation where an author's comments are taken out of context and used in another forum. Thus, although cyber-rape started out as an invasion of privacy issue, it has since evolved into an intellectual property concern, and it is in this area where I've seen it become a problem for teachers and students. Much of the problem with intellectual property and copyright violations on the Internet has to do with the ease with which networkers can forward a copy of an electronic message. On almost every communications software package in use today, forwarding a copy of another person's message is simply a matter of pressing the "f" key and typing in an e-mail address. The process is so deceptively simple that many people never consider taking the time to ask if, by forwarding the message without permission, they might be infringing on the original author's copyright.

The problem is further compounded by the fact that different discussion groups can have radically different policies regarding the use of e-mail messages on the group or "list." On a few lists, "messages" sent to the list have the same copyright status as articles published in magazines, and in fact, the lists have registered ISSN numbers, just like magazines. For example, John Unsworth's *Journal of Postmodern Culture* list (PMC-L) actually has an editorial review board and all the other mechanisms found in traditional scholarly print publications. Other lists impose restrictions on the ways messages may be used; for example, UTEST, a list I oversee, is intended to be a "safe space" where professionals in the evaluation field can share anecdotal information and try out new, sometimes inchoate ideas. UTEST's messages may not be forwarded, archived, or redistributed outside the UTEST list. The copyrights on UTEST's messages are owned by the authors, and there are clear limitations imposed on the messages to ensure that the authors' copyrights will not be violated. But lists like PMC-L and UTEST are exceptions; the vast majority of lists have no clearly articulated intellectual property policy, or a listowner will state that original authors of messages retain ownership of their copyrights even though the messages are publicly distributed by the list and may even be stored in the list's archives.

Students can run into two difficulties here. First, if they get on a list like UTEST and forward its messages to other more public groups, they are not only violating the list's policies, they may also seriously affect someone's career. For example, forwarding a copy of an unpublished article can damage the author's chances of getting the piece published. A more common problem, however, is when students write papers using ideas and quoting text from e-mail messages without giving credit to the original authors. Students often tell me that they assumed that because the messages were "just out there for anybody to read," they could use them without citations. Or they admit that they just didn't bother to cite the original authors because they didn't know how to include an e-mail message in their list of "Works Cited." Thus, in addition to the normal instruction I provide my students regarding plagiarism, I also now add a unit on the appropriate use and citation of e-mail messages.

WWW Graphics

The number of students I've seen struggling with intellectual property issues involving text pales in comparison to the number of times I've seen students "ripping off" World Wide Web graphics to use on their own home pages. Again, the pervasive attitude seems to be "if it's out there and I can get it, then it must be okay."

Of course, this attitude is wrong; photographs and artwork are also subject to copyright and may not be reproduced simply because they are available.[11] However, unlike the copyrights on verbal texts, this has been an extremely difficult point to get across to students. Even though we discuss this issue in class, my students continue to download graphics from archives on the Net when they find images they want. In many cases, they don't consider that someone may have illegally scanned a piece of artwork from a book and stored it in the archive. Even if they do take this into consideration, they mistakenly assume that the person who first scanned the artwork was the only one accountable, and don't realize that they and their institution are equally liable.

The threat of litigation is causing many institutions to take this problem more seriously. At my school, I serve on a Web Task Force that is attempting to find solutions to this problem. An obvious solution we considered was the creation of a Web "police force" that would review Web pages to ensure that they didn't violate copyrights. However, while this may be possible at a smaller institution, the size of our school made this option too expensive, for there are literally thousands of constantly changing Web pages stored on a variety of machines at our site. As a result, we have taken an alternative tack. First, we are creating an approved graphics archive for our users, which will allow them to obtain high-quality photos and artwork without violating copyrights. Second, we have begun a campus-wide education campaign that we hope will sensitize our users to this problem. And third, we have begun creating Web page templates for our users to encourage them to follow standardized page designs and to avoid graphic archives with illegal reproductions.

These three initiatives will not entirely eliminate copyright violations on our system, but it's far more cost-effective than hiring a full-time "police force." Also, it's the sort of "good faith" effort that we hope will protect us from costly litigation.

"wareZ" ftp Sites

Among the services that attract large numbers of people to the Internet are the shareware and public domain software archives it makes available. Using the Internet's "file transfer protocol" or "ftp" utility, networkers have legal access to gigabytes of inexpensive or free software. Unfortunately, the same network tools that are used to make this software available are also used by a black-market underground of software pirates to make stolen software available on the Net.

Essentially, what these software pirates do is download copies of popular commercial software packages, such as Microsoft Word, WordPerfect, or PageMaker, to an ftp site. Anyone who knows where the files are stored may obtain a copy of the software without having to pay the manufacturer. Because IRC channels are so difficult to monitor, the software pirates connect to them and, using a special counter-culture language all their own, they share information that explains how to access the pirated software, or "wareZ."[12]

Students who learn of a wareZ ftp site and download its contents to the school's computer—or, worse yet, create a wareZ ftp site on the school's system—are creating a very serious problem for the school and themselves. The software industry loses millions of dollars each year to piracy, so vendors are thus predisposed to prosecute individuals and institutions that allow large numbers of people to steal their property. Network administrators must, therefore, constantly monitor their sites for wareZ, and students with ftp access need to understand that, even though wareZ have in a sense already been stolen from a company, copying wareZ from an ftp site is also considered stealing and subject to prosecution.

Commercial Uses of Tax-Supported Computing Resources

When most people think of computers and ethics, the first problem they usually think of is "hacking," the inappropriate access of secure databases. Movies like *Wargames* have sensitized us to the problem of hacking someone's system and to the fallacy that roughly goes, "If I can access it, then it must be okay." However, I've only had one student get in trouble for hacking. Most students know when they are hacking, and most school administrations know how to deal with it. There are, however, less obvious areas where "unethical computing" has been a problem for me and my students.

The Internet is often described as the most important advance in publishing since the invention of the printing press. In theory, anyone who can send an e-mail message or create a Web page can potentially reach an international readership estimated at thirty-five million people, and this number is growing. This kind of connectivity and advertising potential has attracted a large number of commercial companies, all seeking ways to reap new profits. It should come as no surprise, therefore, that a few of my students have also found ways to turn the Internet accounts the school provides them to financial gain. In one case, an individual used his access to the Net to create an ad hoc mail-order company selling his artwork. In another case, a student used his Web pages in order to put together advertisements for a local rock band. In a third case, a student approached our Web Task Force with the idea of creating Web pages for the town of Clemson's local businesses and storing them on the university's system. Like the rock band's friend, she didn't expect to profit personally from these pages; she just wanted to do a research study on the commercial potential of the Web.

Each of these is an example of a situation in which students can turn a school's instructional computing resources to commercial ends, putting the school at odds with local businesses. For example, even though neither the university nor the student stood to profit from putting up Web pages of local businesses in the area, there are a number of Internet service providers who stood to lose money. These companies currently charge other businesses between $80 and $90 per hour to design Web pages and another $50 per month per megabyte to store and maintain the pages on their systems. If they had learned that their tax dollars had gone to support Clemson's instructional computing network and that that network was then being used to provide the same services they were trying to sell to their clients, they would obviously have had a grievance with the school. Thus, as the Internet begins to break down the walls that divide our classrooms from "the real world," teachers and administrators need to be aware of these sorts of potential problems and develop policies which prevent instructional computing resources from being used for alternative purposes.

Privacy/Electronic Surveillance
The last "bomb" I wish to discuss deals with how teachers and administrators monitor network use at a site. Given the number of ways I've shown that things can go wrong, I fear that it would be too easy to conclude that students' network activities should be constantly policed and that teachers and/or system administrators might decide to routinely use their superuser privileges to read individuals' e-mail messages and files. As more and more laws and lawsuits are targeted at system administrators rather than users, I'm concerned that our commitment to free speech and an individual's right to privacy will falter. Importantly, the abuse of what Joseph Janangelo calls "technopower" and the creation of "technoppression" by educators may just as easily put a school at risk of litigation and parental complaints.[13]

One of the questions I am often asked as a system administrator is: How much access do I, with my superuser privileges, have to people's personal messages and files? The answer is that there are a number of log, accounting, and archive files that make it possible for a system administrator to recover virtually every keystroke a user types. On the UNIX systems I maintain, for example, I could create a shell script to check every e-mail message on the system for specific words, such as "sex," "wareZ," or "fuck." Furthermore, by changing the command to delete a file so that it actually only moves the file to a hidden directory which only

I can access, I could even go so far as to configure a system so that users couldn't even delete those files and messages they didn't want me to see.

As I hope this makes clear, administrators can configure a system so that virtually no activity escapes their surveillance (though I hasten to add that personally I have never done so). However, although a system can be configured so that its users are subject to constant, inescapable scrutiny, we still must ask whether it *should* be so configured. How would we, as teachers, feel if we learned that administrators at our school had been receiving routine reports on how much time we spent "doing our jobs" by sending e-mail messages to our students or how much time we "wasted" using MUDs? How would we respond if this type of information had been secretly collected by some of our colleagues and was then used to build a case for dismissing a teacher they didn't like or respect— a situation which Janangelo reported to have happened?[14]

Obviously, most of us would consider this kind of administrative surveillance intolerable, and in fact, the Senate sought to make it illegal in the 1993 Privacy for Consumers and Workers Bill, which ruled that no employer could subject employees to constant and secret electronic surveillance in the workplace. Also, the Privacy Act of 1974 provides that agencies shall "maintain no record describing how any individual exercises rights guaranteed by the First Amendment unless expressly authorized by statute or by the individual about whom the record is maintained or unless pertinent to and within the scope of an authorized law enforcement activity."[15] In addition to these federal laws, several states also have enacted legislation which makes it "a crime for a person or company to eavesdrop or record confidential communication without the consent of both the sender and receiver."[16] Thus, computer users *do* have a right to expect that their messages will remain private and that their First Amendment rights are not violated by despotic system administrators. Administrators and teachers do, of course, need to have some means for debugging problems and maintaining the security of their networks; however, a school's policy on these matters must recognize that students have a right to know what kind of data is being collected, and how that data will—and will not—be used.

Conclusion

Despite the problems and "horror stories" I have focused on here, my goal in this essay is to encourage rather than to discourage more teachers and students to use the Net. All too often, I work with teachers who, like me, were forced to become network administrators for their schools or departments because there was no one else willing, or because the principal pointed at them and said, "You're going to be our technology person." And too often, these teachers and their colleagues have become disillusioned with the Net because they blundered into one of the "bombs" I describe here. I hope that by providing at least a partial map of the mines out there, teachers and administrators will see that it is possible to defuse or to avoid these trouble spots. The Net can be a dangerous place, but the risks can be reduced with careful research, reasonable security systems, sound and clearly articulated policies, and user training. And the benefits both for the teachers and their students certainly make it worth the effort.

Notes

1. Susan Romano, "The Egalitarianism Narrative: Whose Story? Which Yardstick?" *Computers and Composition* 10 (1993), p. 6.

2. J. Katz, "The Age of Paine." *Wired* (May, 1995), pp. 154–158, 210–214.

3. Tom DeLoughry, "Gatekeeping on the Internet." *Chronicle of Higher Education* (Nov. 23, 1994), p. A21.

4. Lance Rose, "The CompuServe Case—A Federal Court Recognizes Sysop Rights." *Boardwatch* (December, 1991), p. 30.

5. Ibid.

6. Hahn, H. and W. Murdock. "Net.imperative: Anonymity." *Boardwatch* (May, 1995), pp. 66–69.

7. John Quarterman, *The Matrix: Computer Networks and Conferencing Systems Worldwide* (Bedford, Mass.: Digital Press, 1990).

8. Howard Rheingold, *The Virtual Community: Homesteading on the Electronic Frontier* (Reading, Mass.: Addison-Wesley, 1993), p. 74.

9. Mike Marshall, June 15, 1995. Telephone interview.

10. Tharon Howard, "Who 'Owns' Electronic Texts?" *Electronic Literacy: Computers in the Workplace* (Urbana, IL: NCTE, forthcoming).

11. Ibid.

12. Marshall, *op. cit.*

13. Joseph Janangelo, "Technopower and Technoppression: Some Abuses of Power and Control in Computer-assisted Writing Environments." *Computers and Composition* 9.1 (1991), pp. 47–64.

14. Ibid.

15. Privacy Act of 1974, 5 USC Sec. 552a (1974).

16. Deborah Branscum, "Ethics, E-mail, and the Law: When Legal Ain't Necessarily Right." *MacWorld* (March, 1991), pp. 63.

Bibliography

Branscum, Deborah. "Ethics, E-mail, and the Law: When Legal Ain't Necessarily Right." *MacWorld* (March, 1991), pp. 63, 66–70, 72, 83.

Communications Decency Act of 1995, S. 314, 104th Cong., 1st Session, 1995.

DeLoughry, Tom. "Gatekeeping on the Internet." *Chronicle of Higher Education* (Nov. 23, 1994), A21–22.

Hahn, H. and W. Murdock. "Net.imperative: Anonymity." *Boardwatch* (May, pp. 66–69.

Howard, Tharon. "Who 'Owns' Electronic Texts?" *Electronic Literacy: Computers in the Workplace*. Urbana, IL: NCTE, forthcoming.

Janangelo, Joseph. "Technopower and Technoppression: Some Abuses of Power and Control in Computer-assisted Writing Environments." *Computers and Composition* 9.1 (1991), pp. 47–64.

Katz, J. "The Age of Paine." *Wired* (May, 1995), pp. 154–158, 210–214.

LaQuey, Tracy. *The User's Directory of Computer Networks*. Bedford, Mass.: Digital Press, 1990.

Marshall, Mike. June 15, 1995. Telephone interview.

Privacy Act of 1974, 5 USC Sec. 552a (1974).

Privacy for Consumers and Workers Act, S. 984, 103d Cong., 2nd Session, 1993.

Quarterman, John. *The Matrix: Computer Networks and Conferencing Systems Worldwide*. Bedford, Mass.: Digital Press, 1990.

Rheingold, Howard. *The Virtual Community: Homesteading on the Electronic Frontier*. Reading, Mass.: Addison-Wesley, 1993.

Rickard, Jack. "Communications Decency Act Passes Senate Commerce Committee." *Boardwatch* (May, 1995), p. 67–70.

———. "*Playboy* and *Penthouse* Bare All on the Web," *Boardwatch* (May, 1995), p. 42.

Romano, Susan. "The Egalitarianism Narrative: Whose Story? Which Yardstick?" *Computers and Composition* 10 (1993), pp. 5–28.

Rose, Lance. "The CompuServe Case—A Federal Court Recognizes Sysop Rights." *Boardwatch* (December, 1991), p. 30.

Selfe, Cynthia and P. Meyer. "Testing Claims for On-line Conferences." *Written Communication* 8 (1991), pp. 163–192.

Beverly Paeth

Writing Conferences and My Chapter 1 Students

Holmes Jr. High is located in Covington, a town of approximately 50,000 residents, located on the banks of the Ohio River in northern Kentucky. It is part of metropolitan Cincinnati, with all the problems of a big city: poverty, drugs, teen-age pregnancies, crime, and violence.

Packets. Read the "story," then proceed to answer a multitude of questions. Questions about finding the main idea, using context clues, drawing conclusions, story sequence, identifying the main characters, inference, cause and effect, metaphors, similes, phonics, and vocabulary. True or false, multiple choice. Finish packet one and go on to packet two. Sound boring? It was. But that's what my junior high Chapter 1* students did my first year with them. They were bored and I was bored. Month after month I felt there was no real improvement in their writing because we didn't go beyond answering a few short-answer questions and writing acrostic poems and paragraphs on teacher-assigned subjects like "My Favorite Christmas." There was little or no improvement in my students' test scores. My conclusion at the end of the year was that teaching "basic skills" simply did not work.

Before taking this teaching position, I had been away from education for eighteen years while I stayed home to raise two sons. My only previous teaching experience had been in an inner-city school on the west side of Chicago, where I had taught students who had finished kindergarten but were not quite "ready" for first grade. The curriculum consisted of teaching colors, learning how to print the letters of the alphabet, learning numbers, simple addition and subtraction, and phonics. In science we planted seeds, and in social studies we studied "community helpers" (firefighters, police officers, mail carriers, nurses, etc). However, when I decided to give full-time teaching another try in 1990, the only position

---

*With the passage of the Improving America Schools Act of 1994, Chapter 1 was officially changed to Title I, effective July 1, 1995.

open in my district was that of an eighth grade Chapter 1 reading teacher. I took the job reluctantly, hoping to transfer after the first year to an elementary school where I would be more comfortable.

My first year was the year from Hell. I was hired late, so the students in my class had substitutes for the first two weeks of school. When I walked into the classroom, except for students and desks, it was empty. There were no books and no teacher's guides. I was simply told that I should develop the curriculum on my own, and that I could order any materials I needed. This freedom, theoretically, was a teacher's dream, but frankly, I didn't have a clue about eighth graders, Chapter 1, or the junior high curriculum. I decided to ask the seventh and ninth grade Chapter 1 teachers for help. They gave me skill packets and some old materials that were stuck in the back of their metal storage cabinets. Now, I figured, I was loaded down with enough stuff to keep my students busy. But I wasn't satisfied and the students weren't satisfied; every evening I went home and complained to my husband that I wasn't cut out for junior high. Some of the kids were insolent; they were verbally abusive, they tried to sleep during class, and they really couldn't care less about school or reading. They acted like the last thing in the world they wanted was help, and I felt like a failure. I was in over my head and I knew I had to do something different if I was going to stay in the teaching profession.

Looking back, I realize several important events happened in a relatively short time that changed my life as a teacher. The first came in a graduate class on literacy I took that spring to update my certification. My professor, Alexa Sandmann, introduced me to whole language, the theory of creating "community" in the classroom, the use of trade books (i.e., fiction and non-fiction books in general circulation, neither basal readers nor the "classics"), developing a reading and writing workshop, and the writings of Donald Graves, Lucy Calkins, Regie Routman, and Nancie Atwell. Dr. Sandmann knew about my struggle with these eighth graders, so she handed me her copy of Atwell's *In the Middle* and told me that I had to read it.

I ended up reading the book cover to cover several times. Atwell's ideas about making an eighth grade English class into a reading and writing workshop made perfect sense to me. Giving students time to read and write and authority over the books they read and the topics they write about was exactly what I was looking for to get my reluctant students actively involved with "real" reading and writing. This seemed infinitely more meaningful—and appealing—than wading through packets and writing assignments chosen by some third party.

Along with *In the Middle* and my literacy class that spring came a third event that helped shape my future—the arrival of eight Macintosh computers. They were delivered to my classroom one afternoon, entirely unexpected and without explanation: they just appeared. A computer technician set them up and walked out the door, and I was on my own. I told my students that either they could wait to use them until I learned how, or we could learn to use them together. They decided we should learn together, and we did. Since it was close to the end of the year, we didn't explore much beyond the basics: keyboarding, beginning word processing, and *Carmen Sandiego in the USA* (the only software besides word processing I had at the time). But it was a beginning, and it changed my classroom. I discovered right away that student behavior improves tremendously when students are using computers. Students enjoy using them partly on account of their novelty. They are different from pencil and paper and worksheets, even though they can serve the same purposes. I also learned that students, given the chance, can be great teachers. When I couldn't figure something out with the computer, the students usually did. The school year ended much better than it began and I didn't apply for the transfer. I decided to give junior high another year.

I also decided that summer to restructure my classroom totally. I was determined to custom-design a reading and writing workshop for my students based on Atwell's model. I started to build a classroom library of trade books and I started reading young-adult literature. I familiarized myself with the authors that my students would be reading. I wanted the computers to be used as a tool for our writing workshop: there would be no computer games. Students would keep a reading dialogue journal, a weekly written dialogue with me about what they were reading. The packets would go to the back of my metal cabinet. I felt optimistic. I had a plan now. I was ready for year two.

To my surprise, my plan worked. Eight more computers were delivered in September, compliments of Chapter 1. Now every student had his or her own computer. The reading and writing workshop was a success, and was also much easier than I expected. Students were reading books, keeping reading dialogue journals, and writing. Everything improved: writing, reading, behavior, and—most importantly to administrators—test scores. I no longer felt eighth graders were troublesome. The only area that I believed needed some fine-tuning was their writing. My students wrote, but it was difficult for them to see a purpose for it. Coming up with topics on their own was a struggle for most of them when they wrote stories. Just about all my students noted in their year-end evaluations of the class that they liked the reading workshop better than the writing one. I had them sold on books: I presented mini-lessons on books and authors; I surrounded the students with books of every genre; and I read in class individual chapters and several entire books. I had succeeded in capturing their interest with books, but they would not take the next step and start writing their own poems and stories.

The following summer, event number four happened, again entirely unexpectedly. My school district's General Director of Federal Programs and Testing sent me an application for a telecommunications writing grant that would be awarded to five teachers in our state. Because I taught in a classroom full of computers, she thought the grant would be perfect for me. I wasn't so sure. I waited until the last minute before sending in the application.

I had several pressing concerns when I applied for the Kentucky Telecommunications Writing Project (KTWP) grant. My biggest worry was that if my application was selected, I would have to change the structure of my class, which I felt had been successful the year before. I was in the process of working out the "bugs" and I wasn't sure I wanted yet another change. Time was also a concern. I had my students for fifty-five minutes a day and it was already difficult enough to squeeze in the reading and writing workshop, mini-lessons, journals, and conferences in that amount of time. Where would telecommunications fit in? Then I figured that there was really no reason for alarm: Holmes Jr. High had little chance of being selected as one of the five sites in the entire state. But apparently my chances were better than I thought. Shortly after returning home from vacation that summer, I was notified that I was one of the teachers who had been chosen.

Panic set in. Now I had doubts about what my Chapter 1 students could really contribute. We would be the only Chapter 1 class on the network. I taught five classes a day with eight to twelve students per class, with the part-time services of an instructional assistant. I knew that my incoming students would not be accomplished readers or writers. Other nagging questions kept me up at night: Would the students at the other sites realize that my students lacked writing skills? Could we keep up with the more sophisticated writers and the older students at the other schools in the project? Could I convince my students to write more than a line or two at a time? Would this project benefit my students, or was I setting them up for more failure—the failure that had followed them from grade to grade? Most importantly, how was telecommunications going to fit in with my curriculum? How much extra time would the technical side require? I had only a year of experience with computers. I had no idea about what a modem did and I wasn't sure I wanted to find out. I always believed in learning only what I absolutely needed to know about technology. Now I was in a project that emphasized technology. I really wondered what I had gotten myself into.

At the same time, I was eager to accept the challenge, in part because I wanted to prove that my students were up to it. Chapter 1 kids are not usually involved in projects that are on the cutting edge of educational trends. I have seen Chapter 1 classrooms where students do little with computers besides play "educational" games that emphasize drill and practice—the same old "developing basic skills" approach. Investigative, student-centered, active learning is usually the hallmark of advanced programs, not those designed as "remedial." I have heard many a teacher comment about wasting money and technology in Chapter 1 classrooms. After visiting my classroom, one advanced program teacher remarked to me, "Can you imagine what my students could do if they had that equipment?"

"The same things my Chapter 1 students *are* doing with that equipment," I thought to myself.

As I've noted, one of my main goals with telecommunications was to provide my students with the incentive to write, an incentive that was missing the previous year. I wanted to provide my students with an audience and a purpose for writing. I believed that getting a response from the other sites on the network would be more beneficial than getting a response from me and the students in our classroom at Holmes. KTWP was quite heterogeneous, including students of varying abilities who ranged in age from fourth graders to eleventh graders. This larger "classroom" included not only students in Louisville, Lexington, Paducah, and rural Hi Hat (in eastern Kentucky's Appalachia), but also Mike Rosenberg, our on-line poet-critic from Arizona, and students studying to be teachers at the University of Florida. My students could also benefit from having a group of teachers (at the different sites) in addition to the one they had at Holmes. There were many new voices and opinions out there in cyberspace.

I decided from the beginning that all my classes would be involved with this project. I did not want to limit it to one or two classes, as most people suggested, because I wanted all my students to have the opportunity to benefit from the work we would be doing. At times, it was difficult to have fifty students participate, but the benefits outweighed the negative aspects.

One of the first challenges I faced was getting students to "buy into" telecommunications. That September, the students sat quietly staring at me as I tried to explain telecommunications to them, and how we would use it with our reading and writing workshop. Most students liked the idea that they would be using computers, but when I got to my sales pitch about writing, they all complained, "We have to write?" They wanted to hear about computer games, not about writing to conferences and working on pieces for portfolios.

My students surprised me in some ways. They were predictable in others. Along the way, I learned more about technology than I ever wanted to know. Yes, the project took a great deal of time and commitment on my part. That first year, both teacher and students started on a journey into the world of literacy, technology, and community. I can't imagine ever going back to those dreaded packets.

Despite my early concerns, my students did make a substantial contribution to the on-line writing. They added distinctly different voices and a richness to the network. Some of them had problems at home and at school that are common to kids growing up in an inner-city environment. Most of the time they were blunt, but their frankness stimulated some of the most interesting discussions on-line. All of the on-line writing was filed into conferences, or topic areas. Setting up separate conference areas for various topics helped to keep notes organized for both the readers and the writers. Students played an important role in creating the conferences and establishing their tone. One example of this was the conference called "Autobios." We teachers had envisioned "Autobios" as a "pen-pal" type of conference. However, the second note posted on the conference the first year of the project was from an eighth grade student of mine named Bridgett, who wrote about her problems at home and her problems with drugs. At first, I hesitated about posting Bridgett's note on the network, wondering if this was the direction the conference should take. But I finally decided that the students needed to take ownership: it was their conference, their project.

> Hi! My name is Bridgett. I am fourteen years old. Well I had a bad problem with drugs and alcohol. I never came to school and the law was always looking for me for any reason. After they caught me and brought me home, they went out the front door and I went out the back door. I would always blame my stepdad for me not wanting to come home. I never realized I had a problem with drinking. I thought everyone else had the problem. I would yell at my mom, I would tell her I hated her and that I wished she would die. I

thought my mom hated me so I would run away to make things worse. I thought it would be better out on the streets with not knowing where my next drink of beer was and the next joint to smoke. I just thought I was a big shot. I thought I had all the friends I needed to do drugs with.

Well one day I was tired of doing it so I went up to my aunt's and she asked me if I was done running and if I wanted to go home. About that time my mom called and she asked me to come home to talk with her. I wanted to go home bad. I told her I would think about it. When I decided to go home, I was scared. When I got there my mom and her boyfriend (my stepdad) said that they were either going to send me off or get me some help, they asked me what I wanted and I told them "help." We called up the hospital and they told us to come up at three. That gave me enough time to get cleaned up. We went up there. I was like, "Aw this place will not help me, when I walk out the door I'll get some beer and get messed up where I can't walk."

Well I look back on my life and see these people did help me and if they didn't, I would not be in school now. What they did to help is that they took me to AA and they were there for me when I needed someone to talk to. I also learned I can have a good time without using. If they didn't help me I would not be sober today.

Response to Bridgett's note from other sites was immediate and set the tone for "Autobios" for the remainder of the year. Rather than the typical pen-pal stuff, we heard from real kids discussing real problems. Bridgett received many notes and she made a number of connections with other students on-line. One that touched Bridgett—and everyone else who read it—was from a sixth grade student in Lexington named Bambi.

Dear Bridgett,
I hope you have found a solution to your drinking problem. My mother had a drinking problem and she tried to hide it from me and my father. When my father found out about it he tried to help my mother to stop drinking but she never did because she didn't want to give it up. Sometimes I still think that she loved the drinking more than me her only daughter. Now I have to be careful to not take that first drop of alcohol because alcoholism is in my genes.

My mother drank when she was expecting me and when I was born I was very tiny. I was often sick during my first year. My mom used to leave me by myself when I was very young while my dad was at work. She would visit bars and beg drinks from men. She was picked up by the police with me in the car. They would call for my dad to come and pick me up. If he was not available they would call my neighbor Thelma and I would stay with her for long periods of time.

After my dad died when I was six, I was picked up at 10 at night making a phone call to one of my mother's boyfriends. I was then taken away from my mom and put in foster care. The lady that kept me when I was small promised my dad she would take care of me. She was the mother my mom could not be because of her drinking.

Thanks to the court I now live with my soon to be adoptive parents Harold and Thelma. Even though my mom could visit me once a week she did not. Everything that my dad left me that my mom could get, she would sell it to have money for drinking. Even when I had nothing to eat, she did not care because she had what she wanted, her alcohol. My advice to you is to go get help. Go to the AA because I don't want your daughter's dreams shattered like mine were. If you can't get help at AA get help somewhere.

Always know that there is a 12-year-old girl in Lexington, Kentucky, that cares very much and hopes your problem will soon be solved. There are other kids with your problem and together they learn to live without drinking.
Sincerely,
Bambi

Unfortunately, Bridgett continued to have serious drug problems during the year, along with frequent absences. But the one thing that she did care about was writing to other students who had sent her letters of support.

After Bridgett opened the door on the "Autobios" conference, students continued to use this conference to write about the serious issues that confront adolescents today. They wrote about divorce, suicide, rape, and the death of loved ones. My at-risk students were directly involved in establishing the tone and direction of "Autobios" and helped make it one of the most successful on the network the first year.

KTWP started with only a few conferences, but we soon realized that we needed to expand the number of choices. Popular ones besides "Autobios" were "Sports," "Issues," "Communities," "Diversities," "Fiction," "Poetry," "Critics' Voices," and "Music." We started KTWP with only a few conferences. But when students started writing about what they were interested in, we soon realized that we needed to expand the number of categories. My students, along with those at the other sites, wrote about their schools and neighborhoods in "Communities." They offered opinions about college and professional teams as well as their school teams in "Sports." Students reviewed everything from plays to movies to "ramen noodles" in "Critics' Voices." Teenage pregnancy was a hot topic in the "Issues" conference, along with issues related to race in "Diversities." Most of my students tended to stick with conferences in which they could write from experience. Posting writing on "Fiction" or "Poetry" took more courage because of the possibility of getting critiqued. But surprisingly, my students weren't reluctant to reveal their innermost thoughts and family secrets on-line in "Autobios."

I downloaded all the notes from each conference, laminated them, and filed them into spiral notebooks for students to read during class time. However, because students could not possibly read all the notes that were posted on-line in class, I made pocket folders for each conference. Students could "check out" the folder of the conference they were interested in and read the notes at home.

What surprised my students was that for the first time in their school careers they had a choice about their writing. They were no longer given assignments. I incorporated KTWP as part of our writing workshop and it became one of the options students had when deciding what writing they would do. Students wrote about what they were interested in and what they cared about. I didn't tell them how long a piece had to be and I didn't set a deadline for its completion. The important thing to me was that my students felt the writing was theirs and that their work would be ongoing. Some students wrote short little notes to conferences such as "Sports" and "Music." Sometimes they asked questions of other students on the network or merely offered an opinion:

> To: Music Mike Rosenberg
> From: Dwayne Page
> Holmes
>
> Whaz'up? I like rap music too. I think gangster rap doesn't send a bad message. If you are going to listen to gangster music you should be able to handle its lyrics. Some gangster rap tells you how it is growing up where they live at. Some rappers like to tell you what will happen if you sell drugs or if you are in a gang. Most rappers will have a song on their recordings about growing up in the hood. Ice Cube will put a song out about bad cops. But not all rap talk is about violence. Some rap talks about young mothers and fathers raising up a baby. And some tapes will tell you what will happen if you have unprotected sex.

Only occasionally did my students post polished pieces of writing. Instead, they used telecommunications to connect with students who were ostensibly quite different from them. To their surprise, they discovered a common ground. Week after week, they learned that kids from eastern or western Kentucky were a lot like kids in Covington. Some of my students liked the freedom that they discovered by writing to students who didn't know them, who wouldn't judge them as friends and acquaintances might. It was, in a way, like calling in and commenting on a radio talk show. The relative anonymity was a benefit to them. Gary (who often took pieces of writing home for his father to help him revise and edit) wrote in his year-end evaluation:

> This year was fun. We got to do a lot of stuff like write to people that we don't know. I like writing to people that I don't know. I think it is better if

you don't know some of the people that you write to because they don't know who you are and they only know a little about you that's if you tell them.

But while some enjoyed anonymity, others complained that they didn't like writing to KTWP because they never got to meet the kids they wrote to. This was especially true of students who seldom posted notes:

> I like the writing to people but I think it would of been better if we could of met them in person because if we know what they are like then maybe we can have more things to write about.
> Bobby

> I wasn't too fond of writing to KTWP, it was ok, but I didn't like writing to people that I didn't know. It made me feel weird. I don't know why, but I do.
> Randi

One of the most important aspects of this project for all students, especially for those who were considered at-risk students, was the exposure to students who were accomplished writers. Because of this project my students were motivated to improve their own writing, and often attempted to copy the style of the more accomplished writers in the project. I made it a practice to read them stories from a girl who identified herself only as Maverick, a prolific writer of suspense stories from Lexington who posted her work serially (see Nancy Stout Bell's essay on "Maverick" in this book). I made sure to point out a particularly wonderful description or passage. The first thing the students wanted to know, of course, was what grade Maverick was in. When they found out she was in eighth grade just like them, they were impressed. They expected her to be much older because of her ability to tell a good story.

Soon students were checking for more writing from Maverick. At the same time they began writing their own fictional stories, often adding the same colorful language and trying to imitate her style. One of my students, Jena, also wrote a story in serial form. Here is an excerpt:

> Where was Ashley? She disappeared. When I came back she wasn't lying there anymore. She wasn't even in the room. I thought about it for a minute and realized it must have been my imagination. No one could get up and walk away if they had collapsed or passed out or even died. You just couldn't get up and walk away.
> My imagination was running away with me again. I tried to shake the thought of Ashley out of my head but all I kept seeing was her lying on the floor and blood dripping from her neck. I looked all around once more but I couldn't find Ashley. It's like she had disappeared. Vanished.

After reading several of Maverick's pieces, another student, Adam, wrote a three-page story about an antique typewriter that had magical powers, adding the kind of detail and description that had been absent in his earlier pieces:

> One bright and sunny morning, Brian got up around 8:30. He spent the night at his grandma and grandpa's house. Brian was going to help his grandma and grandpa clean the attic that hadn't been cleaned in fifty years. At noon he went up to the attic to go ahead and clean it. It was dim, cold, dusty, and had cobwebs in the corners of the walls. There was a big chest filled with old clothes and an old hat rack with two hats on it. In the far right corner of the attic was a square cardboard box. Brian lifted up the lid to see what was under it. There sat a typewriter. His grandpa came over and told him that he used it when he was a reporter for the *Seattle Times* and he said his dad was also a reporter too, way back then. Brian's grandpa came over and handed the typewriter to him and told him to keep it.
>
> Brian took the typewriter and ran down the attic stairs and into the family room. Brian was going to write a fictional story. Brian slid in a piece of paper and started out with, "One cold and foggy day." In about five minutes Brian looked out the window because it made him think better and noticed that it wasn't sunny out anymore. It was foggy. Then Brian opened the window to see how cold it was. A big brush of cold air came from the window and hit Brian in the face. Brian shut the window and sat back down.

Reading good writing from other students on-line, combined with extensive reading of young-adult literature, inspired my students more than any of the lessons on writing that I had used in the past. However, change did not come overnight. It took months of modeling, reading good writing, and lots of encouragement before my students started believing in their own abilities as writers and finding the courage to start taking risks on-line. In February and March I began to see a distinct change in student writing. By this time my students had read at least eight trade books during reading workshop, they had heard me read numerous poems and short stories, and they had read lots of on-line writing. Then everything began to click. They began to work steadily on one piece of fiction. They tapped away at the computer keys without stopping. They wrote long, complex stories that seemed to ramble forever. They began to add detail and description. The hardest part for most students was coming up with good endings because they didn't seem to want to stop.

One student, Georgette, got interested in poetry, at first because she knew she would receive a response quickly from our on-line poetry critic, Mike Rosenberg. Georgette found she could express her feelings more easily through that medium, and soon she was encouraging her whole class to write poems, not stories. Before long everyone in that class was trying their hand at poetry and coming to Georgette for advice. She became the class expert, quoting Mike as she dispensed advice: "Show me, don't tell me." The poetry was not great, but the important thing was that Georgette and the other students began to explore other genres of writing and to see themselves as writers. Georgette sent this note to Mike along with one of her poems.

> I am going to take all of the poems that I have written and put them into a book so I can have all of them one day published in a poetry book or something. I hope you think that is a good idea.

She also wrote Mike to explain the process she uses when writing her poems and to thank him for his help:

> I would like to tell you how I go about writing my poems. When I have nothing to do around the house (and that is almost every day), I sit on my bed with my pen and paper and think of some ideas to write poems. When I finish them I put them into my poem folder where they are kept until I get to Mrs. Paeth's class and type them and send them to you. Then I read the things you tell me, revise them, print them out and put them into my folder. I have all of my poems in the folder. I can't believe that I have saved them ever since the beginning of this year. That is amazing!
>
> I really appreciate you helping me when I send my poems to you because I do want to be a good poet and you are the one who is helping me along the way to success. I just want to thank you for your time and effort that you have put into these poems that I have sent you.

Every once in a while, issues came up that we, as an on-line community, needed to address. One involved a student named Antonio who started the year as a novice writer. He was argumentative and competitive. He wanted good grades and, although he was a Chapter 1 student, he consistently made the B Honor Roll because he had an inner drive to be successful and to go to college. Although he nearly drove me crazy with his complaining and bickering, we had a common respect for one another. Antonio, however, never wanted anyone to read his work. He would cover his work by throwing up his arms in front of the computer screen when classmates walked by so they could not see what he was writing. He had little or no confidence in his writing. Once I displayed a piece of his writing in the classroom, thinking he would be elated, but he was horrified, and taped a blank sheet of paper over it, asking me to please take it down.

Sometime later, a crisis occurred when I gave the class the assignment of either posting a note to a conference or writing a response to someone on-line. Antonio wrote a response, but "lost it" somehow on the computer. In desperation to complete the assignment, he decided to send to the "Fiction" conference a short fiction piece that he had worked on earlier in the year. He carefully edited it himself. He was nervous about posting his story on the network, but he didn't want to get a zero on the assignment.

> Once there was this time that I had to go home by myself and I was scared. As I was walking down Madison Ave., there was this dog. I was going to run but it felt like my legs were broken and that I could not move. Somehow I saw a car out the side of my eye. I was thinking that if I can make it to the car I would be safe. As I was getting on top of the car the dog had grabbed the bottom of my leg. I was going to scream but my mouth could not even open. It felt like I had glue on my lips.
>
> The dog tore my pants leg and got a little of my skin. I was on top of the car. I thought that I would be safe. The dog was looking at me, pacing left and right. And then all in one motion the dog jumped on top of the car. When he jumped up, I jumped off. When I got off the car I was running as fast as I could. At first I could not see the bulldog then it came behind a tree and grabbed my leg. If the dog wanted to he could have took my whole leg off. I started petting it and the dog followed me home and now I have a dog.

A few days later this response came from a seventh grade student in Lexington.

> Dear Tony,
> This was a good story, but some parts weren't descriptive enough. Some parts had grammatic errors in them. Read your story over again and see how it sounds. Also, next time you write a story have your peers check it when you're done. They can tell you how the story can be improved.
>
> Sincerely,
> Chris

When I saw this note I didn't know what to do. I knew Antonio and he did not take criticism well. I also felt that I would have trouble getting him to write the rest of the year if he read Chris's note. Even though Chris meant well, Antonio would not see it that way. I decided to write about the issue in our teacher's journal (a conference closed to students) and get some feedback from others in the project:

> I think students should be able to send stories and poems to "Fiction" but not necessarily get critiqued unless they ask for it. I want students to have a place to send fiction writing and I don't want them to be afraid to send it because someone will read it with a critical eye. Some of my students want and can handle peer evaluation and some just are not ready for it yet.
>
> I don't want you to take this personally because what your student wrote wasn't a put-down, I just think my particular student will see it this way. I'm

glad your students are reading our stuff and responding to it. I just don't know how to approach my student with this note. Anyone have any suggestions?

Jane Eaton, a teacher in Lexington, responded:

Until now, I had only positive thoughts about the anonymity that [writing] on-line has given our children. I thought of it as a mask that they can use while testing the waters or revealing their most delicate thoughts. After reading your note and the note that our student sent, I see another side to the picture. Nancy (Bell) had been going over peer editing again in her classroom and obviously Chris was inspired. He will be a fine lawyer or accountant—in other words, a detail man. Instead of another kid, he saw a project that he is good at. He is a kind child and would never consciously hurt anyone. But at the moment, he was reading a disembodied piece of paper. This gives me pause. . . . I agree with your action in withholding the note. That is still our job in monitoring what is going on on-line.

You know what is best for that child.

I never did give Antonio the note because I decided in the end that it would do more harm than good. He had been, as Jane said, "testing the waters," and he needed to be handled with care. Antonio turned out to be one of my most prolific writers by the end of the year. Slowly, with lots of encouragement, he started to take more risks with his writing, began using similes and metaphors whenever he had the chance. His writing still needed editing, but his overall improvement in content and attitude was remarkable. By the end of the year he asked me to display his writing on bulletin boards. Here is a small section of a five-page story that he wrote near the end of the school year:

As the door opened, the school door hinges were creaking hard. The kind of hard that made your ears hurt like somebody was taking their fingernails across the blackboard. The teacher came in. She was an old lady like most teachers are. She had all gray hair with teeth that lined up in a row like men are on the front line in a war. She had gray eyes that made you want to scream. And she was so skinny that she looked like an anorexic person.

She came in and slammed down her books on the table. She did not say nothing. She just looked at all of us like we had done something to her. Finally she said, "Look class, I have heard a few things about you that I don't like." She looked again.

"So don't think just because I'm a sub that you are going to get out of hand. And if you want to be bad, I can be bad too because I might be old but I still know how to put you kids in your place."

The room was quiet, quieter than we have ever been that whole year. One of the kids next to me said, "She's a bitter old lady."

I answered back, "Tell me about it. The Grinch is nicer than her."

Apparently she heard what I said because she said, "Tony do you have something to share with the rest of the class?"

"No," I muttered out.

"Well, be quiet and don't say anything else for the rest of the day."

I was feeling kind of embarrassed because I was her first victim and whoever a sub jumps on first she is going to be watching for the rest of the day.

After that the whole class was quiet. You could hear a roach come across the floor.

At-risk students are not like other students. In general, they have little self-esteem and their egos bruise easier than most kids because of years of failure in the classroom. I do very little peer editing with my students because I have found that it does not work well with the students I have. Teenagers who are at-risk, may have failed a grade or two, are not willing to share their work with others, especially right away. The thing my kids fear the most is that when they enter my classroom they will have to read aloud in class or show someone their writing. It is only after we build some trust that any sharing can occur, and then usually only between students who are on good terms with one another. If I praise a student, he or she will become more willing to show others.

Part of the responsibility of working with at-risk students is to build up their self-esteem. Telecommunications can help in a number of ways by creating opportunities for students to be responsible. My students opened conferences and collected and posted notes for the class, edited their own notes, and kept logs and notebooks. They also made the decision to publish their writing—on their own. If we give students the opportunity to be successful, most of them will be. Several of my students even arrived at school a half hour early to capture, edit, and post notes each day. Students who never got involved in school projects volunteered to work on a newsletter we were doing with students from the other sites on the day off for President's Day.

I let my students know from the very beginning that first year that I needed their help, that each of us was both learner and teacher. My students didn't disappoint me. They freely gave me advice on everything, from how to hook up the fax machine to how to relax when I had to give a workshop for other educators. They were prepared when I came into the classroom, threw up my hands and said, "I need your help." One student even commented, "We are always getting you out of trouble."

Chapter 1 teachers typically have classrooms filled with technology. The important question is how to use that technology to improve the curriculum and help the at-risk students do meaningful work instead of electronic worksheets. KTWP helped me to discover ways to get my students involved with different types of writing with a purpose beyond pleasing the teacher. Because the focus of KTWP the first year was for each site to do a community-based writing project, my classroom expanded to include the community. My students used computers to produce parent newsletters, and to design, write, and publish children's books that were distributed in the community; they designed a survey to find out the reading habits of our junior high students; they wrote letters to authors, and completed a Christmas writing project with primary students in our district; and of course, they used technology to communicate with other students in the state. In addition, they made videos documenting our projects that were shown on local public access TV; they planned and conducted a candy sale to benefit the local community center; and they worked on the construction of a house for Habitat for Humanity.

Looking back, I hated to see that first year end. I had asked a great deal of my students but whatever I asked, they did.

That first year culminated with our reading program being recognized as an exemplary Chapter 1 program by the U.S. Department of Education Compensatory Programs, the only Chapter 1 program in Kentucky to win national recognition that year. The award was based largely on the work we did in KTWP, the community projects we did during the year, and student performance on state-wide testing. Much to my surprise, my Chapter 1 students out-performed their non-Chapter 1 peers on the reading portion of the state assessment test.

Was it all perfect? No. We had our share of problems. At times the work and the management of the work was overwhelming. It was a challenge to incorporate KTWP into my existing curriculum. We had to cut back on reading time to allow for writing projects. The students and I had to be flexible in order to accomplish all that we set out to do. Some projects were done on Saturdays, such as the work we did with Habitat for Humanity. I also had a Macintosh PowerBook that students could take home to write with. My Chapter 1 assistant, Jennifer Turner, was a lifesaver. She worked with some students while I worked with others, and she also handled all the paperwork and record keeping that is routine in every Chapter 1 program. The two of us spent a great deal of time, especially the first year, organizing the on-line writing into notebooks, working on the community projects, and corresponding with the other teachers in the project.

It was much harder to capture the "community" feeling the second year of the project. I felt I was past the novice stage with KTWP and telecommunications; I was probably "high apprentice" and on my way to "proficient." The pressure of the first year was over. I started the second year knowing what I was doing; I didn't need the help of the students as much. I didn't feel that we needed to do project after project. I relaxed and realized that if something didn't get done, it didn't get done. We concentrated more on writing. My students the second year may have become better writers, but I missed the spirit and camaraderie of the first year when we really were overachievers. I doubt I will ever have another year teaching like that one. We had a great deal of fun because we were so busy being a part of something new and special.

Not all students were enthusiastic about telecommunicating. Some students posted one or two notes and never received an acknowledgment. Response seems to be the key element to the success of any telecommunications project. One student who felt frustrated wrote to KTWP:

> My name is Nicole Runion and I wrote to a student about two months ago and every day I ask my teacher if she has written me and every day the answer is no. My teacher Mrs. Paeth told me to make a complaint so I am. I thought this would be fun but now I know it is not fun at all. I don't understand how everybody got so excited for nothing. They won't get written to.
> I hope that students can be encouraged to write more.

The teacher's enthusiasm is also important, and it's sometimes hard to maintain. I needed to be a cheerleader to get my students to want to read books and to get involved with KTWP. There were times when I felt that teachers, including me, lost some of their enthusiasm. When that happened, student interest waned and the project suffered. Like anything else in education, the bottom line is that if the teacher doesn't buy into it, the students won't.

When I think of my Chapter 1 students and KTWP, I am reminded of Frank Smith's term, "the literacy club." He uses it to describe a community of students who are users of written language. I believe that my first priority as a Chapter 1 reading teacher is to get my students "admitted to the club"—to see themselves as readers and writers. As Smith says in *Reading without Nonsense*, "There are no dues to be paid, no entry standards to be met. A mutual acknowledgment of acceptance into a group of people who use written language is all that is required." There are definite advantages of being a part of the literacy club,* which to me parallel the

---

* Smith describes these advantages as follows: "Students see what written language does. Children are admitted as junior members, they are not labeled. Members help newcomers to become experts. Students are quickly admitted into a full range of club activities, as they make sense to them and are useful to them. Children learn to identify themselves as members of the literacy club. They see themselves as readers and writers. All learning takes place without risks."

advantages of participating in this telecommunications project: students see written language being used; they are not labeled; and the older or more distinguished writers help novice writers to improve. Students also see themselves as part of a community of readers and writers where it is safe to take risks.

One of the things that I learned through the project is that we need to give at-risk kids the same kind of challenges that we give our best students and that the at-risk students must become responsible for their learning. Telecommunications has done that in my class. Most students see themselves as equals with other students on-line. In telecommunications, multi-grade and ability levels can work together successfully. In this project we had students who ranged from novice to distinguished.* It was truly inclusive.

When I reflect on the last few years and how my classroom has changed, I see my at-risk students being successful and emerging as members of the literacy club. Not all students achieve the same level of success, but for many it is their first success in school. It is a far different classroom today from the one where students worked on skill packets and never wrote more than a paragraph or two, and then only under duress. When KTWP is over, I will continue using telecommunications in my class. Learning does not have to be boring, it can be fun, as these student notes indicate:

> This year has been the greatest year for me. I learned a lot about computers and I learned that reading is important. I read over thirty books this year. I like doing writing, doing KTWP and doing KTWP projects.
> Sharon Rowekamp

> I thought that KTWP was a pretty good program. When I first started in this classroom I did not think that I would like it. I thought, "There is no way that I will like reading and writing this much!!" But it turns out that it was a pretty fun classroom, we got to do a lot of fun projects. I also read and write more often then I did before. We also got to write to a lot of different kids, that was pretty fun. We wrote about different subjects.
> I liked that.
> Melissa Eldridge

> Well I really like writing because it shows that I have some secret abilities inside and writing helps me to get them out on paper. I also like to get ideas from authors like R. L. Stine, S. E. Hinton, and Beverly Cleary.
> John Marshall

---

* The Kentucky Holistic Scoring Guide assesses student writing portfolios according to four performance levels: Novice, Apprentice, Proficient, and Distinguished.

I loved your classroom, it was my favorite class. When you let us pick our own books I thought you were joking, but you weren't and I liked that.

Writing is fun and great. What I mean is that I'm a better writer than before. Journals are great because what I write down in it only you can see. When I was able to write my own children's book, I just loved the idea that a child would sit down and really read a book that I wrote, WOW!

I've improved as a writer, just think of some of the stuff that I've done this year. I've also become a better reader and a lot better speller.

I liked having a computer in the classroom, it's lots of fun. KTWP was my favorite of all things. I liked it when other kids could write us back and then send it to us through a fax machine or modem. That's so neat, it really is.

Sabrina Vurchio

Bibliography

Atwell, Nancie. *In the Middle.* Portsmouth, N.H.: Boynton/Cook, 1987.

Smith, Frank. *Reading without Nonsense.* New York: Teachers College Press, 1985.

Nancy Stout Bell

Maverick

JULIE WAS NEW in our eighth grade class. This was highly unusual because our K–8 school rarely admits students for one year. The authorities at Saints Peter and Paul, a private Catholic school in downtown Lexington, Kentucky, felt that a foundation for a Catholic education could not be built in one year. Most of our students had attended Saints Peter and Paul School for most of their educational life. In their eight years together they had become a close-knit group; they treated each other more like brothers and sisters than fellow students. But this new student had just moved to Lexington, she wasn't transferring from another school in town, and her parents did a bang-up job convincing our principal to admit her. It was exciting, and unexpected, for the eighteen returning students to see a new face in "their" class.

She was also "different." She was from Wisconsin, not central Kentucky like the rest of them, and she and her brothers had spent the last year in homeschooling because her parents did not feel that their previous school had been right for them. Her family had moved to Lexington because her mother was a well-known equine artist and sculptor and many of her clients, and potential clients, lived in the area. When her parents found out about Saints Peter and Paul, they decided that it would be best for Julie and her siblings to return to a classroom so that they could interact with other kids.

At first, Julie was a great observer. She would watch and listen to the other students, but seldom joined in their conversations. Months later, she admitted to me, "I knew everybody before I gave them a chance to know me." She quietly went about her business, turning in excellent work and completing all her assignments, participating in discussions only when asked.

The class was participating in a telecommunications project with four other schools in Kentucky, which had been selected for the Kentucky Telecommunications Writing Project (KTWP), an experiment in telecommunications and student writing. Participating teachers were communicating on a regular basis, discussing everything from classroom victories to "what do you think?" The students were sending on-line letters about what they were doing in their lives and topics of interest to them. They had also begun posting their own poems and stories. They would anxiously await replies from the other students on the network, who would respond with more letters and more stories.

Julie watched the other students and chose not to participate. But then, on November 5th, she suddenly entered her first fictional story into the log book, the book in which students write the file names of work they have done and want to be sent on-line. When five or six entries were made into the book, a teacher or student, whoever had a spare moment, would send the notes on-line by uploading from each student's disk. Julie signed her entry with the adopted pen name of Maverick—which she would never explain to her fellow classmates or teachers.

To: Fiction
From: Maverick Kasper
Topic: Fiction
Date: Nov. 5

The Dragon's Lair

She trampled blindly through the Dark Forest. Her heart was pounding against the cage of her ribs. The twigs cracked beneath her like dry bones. They were hunting her down. They were the predators and she was the prey. She was terrified, and alone. The entire Orcan army was after her, a child, Shana the Thief. She could hear the shouting of those horrible, gruesome creatures. It rang like a bell in her ears. She leaped swiftly over a rock and came to an abrupt halt. In front of her was a cave. Even in the darkening twilight she could see clearly the craggy entrance.

With a single glance behind her, she plunged into the unknown depths of the cave.

Once inside, she tried to sustain her heavy breathing. She could see nothing, but there was not anything to see except black nothingness. A tremor ran through her. Suddenly they were at the cave. She could almost see their green, warty skin, their gleaming, unblinking eyes; they were like repulsive beasts only wanting to taste the blood of their enemies. And Shana was their enemy.

"The little thief just walked right into the Dragon's Lair," one raspy voice sniveled.

"No one survives the Dragon's Lair," another Orc responded with a blustering grunt.

The shocking statement almost knocked her over. Suddenly, an overpowering stench reached her. It was putrid, and could only be the scent of a dragon. So the Orcs were truthful in their words, and she was trapped in the same cave as a dragon. She was terrified. It was an extreme, dreadful feeling of helplessness, one she had never before known.

"We'll keep watch here tonight to make sure that little wench doesn't get out alive," one Orc sneered.

Just then a bloodcurdling roar filled the cave and echoed against the rocky walls.

The darkness, the terror, knowing she was alone. Shana knew that there was almost no chance of getting out alive.

The sounds of the Orcs were cut off by a low booming growl. The odor of the dragon was nauseating. A sudden clicking of its claws against the rocks of the cave startled her. She didn't dare move. She recalled the old saying that if you don't move a dragon cannot see you.

Suddenly, she saw them. They were two flinty red eyes that cut through the darkness. They stared imperiously down at her from thirty feet in the air. She realized that the old saying was senseless. It knew where you were even if you didn't move.

Her whole body was numb with fright, her blood ran cold. She rose slowly to her feet and fingered a small dagger, which was her only weapon against this fire-breathing beast. Sweat dripped off her like raindrops, but she couldn't feel it, and she couldn't feel her body shaking. She could only see the red of the dragon's eyes in the blackness and feel only that the end was near.

The only chance she had to survive was to use her thief skills. She squeezed shut her eyes and concentrated with more might than she knew she had.

All this time, these endless seconds, the dragon hadn't moved.

Suddenly, it let out a fiery ball of flames. She couldn't see, but she heard a rustling and dived to the cold rough ground.

The flames exploded against the wall of the cave not far above her. The dragon, disappointed, lifted an enormous leg to crush her.

She could feel the vibrations of it leaving the ground, and rolled over to the rocky wall at the side of the cave. Blood oozed out of her cuts and scrapes and she bit down hard on her lip to keep from screaming out all the agony that was inside of her.

The dragon smashed down his foot where she had been. It realized she wasn't there and was more furious than it had ever been. To show its wrath the dragon exhaled a large fireball aimed for her.

Feeling the sparks flying toward her, she threw herself across the cave and slammed against a large rock, wincing.

Again it missed and hit the cave with such immense strength that great boulders had begun to fall.

Shana the Thief opened her eyes to almost see the massive, monstrous beast make a powerful lunge at her. She closed her fingers around the dagger and threw it at the creature's heart. Its mark was true.

A piercing shriek, the dragon's last, cut through the night.

Shana the Thief had triumphed in the Dragon's Lair.

Soon Julie was on-line again. This time she was replying to another student's work.

To: Tommy Gatton, SPPS
From: Maverick Kasper, SPPS
Topic: "The Mistake"
Date: Nov. 18

I read "The Mistake" and I thought it was really good. I liked your story about Angella a little better, though.

I liked the way you made Alex's life so close to perfect. He was happy, doing well in school, had lots of friends, and yet he had a terrible secret that was the only flaw in his life.

If I were he, I would have been depressed with the fact that my life was just the result of an experiment. I would like to think my life was more than just an error created in a laboratory.

Did you ever see "Twins"? Danny DeVito was also a mistake. He was the outcome of a "milkshake" as he called it. He didn't know it until he met his brother Arnold Scwartzenagger (not spelled correctly) and together they found out. It made Danny DeVito's life worse than it already was.

Your story reminded me of a plot from a good Steven King novel. I look forward to reading more of your stories in the future.

Christmas break came and went. Julie returned to school and promptly entered three fictional stories into the log book. While the other students had spent their holiday sleeping and watching television, Julie had spent hers writing. A fourth story, "Alyssa," came out several weeks later.

To: Fiction
From: Maverick Kasper
Date: Jan. 31

Alyssa
Alyssa's heart was pounding against her ribs. Harder and harder. She could feel it in every inch of her body. Gazing behind her, she knew they were following her. Alyssa dodged into a desolate alley and ducked behind a trash can, breathing hard.

Footsteps sounded. In the alley. Not far away. Closer. Closer. They were coming. Coming for her.

Alyssa wrapped her arms securely around her slim shoulders, it was the only protection she could offer herself. She was afraid. Deathly afraid. Afraid of them.

They looked around. Searching. Watched. Observing anything that moved. A stray leaf. A hungry cat. Maybe she wasn't there. Maybe.

"Aaachhoo!" Alyssa's heart stopped. It had been hers. The sneeze had been hers. Ahh! So she was indeed there. They would surely get her now.

Alyssa peeked out from behind the trash can. Suddenly she was staring them right in the eyes. Staring into those round glistening eyes. She must run. She must run faster than she had ever before. But her knees were weak. She could not move. They were coming. Coming for revenge. A revenge they would stop at nothing to get.

Alyssa was suddenly on her feet and over a wall in one motion. She'd never know how she'd been able to do it. But she couldn't think of that now. She must only think of her life.

They would get her now. Surely they would get her. What's this? Over a wall? Well, all right. If she wanted to play hard to get, so be it. They would be able to do it. Surely they would.

Alyssa's breath came in short gasps now. She was terrified. What had she done? Done to them? Certainly it couldn't be—Oh, no! Was it what she had done last Halloween? The mask. . . . The woods. . . .

They would get her. No matter what it took. She was a human. Humans tired. But they never did.

Alyssa was out of the city now. Her shoes were pounding against the grass sprinkled with night dew. She wouldn't lose her footing. She couldn't. There it was! Looming big and bright! She was so close. So close. Her house. Faster. She had to go faster.

Oh, no. The refuge. If she got there she would be safe. They had to get her. Now. Suddenly they got a burst of energy and were in front of her.

Alyssa shrieked. She was breathing so hard she had no way to fall. No way to beg for forgiveness. Forgiveness of what she had done.

They sneered. They wouldn't forgive her. Only humans forgave.

Mrs. Reed looked out the back door. Alyssa would be home by now.

"Alyssa!" Mrs. Reed wiped her hands on her apron. But her only response were the crickets at the pond.

Willie, at the window, was pale and shaken. He had seen it. He had seen it all. The things, his sister, the gleaming light. And then it was all gone. . . .

It was with this piece that Julie received a reply from Chris Edgar, a writer and editor from New York City donating his time to respond to student writing. She worked hard to keep an expressionless face, but it was obvious that she was pleased with his response.

To: Feedback
From: Chris Edgar

Dear Maverick Kasper:
"Alyssa" is a great piece. I'm impressed with your writing style here; it has a wonderful starkness to it, which helps give your story its powerful atmosphere of suspense and mystery. I admire the way you handle the narrative, mixing third person with stream-of-consciousness—in other words, the way the reader sees Alyssa from the outside while at the same time hearing her thoughts. It's very effective and is a great way to build tension. (By the way, I very much like your use of short fragmented sentences and repetition— which is at once poetic and spooky.) I would suggest a few small improvements to your piece, which is strong already. (Bear this in mind.) There are a few places where the story moves a bit too quickly. For instance, it seems odd

to the reader that Alyssa gets out of the city so fast, and "they" pass her so suddenly. I think you need to have a little more time elapse, to have some things happen in between. Likewise, there are a few places where you make things too ambiguous, or try to be too mysterious, for instance, the references to Halloween—be careful of dropping red herrings, particularly in suspense-type stories. Once you get the reader you need to avoid distractions. But these are minor things. All in all, I loved "Alyssa," and I very much look forward to reading more of your work.

The next day Julie posted yet another story. Her classmates were now reading her work before she sent it on-line to other students at other sites, and she was generating stories as fast as they could read them. The more her classmates asked, it seemed, the more she wrote. Finally, on February 15th, Julie received her first responses from KTWP students at other sites. When I gave her the notes she retreated to a corner of the room and read:

To: Fiction, for Maverick Kasper
From: Megan Jacobs, Brown School, Louisville
Date: February 15

Dear Maverick,
I read the story you wrote called "Abby's Tree." I think it's really good and I like the way it's written. It's mysterious and has a neat plot. I am a writer myself; but I haven't written many mysteries. The part of your story I read was the beginning up until the part where she climbs the tree on August 5. Is that the ending? If it's not, we don't have the rest of it here. And I would love to know what happens next (if you wrote any more on that story).

There was a story I wrote in December for school, and when I read "Abby's Tree" I thought it was unbelievably similar to mine. Mine was about a little girl who had a huge oak tree in her backyard that she loved and said it was her best friend. The tree never let her fall out of it because it seemed to like her. You probably don't believe this because it's such a big coincidence, but it's true. Another weird thing is: the girl in your story is named Abby, and the girl in mine is Ashley. Their names are even alike! We wrote stories that were so similar even when neither of us had read each other's stories before. The parts I just mentioned are alike, but the stories are different, of course. Would you like to read mine? If you would, just tell me and I'll send it to you.

To: Maverick Kasper
From: Wednesday
Topic: Fiction (What about Marty)

I read your story "What about Marty" and thought that it was really interesting and good. Are you going to write any more to the story? If you do, please send it, I would enjoy reading it. The only thing is, what really did happen to Marty, is he suspended in another dimension, or something? Also what is that light and noise, I mean I know it trapped Marty and almost trapped Ian but where did it come from? I liked the plot and thought that it was good and a lot better than anything I could write. How did you come up with the story? Please write me back.

These responses seemed to catalyze Julie's writing even more. She later told me that when she first began writing stories to post on-line she was not concerned with others' opinions of her writing. She already saw herself as a writer and felt she didn't need an audience. But when she found out that her readers liked her stories, she began to work twice as hard on them. She liked the attention and did not want to disappoint her readers.

"I was flattered by the reactions other readers had about my writing," Julie would later tell me. "I did not feel any pressure, but I had never had any reason to write short stories before KTWP. It was my reason to write. My writing seemed to make others happy and I found that if others were happy, so was I."

Julie's writing was changing her relationship with her classmates. The other students, tiring of Julie's aloofness, had quit trying to include her in "the group." However, they couldn't help but notice the quantity of stories she was generating, and would sneak out in the hall to the bulletin board where all on-line work was posted to read her work. Soon, others were bringing in fiction stories they had written and were asking Julie to read them. Julie never told them specific things to change, but would smile, with her head tilted down and eyes turned upward, and say, "Not bad." That one comment from her would spark new energy in her classmates and more stories would soon appear. There had always been several girls and a few boys from the class who occasionally would write stories. Julie became almost a cult figure in the class and students who had never written a story, unless assigned, were bringing in manuscripts for her to read. It became a contest among students to prove that they, too, could write fiction.

Jason liked a challenge, viewed himself perhaps not as a writer, but at least as an intelligent student. The contrast between him and Julie was striking; she the introverted, outwardly subdued student and he the accepted, easy-going member of the class. The relationship developing between the two was hard to miss. Each had a nonchalant style that did not openly solicit the acceptance of the other; yet each was silently encouraging the other to write. Jason tried to imitate Julie's style of writing by using short sentences and leaving unanswered questions for the reader to ponder. It took him several attempts, but he finally posted a story.

To: KTWP
From: Jason Flanary
Topic: Fiction

The Closet

Yeah, I remember Jeremy. He was a good kid. Jeremy was a lot of fun, always there when I needed him. He was like an older brother to me. Now he's gone, and I'll never see him again.

All of us had always known Robert. He was a little on the weird side, but always did his homework, never missed a day of school, and always listened to his teacher. His parents were never home. His so-called "excuses" were they were on a business trip, or they were on vacation.

It was a bright Friday afternoon and Robert and Jeremy were spending the night at Robert's house. As soon as they got to Robert's house, Jeremy right away noticed how run down and shabby it was. It was a real old house with windows broken and the screen door was hanging by a rusty nail. The house was a ugly green color with the paint chipping on the side.

As they stepped in Jeremy noticed an overpowering stench that hit you right in the face. Jeremy asked where the bathroom was and Robert replied the second door on the right.

As he stepped in he noticed the dingy bathroom mirror with a crack down the middle. The shower curtain was hanging by a ring and the window by it was knocked out.

As they stepped into his room he noticed all the blankets and toys all over the floor. Then he saw the closet. I now call it the forbidden closet. What happens next is hard for me to tell, but I'll try. The closet was perfectly clean. There was glistening floor beneath it and varnish shone in the sunlight.

Jeremy said, "What's in here?"

"NO" yelled Robert. But it was too late. Jeremy had already opened it.

The neighbors said they heard someone yell "Oh, my God," at the top of his lungs, and then a loud screech.

We all know what happened to Jeremy, but what ever happened to Robert?

The competitiveness between Jason and Julie that began with her writing carried over into other school subjects. They seemed to challenge each other in a way that I had not seen before in my classroom. Each would respond to the other's successes with more efforts of his or her own. This was all done in a friendly manner, as Julie was now beginning to open up. Julie's classmates were inspired by her and she was inspired by their attention. While acting as a critic by day to others in the class, Julie was hammering away at her computer at home every night. She produced story after story, carefully editing each one. Later she said, "I sensed that on the telecommunications network many people did not edit. Editing is so important to good writing and I wanted to serve as a model for others. Sometimes just changing that one word can make or break a story." Julie was a mature and insightful thirteen-year-old and felt a responsibility to share her talents with others. She never lectured, but taught by example.

By the end of February Julie had written four complete stories, but her greatest success came in March when she began posting, in installments, a piece entitled "The Eleventh Hour." She told me she began to write it because her parents were concerned that she always wrote gruesome stories and she wanted to show them that she could write in a variety of genres. But when she got going, it too turned gruesome—but not until later in the story, after she had proven her point about her flexibility in her writing. Julie, who believed she could write in any genre she wished, could not resist suspense. She found it boring to write about things in her everyday life, and wanted to experience new feelings through her writing. She also knew her audience—other adolescents like herself—and was writing for them, even though she would not admit it.

To: Fiction
From: Maverick Kasper
Date: March 7

This is a story that was rather long so I will send only about a page at a time. I really enjoyed writing it and hope to hear your thoughts too. Well, here's the story.

The Eleventh Hour
Becca shivered as she stared out the window of the taxi. Rain was pouring down on the dark abandoned street. Why had she even thought to baby-sit the Sawyer kids? Her friends had told her not to.

Letting her off after she paid him, the cab driver sped down the road back to town. Looming at the end of a long driveway behind a locked metal gate was an enormous mansion. Becca gulped down the lump in her throat. Pulling her jacket tighter around herself she started to the gate.

There was no way of turning back now. The trees were ebony and glistening from the light of the moon. The breeze was cool and clean. The rain had stopped now and the sky was clear. Clear and black.

Becca wanted to get to the house as soon as she could. She felt as though someone was watching her every move. Someone dangerous. How could she get past the gate?

An owl gave its lonely call. Crickets answered in chorus. A chilling breeze blew over the damp grass and through the trees. And Becca was a part of it all. But she didn't want to be.

Suddenly, the gate unlocked and let her in. Becca opened her mouth to say something, but she couldn't speak. She walked uneasily toward the house, dragging her feet as she went.

The house was massive. Many windows stared darkly at her. There did not appear to be a light on anywhere in the house. A feeling of terror in the pit of her stomach grew until it filled her entire body. Why was she doing this? She didn't need the money. But something drew her to this place. A strong force. A very strong force.

Not able to put it off any longer, Becca reached the door. She felt eyes boring into her back. Turning around to face them, she saw only darkness, the trees blowing, and the moon which was the only light in the sky.

Becca knocked softly on the door. She could barely hear her own knock but obviously something did. The door opened to reveal a dimly lit hallway. Dimly lit with candles that were attached to the wall. Becca looked around warily, her heart throbbed like a butterfly caught in a net.

Nobody was there. Then who had opened the door? Becca would never know.

When she took two steps into the hall, the door shut behind her. Becca shivered.

"Hello?" Becca's voice echoed in the large hall. She could see a closed door and a winding staircase. But that was all there was.

To be continued. . . .

A response to her story came within the week.

To: Maverick Kasper
From: Jason Flanary
Topic: Fiction

Dear Maverick,
I have just read the first part of "The Eleventh Hour." It seems to be your usual, scary, horrifying tale that you like to compose. I know I'm late in reading it since it's been out since March 7, but it looks good so far.

Anyway, I would like to know why your stories are right out of the stories from "Tales of the Crypt." Could it be because of the mighty ghost "Tom" that lives in your house, or is it just the way you are? My question is what is so bad about the Sawyer kids and why is Becca so scared?

Julie's classmate Jason had read her story, along with the other students, after it had been posted on the bulletin board in the hall. Our students would simply post a note, send it on-line, and have it received just like any other note from another site. Jason's note was one of the first negative notes Julie had received. It was obvious from her facial expression and body language that she was mad. Her reaction: she fought back with more writing and more editing. I later asked her how she felt about Jason's note and she told me that at the time she was upset because she felt he didn't really care about the story, he just wanted to get a rise out of her. When I pointed out that that is exactly what he did, she laughed and said, "But I wrote more stories!"

Julie put great thought into the pacing of the release of her serial story. She wanted her readers to want more. She could sense by the reactions of the other students that she had them right where she wanted them. Her next installment came out one week later, and then was quickly followed by Part III.

To: Fiction
From: Maverick Kasper
Date: March 7

This is Part II of the story. I've already sent the first part so you might have to catch up.

The Eleventh Hour
"Yes?" Becca jumped a mile when she heard that. Looking around she saw a pair of green eyes fixed on her.

"I'm Becca Kassner. The baby-sitter. You called me for a job. Tonight." Becca's voice wavered.

"Of course," the lady walked down the stairs and turned on a light. Brightness filled the hallway and it didn't look nearly as bad as it had.

"Thank you ever so much for coming." Mrs. Sawyer was actually quite pretty. But there was a feeling on her face covered up by the smile. A feeling that Becca had felt when she had stepped out of the taxi.

"My name is Eleanor," she smiled.

"Hi." Becca gave a forced smile and the fear was almost gone now.

"Jason, my oldest son, will be home tonight around nine or so. He has a key so keep the doors locked. Always. Always keep the doors locked." The way she said it made it vital to Becca.

"All right, well, I must be off. The kids are in the kitchen, first door on the left, through that door. I will be back by midnight." It didn't seem to be Mrs. Sawyer that was talking. Becca locked the door behind her and turned to meet the kids.

Cole would be twelve, two years younger than herself: Minty was a little girl of ten. Skye and Kit—the twins—were eight. Tucker was just five.

Through the door. First on the left. Inside she saw five solemn faces. Almost hidden by shadows. Five pairs of blue eyes. Sitting so close together. Too close.

"Are you playing 'Quaker meeting'?" Becca joked and flicked on the light.

Minty leaped off the couch and hurriedly flicked it off.

"Why did you do that?" Becca demanded of her.

They all stared at her again. Their stares were blank and meaningless. Cole ran a hand through his tan hair and a sparkle appeared in his eyes.

"Because it comes every night. The eleventh hour. It comes. And it might know where we are if the lights are on." Cole felt a little better when they were off. But it knew where they were despite the lighting.

"It? What's it?" Becca's voice got small and her heart skipped a beat. The eleventh hour? Why didn't they just say ten o' clock?

"We don't know. We never know. We keep telling Mother to move us, but she just says it will find us wherever we go."

What was happening to these kids?

(To be continued . . .)

"The Eleventh Hour" also had an impact on students at other KTWP sites. Donterius, a Chapter 1 student at Holmes Jr. High School, had started the year with great enthusiasm for the telecommunications project. He jumped right in, wrote a few letters, but quickly lost interest when no responses came back to him.

School had become a struggle for Donterius; he lived in a housing project in one of the roughest sections of his community and the distractions his neighborhood offered were tough opponents for his school work. He didn't like to turn in his assignments and he had failed his reading/writing class the last two quarters. One day his teacher, Beverly Paeth, began to read aloud the first installment of "The Eleventh Hour." Donterius listened carefully. His interest was piqued. He asked his teacher if she would make him his own copy of the story. She did, and he read it over and over. Then Bev told him about Julie's other stories from earlier in the year, and he wanted copies of those too. He read them all with the same intensity that he had read Part I of "The Eleventh Hour." His interest in coursework returned as he went from a student who came into the classroom complaining that he had nothing to read, to one whose first words would be, "Did you get another part to the story today?"

Donterius could not stop talking about Julie and her stories. He was impressed that someone his age could write "stories like that" and felt a personal connection with her because of the network. One day Donterius walked into his classroom, turned on a computer and wrote a letter to Julie.

To: Maverick Kasper, SPPS
From: Donterius Salter, Holmes
Date: March 25

Hi my name is Donterius Salter of course you knew that because my name is at the top of the letter. I am a big fan of your writings and think that you could be a really good writer some day. I was talking to my teacher Mrs. Paeth about two days ago telling her how much I like the way that you write and that you should take all of your writings and make them into one book. I really like your story "The Eleventh Hour." I think that you should write more books like that. I really can't wait until you get finished with "The Eleventh Hour" because I am really getting into that story. Well I got to go because my words are getting short so Byeeeeeee.

Encouraged by Donterius's note, Julie published the final installment to "The Eleventh Hour."

To: Fiction
From: Maverick Kasper
Date: March 25

Finally, the last part of the Eleventh Hour. Part V, I believe. Please write any responses you may have.

The Eleventh Hour

The next morning the kids quickly marched down the driveway and into the waiting cab. They would be safe now. They had to be.

Watching them safely hidden by the leaves of the forest, their father cried softly.

James Sawyer finally reached his luxurious home. It was nearly ten o'clock. Nearly the eleventh hour, as he and his kids always called it. His six kids would be at home with his loving wife. He was a scientist. And today he had made the most amazing discovery that he couldn't wait to share with his wife.

"Eleanor!" He lifted his wife high in the air and kissed her passionately on the lips.

"James, what is the occasion?" Mrs. Sawyer smiled.

"Do you remember the formula your father created? The one that cures cancer? As you can recall, it didn't work out very well because of its side effects. Well, I perfected it!"

"No! James, you didn't mess around with the same ingredients my father used, did you? The Phyodermic Acid?"

"Yes, but you see, honey, he just used the wrong amount of it. But I found—"

"NO! He used it and it killed him! And my mother!"

"But dear, I already used it and it worked."

"Get out! Get out of my house! Now! If I ever see you again I'll kill you! When my father used it he went crazy and killed my mother before he could be stopped! And then only by death! Don't go near the children! Ever! Go!" Mrs. Sawyer's eyes were wild and filled with fury.

James walked silently down the street to his lab. His heart ached with the love that he had lost. Opening the door to his lab he madly grabbed the Phyodermic Acid. Highly dangerous if not used correctly, he often noted. He never knew the exact outcome of it, but this time he didn't even think about it. He didn't care what happened to him now. Pulling off the top of that bottle, James gulped down the entire dosage.

The clock struck the eleventh hour.

Looking in a mirror he saw himself transform. His body started to lengthen, his teeth turned into long yellow fangs, his skin turned black and glossy, muscles became larger, and his eyes turned from bright blue to glowing demonic yellow.

With her writing she also sent a personal note to Donterius.

To: Donterius Salter, Holmes
From: Maverick Kasper
Date: March 30

I'm glad you like my story. I have one or two other stories similar to that one lined up to send. I just can't stop writing these horror/suspense stories. Take The Eleventh Hour for example. I started out with the firm state of mind to make it a normal story, without any gruesome writing or anything like that.

As you can see, I failed. But it's still a pretty good story. My little brother read it and he said that it was one of my best. I'm not so sure but he seems to be right.

Thank you for writing to me and I hope to hear again from you soon.

Donterius resumed work on an unfinished story that he had begun in the fall. His story took on characteristics that had become Julie's trademarks: the one-word sentence; the repetition of words; gruesome details. He was now reading books by R. L. Stine because his teacher had told him that Stine's style was similar to Julie's. Donterius wrote one more time to Julie:

To: Maverick, SPPS
From: Donterius, Holmes Jr. High
Date: April 13

Hi, I am glad you wrote me back. I have wrote to KTWP but I never get a response. If you could I would really like for you to send me those other stories that you wrote. In my last letter I asked you if you wanted to take all of your stories and try to make them into one whole book. But in your letter you didn't say anything about it. . . . Why?

I have been writing a story for quite a while and I was wondering if I could send it to you and let you take a look at it because I have been having some problems with it. I will send it to you when you write back saying yes or no. Well that's all I have to say for now, hope you write back soon.

Julie ended the year with another installment story and Donterius was still working on his story to send to Julie. School dismissed for the summer break and regrettably Donterius never managed to send his piece to Julie.

It wasn't until a year later that I sat down with Bev Paeth and learned of the full impact that Julie's writing had had on Donterius. Julie was a writer, and the telecommunications project gave her an audience for her work. Julie will always write. She wrote to please herself, but the acceptance of other students encouraged her.

I told Julie what Mrs. Paeth had told me about Donterius. Thinking she would feel a bit smug about her influence, I was surprised when she said, "Oh yeah, I remember Donterius. I named my cat after him." I asked her why she had done that since she had never met the boy and had only written to him a few times. "Of all the notes of praise I got that year on my writing, Donterius's was the most sincere," she said. "I truly felt he liked, REALLY LIKED, my writing. He gave me hope that one day I really could be a writer." What had she "heard" in Donterius's notes that I had not? Here I was thinking how special Julie had been for Donterius. I'd been mistaken. Donterius was special to Julie.

A year has passed since Julie was in my English class. She graduated with her class and went on to Lexington Catholic High School. I see her occasionally and always ask her about her writing. She tells me that she has finished her first novel, but now spends a lot of her time writing poetry. Finding time to write has become a problem, too, with the demands of high school. Julie has also joined the volleyball team and is moving towards acting and drawing as an outlet for her artistic talents. It's interesting to note that she no longer calls herself "Maverick." She never would reveal why she chose that particular name, but I have a suspicion it had to do with the literal definition of the word; she felt that her writing was unorthodox and the name fit. However, Julie's writing made her accepted and I suppose she no longer needs the façade. She's content to be herself, writing whenever she can, and calling herself Julie.

Donterius repeated his eighth grade year and is now a freshman at Holmes High School in Covington, Ky. He is doing well in school, has a part-time job, and is "stayin' out of trouble." He says he thinks about Maverick and her stories and would really like to meet her someday.

Bette Ford

Going On-line

I TEACH composition and literature at Jones Junior College in Ellisville, Mississippi. A few weeks ago, Deana, a student in one of my freshman composition classes last spring, dropped by my office just to chat. During that conversation, she reflected on some of her best times in that class. Among her favorite and most rewarding activities, she said, were the e-mail exchanges we had with students in Alaska. When I asked her what made these experiences special, this was her response:

> Well, it's just encouraging to learn that people in Alaska have things in common with us. Some of their family stories remind me of my own. But some of their everyday stuff, like ice fishing and dog sledding, is new and exciting to us.

Deana is not alone in these sentiments. Computer conferencing seems to turn most students on.

However, many of my students don't know the rugged roads I traveled before I became reasonably comfortable turning on a computer. Only a year earlier, during my final summer in the M.A. program at Bread Loaf, I almost panicked to learn that my old faithful electric typewriter had been damaged beyond repair during shipment to Vermont. Somebody tried to convince me that even with the very minimal computer experience I had—a six-session introductory course dealing mainly with the evolution of the computer—I could learn word processing quickly enough at the Bread Loaf computer lab, known as the Apple Cellar.

I gave it a try. But my learning was not quick. As a matter of fact, I required the attention of every technical assistant in the Apple Cellar just to open the word processing program on a computer. They were all sympathetic to my technical illiteracy, assuring me that I would soon be fine. However, I was not that sure. Fearing that I would still be trying to figure out how to save or delete or print on the day my final papers were due, I decided I would rent an electric typewriter. I needed old-fashioned security—in my room.

However, I did not realize how *really* old-fashioned typewriters were. After my fingers had failed in their walk through the Yellow Pages, my feet took to the streets of Burlington, Vermont, stopping at every business machine dealer in hopes of finding a typewriter to lease for approximately a month. Over and over I got the same response: they dealt only in computers.

I was at the end of my search that Friday afternoon, and I felt a miserable mix of desperation and defeat. I decided to tell the salesman in the small personal computer store about my plight.

"A whole host of my family members already have tickets to fly here for my graduation next month," I confided. "Unless I find a way to get my papers done, I may not graduate. And I've already fiascoed with computers."

His obvious amusement didn't outdo his compassion. "Let me ask our bookkeeper what happened to a couple of old typewriters we used in the office a long time ago," he said. "If one is still around here and if it's still working, we may be able to work out something to help you."

In a closet in the back of the store, he did find an old electric typewriter, which he dusted off as I completed an improvised rental agreement. After the salesman had loaded the heavy machine into the trunk of my car, I headed back down Route 7 toward the Bread Loaf Mountain, now feeling like a champion of the cause for commercial anachronisms. And, more importantly, I would graduate after all.

However, graduation from Bread Loaf by no means meant separation from Bread Loaf. Networking kept me connected: teacher-researcher projects, one of which I had begun in Dixie Goswami's class, kept me talking with her and other Bread Loafers about what we were learning. At that point we were communicating by phone or by U.S. mail, which we now call "snail mail."

Bread Loaf News, the official Bread Loaf publication, kept me informed of other Bread Loaf programs, including BreadNet, their telecommunications network. I recall especially an article by Ike Coleman and Leslie Owens in the Spring, 1990, issue. Entitled "Teaching the World," the article describes a "world trade" computer conference in which "students around the country and the world shared and responded to descriptions of their communities and their cultures." Via computer, students in small-town Salem, South Carolina, exchanged information about their grocery stores and small shops with students describing bodegas in New York. Students in Port Alexander, Alaska, shared information about ratfish and skates, and students in Deming, New Mexico, described traditional foods in their culture. According to Coleman and Owens, these connections "bridge cultures, helping to break down prejudices."

At a teacher conference a few months later, I met Alfredo Lujan, another Bread Loafer. Alfredo told me about how he and his students used computers for both writing and conferencing. He was encouraging, assuring me that my students and I could do it, too. "That's a joke," I thought. However, just imagining the possibilities invigorated me. I think I also anticipated the enthusiasm of students like Deana. I'd have to try it.

Then reality struck, with flashbacks of my Apple Cellar disaster. But my new aspirations were a much greater challenge than getting graduate papers typed. And although that period of academic anxiety had convinced me that I must get intimate with a computer, I knew the process would take lots of time. Now how could I even think about sending typed messages through phone lines when I didn't even know how to type on the computer? Like typewriters, I thought, computers would surely be obsolete by the time I learned to send electronic mail. Yet my high school seniors needed this opportunity—before they became senior citizens. All the while, I think I was wishing for a patient technology tutor.

Rocky Gooch, Technology Consultant for the Bread Loaf Rural Teacher Network, is an icon of patience. I know, because I have made him prove that virtue over and over again. Three years ago, while Rocky was visiting Mississippi, I sidetracked him to come to my house and connect a modem to the computer I had gotten a few months before. Connecting the equipment took Rocky very little time; he could have been out of my house in twenty minutes. However, I had about a year's worth of computer complications for him to clear up for me—not only about BreadNet, but also about my word processor.

After Rocky had shown me certain operations explained in the manuals, he demonstrated them for me on the computer. For example, he explained that it would be much less expensive to type a message first as a word-processing document and upload it before sending it on-line. After watching him demonstrate the process several times, I still couldn't do it unless he interceded. I decided I would write down each step as he explained and demonstrated it. The manuals just weren't enough. I needed instructions written in the language of the technologically illiterate—my own. This seemed like such a good idea that I had him repeat demonstrations of other features, too, as I wrote them down. Before Rocky left, exhausted but nonetheless cheerful, I had a hefty handwritten manual on a miscellany of computer operations.

"You'll do fine, Bette," he encouraged, as he waved and sped out the driveway. "Just keep playing around with it."

I did just that. However, the computer did not play fair, especially when it came to sending e-mail. For a while, each time I tried to log on I'd get signals such as "not connected to server" or "no matching names found." One night I decided I'd call Rocky long distance and have him talk me through the process, since my contrary computer would obey neither the official BreadNet manual nor my personalized handwritten one. Perhaps it would heed Rocky's commands. This is when I learned that I could not talk to him and send e-mail at the same time—through the same phone lines. (Recalling this incident, I'm also reminded how often even now I start to answer my phone if it rings while I'm on-line.)

Usually, what I was doing wrong or not doing at all was something very simple, such as turning on the modem. More than once I considered giving up—exiting the technology highway. However, images in the distance—enhanced learning opportunities for my students—kept me driving ahead.

I finally made it on-line. I'll never forget how excited I was to see the stamp flash-dance onto the right corner of the address box, indicating delivery of my message to Rocky. The message went something like this: "Rocky, if you get this, it means I'm on-line."

Within minutes Rocky replied, "Congratulations, Bette! You are on-line!"

And in a few weeks, so were my students, conducting their first e-mail conference—a community-based examination of two heated current political controversies in our state (and in other states as well, we learned during the conference). My twelfth grade English classes participated in a cross-state conference on a school prayer issue, which they ultimately shared on-line with students in other states. Here is an example of one of my student group's messages:

> Bishop Knox, a principal in Jackson, Mississippi, has lost his job after allow-ing a student to read a prayer over the school intercom. We were very inter-ested in this controversy, for it involved matters which could affect us directly. We randomly polled 116 students in grades ten through twelve at Hattiesburg High School, asking the following questions: 1) Should students be permit-ted to pray over public school intercoms? 2) Do you believe the increase in crime, teen pregnancy, and sexually transmitted disease is due to a lack of moral instruction in public schools?
>
> Responses to the questionnaire were almost equal across grades. Forty-three percent of all the students said they were for prayer over the intercoms, while fifty-five percent were opposed to it. Two percent were uncertain. On the second question, forty-four percent said there was a correlation, while fifty percent said there was none. Six percent were uncertain. Most students said morals should be taught at home and church, not at school.

The students then took the poll a step further:

We are particularly interested in the differences in these responses and those resulting from our local newspaper's poll of adults on the same issues. According to the newspaper poll, more than eighty percent of adults they questioned favored school prayer and believed moral instruction in school would help reduce crime and problems of teenagers. . . . We also sent our poll results and our analyses to the editor of the local newspaper. Unfortunately, the paper did not publish our work.

Though this very significant inquiry did not make the local news, we were both enlightened and encouraged by responses from other BreadNet students, some of whom had similar conflicts in their states. Computer conferencing gives students the opportunity to let the world touch them with stories both similar to and different from our own. In the words of John, who was in one of my composition classes last spring, "a lot of people don't know we've got it goin' on in Mississippi. We can show 'em on BreadNet."

Another important discovery I've made is the technological resourcefulness of some of my students. I had always known, of course, that they were competent on the word processor. However, some of them had e-mail access at home, even before I began my arduous journey to get on-line. Near the end of our first year, one of my seniors asked me how he could get on BreadNet from home. Wanting to continue participating in the on-line dialogues, he was disappointed when I told him this was probably possible only through teachers with access to the network. He said he'd keep in touch, and the following year he offered me technical assistance whenever I needed it. (I needed it about a week later, and he fixed the problem in minutes.) How naïve I had been to assume all my students traveled the technology freeway as slowly as their teacher! And how much time and sweat we might have saved poor Rocky!

I'm sure I'll always be slow learning new programs, and, fortunately, some of my students will always be far ahead of me. However, through computer conferencing, we're reaching the same destinations across the nation and the world. I'm no longer chasing typewriters. Instead, I'm advocating computer literacy for all teachers and students. I've come a long way down this highway, and I want plenty of company.

Linda Friddle Hardin

Just Cruising

A Personal Road Map for Integrating Telecommunications into the Classroom

IT IS MAY, and not yet 7:00 A.M. as I drive through the South Carolina countryside. My route to school winds through the mist that rises from the meadows and rolling hills along the base of the Blue Ridge Mountains. The best part of the day, I think. Silence, public radio talk of wars far away from our little patch of earth. Housing developments give way to small farms, horses and cattle wandering through lush grass or scratching their necks against grand old oaks that line the road. The woods bordering the Saluda River rush by my windows, then I'm out onto Blind Tiger Road and across the wildlife habitat area of Lake Robinson where an egret is fishing in the marsh. I slow up behind a school bus with kids making faces at me in the windows. I make faces back.

Our school has lots of early arrivals, both teachers and students. Built in the 1950s, Blue Ridge Middle School sprawls across a hillside, now circled by portable classrooms. It is the old high school, and our student body squeezes rather uncomfortably into it now as more urban dwellers seek the country life. I wonder how long this little community will maintain its peacefulness. Here students and teachers have an easy comradeship: violence is only a hard shove in the hall; drugs mean beer or chewing tobacco; no graffiti mar the building.

Yet Blue Ridge is changing, ever so slowly as newer homes overtake the big house/small house/trailer combinations where extended families live together on land they have owned for several generations. When the old people die, the children split up the land and sell it to developers. Already the woods along the river are thinner. Soon there will be no place to plant the beans and tomatoes. Before long, my students won't be able to pick a watermelon from the patch, cut it open, and watch the juice run down their fingers.

The quiet halls are filled with hot spring sunlight. I can hear the clamor of voices behind the door to my room, closed to contain the precious air conditioning. My seventh graders have been coming early for months now, and I can hear the whirs, beeps, buzzes, and rattles from our one modem as students log on to the computer networks that are their roadways out of the Blue Ridge countryside.

"Hey, Mrs. Hardin, the kids in Alaska liked my story," Joey yells, pointing excitedly at the screen. "Some of them were afraid of trying obstacle courses and being attached to ropes, too."

Lorrie shimmies in her seat. "Download that file, Joey. I promised Mrs. Long I'd have a map of Bosnia with all the United Nations safe areas to show in social studies first period." Lorrie is really impatient this morning. "Mrs. Hardin, I've got to have an illustration to make my report easier to understand. Make Joey hurry up!" she demands.

"But I want to read what they said . . . ," Joey protests, as Lorrie muscles him out of the chair in front of the screen.

"Read off-line, Joey. That's the rule. And don't forget to write them back." Lorrie is already typing in her query on the World Wide Web as Joey pulls out his disk and goes off to print the comments of his Alaska reading response group.

Bent over another screen, Shannon and Ronnie are working with a drawing of a comic book character that they want to improve before sending it to some other X-Men buffs in California. "You're sure we can't send colors, Mrs. Hardin?" Ronnie is convinced that color will make or break their cartoon.

"Why not try it?" suggests Elizabeth, who is typing up a draft of her essay into a small battery-powered keypad. "Ask the kids in California what they see, and if it doesn't work, you can zap the color and send it black and white. You didn't have any color when you started, and it was a good drawing then. Who can help me transfer my writing from the electric keypad to the computer? I'm sending my essay to those kids in Santa Fe."

"I'll help you as soon as this map prints out," Lorrie yells. "Now, open a new document, just as though you were going to type. Then, unplug the computer keyboard. The keypad attaches where the keyboard was." Lorrie leans over to peer at the keypad's four-line screen. "Now, the screen says you're ready. Press the Send key on the keypad. See, there's your essay on the computer screen."

I marveled at them. I could not help myself. In September, neither Joey nor Elizabeth had ever used a computer for writing; Shannon and Ronnie had never drawn without paper and pencil, or known that a scanner could capture a piece of art; Lorrie had never thought of Bosnia, let alone known how to find a specialized map; no one had ever heard of the small Alpha-Smart keypads we used for typing at our desks. Nine months later, they were all seamlessly integrating the technology with their reading, writing, and artwork.

Just as I enjoy my morning drive to school, my students like going places via telecommunications. Just as I choose to take the curvy mountain roads rather than the faster four-lane highway, Elizabeth, Shannon, and Lorrie choose their own roads. We aren't high-tech; we are just a small South Carolina country school with no computer lab, just a few computers scattered throughout the buildings. Yet my students have devised ways to make our two classroom computers, modem, electric keypads, scanner, and printer work for them.

For years, I worried that my classroom at Blue Ridge was too isolated and self-contained both for my students and for me. Like my students, I felt isolated in a culture that did not support frequent interactions with my colleagues or with other adults outside the building. Telecommunications helped to change this.

And all in a year's time. In September, I had just returned from the Bread Loaf School of English in Vermont where I had become part of the Bread Loaf Rural Teachers Network (BLRTN). Rural teachers from six states (Alaska, Arizona, Mississippi, New Mexico, South Carolina, and Vermont) attend the Bread Loaf program in the summer and work together via modem during the subsequent academic year. BLRTN enables rural teachers to link their classrooms as well as to have on-line discussions about teaching, educational trends, cross-curricular projects, and professional conferences.

BLRTN director Rocky Gooch says, "Most BLRTN teachers, network leaders, and staff log on frequently because it supports their classroom work and professional development in so many ways." Conversations on the network are organized into conference groups that range from Native American literature to alternative assessment. Conferences with each of the six states feature collaborative research projects conducted by both teachers and students. BLRTN coordinator Dixie Goswami encourages us to integrate telecommunications not only into our normal classroom curricula but also into our personal lives. "When we're doing our job, the technology becomes invisible," Dixie says.

At the time, Dixie and I were discussing the types of literacy our students would need for continued success in school and in life. Certainly, for my seventh graders, the first graduating class of the year 2000, basic literacy will mean far more than the ability to read a grade-level text or compose a descriptive paragraph. They need to learn to talk with those outside the world of Blue Ridge—naturally, conversationally. They need technology with training wheels, where an occasional wreck does not mean that their driver's licenses will be revoked. Right now, they need cruising time, the freedom to admire the scenery and gab with the natives.

When I first began to use telecommunications, I was determined that it would be simply another tool, not a separate course of study. The benefits of telecommunications seemed obvious to me:

• Telecommunications could make individualized learning and personal inquiry the norm for me and my students, not the exception.

• It could expand the physical limits of our school building and the time limits of the school day.

• It would enable us to communicate and to collaborate with other classrooms across the United States, and to access interesting new resources through the use of commercial networks (America Online, Compuserve, or Prodigy) and the Internet.

• It could increase the number of times we wrote each day, and improve the quality and clarity of our ideas.

• My students would bring an infectious energy and enthusiasm to networking, and I was just as excited by sharing ideas, problems, and solutions with colleagues across the country.

I also already knew the basics of using a network. Whether connected to a state, regional, or private network like BreadNet, or to the Internet (the worldwide "network of networks"), I planned to do three main networking activities with my students: e-mail, computer conferencing, and accessing new information resources.

E-mail. Using e-mail, I wanted my students to exchange research and personal writing with other students on BreadNet, on other commercial networks, and on the Internet. As for myself, I wanted to use e-mail to consult with colleagues in my school district and across the country on curricula, technology, and school reform. E-mail would enable us to have conversations with others across time zones and continents and receive immediate responses. My students could provide a service for our entire school by teaching others how to use e-mail effectively.

Conferencing. My students and I would share information in a "global classroom" where we would discuss an issue with other teachers and students as if we were in the same room. We could join organized discussion groups on topics ranging from Native American literature to protection of the environment.

Remote Information Access. Computer networks, in particular the Internet, make information from around the world available to any classroom. After reviewing the materials available in our media center, I knew my students at Blue Ridge needed access to additional resources, such as:

• Research data from college libraries and news services

• Experts in various fields

• Legal decisions and commentaries

• Information on space flights and space science

• Current information about the rapidly changing world picture, including maps and governmental structures

• Important texts such as the U.S. Constitution and the Koran (both available through Project Gutenberg, a non-profit organization seeking to prepare electronic editions of more than 10,000 books by the year 2001).

Conferencing with a KISS: BreadNet

As an enthusiastic beginner, I was ready to undertake a dozen projects. Fortunately my better judgment quietly reminded me to be patient, and to select my personal projects and my students' networking experiences carefully. Adopting the KISS (Keep It Slow and Simple) philosophy of a network-savvy Alaska colleague, Karen Mitchell, I began by finding relevant professional issues, such as alternative assessment techniques, to discuss on-line with colleagues across the country.

I began by reading the work of my fellow Breadloafers as they discussed a wide array of topics in BreadNet conferences created and structured for discussion of teaching techniques and professional issues.

Since Blue Ridge is part of a South Carolina Department of Education alternative assessment project, and I was piloting the National Standards Portfolio Assessment in my classroom, I wanted to hear other's thoughts, especially on portfolio assessment. Robert Baroz of Vermont was also part of the National Standards pilot, and he highlighted the major issues for me when he answered the question, "What makes the need for alternative assessment so pressing?"

Robert talked freely about his problems in assessing his students' progress over time. "The only information I had," he said, "was whatever grade the student had last year for English and the one writing sample to date. I wondered what to do in order to acquaint myself with my students' histories as readers and writers. I knew that I would see more samples of work as the semester continued, but this meant I would not really see their potential . . . until nearly the end of the semester. Was there a better way?"

I saw that Robert had used exactly the same procedures that I had and was facing the same frustrations. Our state's Basic Skills Writing folder gave no better assessment of student work. We had both approached our students' previous teachers to obtain background information on the students' reading and writing abilities. We had learned about the students' behavioral traits, but not about their writing skills. We had no idea what skills the students had mastered, what progress they had made, or what they needed to continue their progress. I was also searching for ways to include students and parents as active partners in assessment.

As I continued to correspond with Robert over a month's time, I learned that Robert had rewritten with his students the highly technical evaluation scales used by the National Standards Project. This had helped students and parents to understand the evaluation scales more clearly. I began to rewrite the portfolio evaluation language myself and try my rewrites in student and parent conferences. One student wrote me a note about our new evaluation procedures:

> Dear Mrs. Hardin,
> I like the way we can talk about my writing now. My mother told me she never really understood what good writing was until we talked about it with our new checklist last week. I have really changed this year. Thanks, Yvonne.

"Thanks, Robert," I thought, as I looked at Yvonne's portfolio. "I was trying to use someone else's words to talk to students about their own work."

Since I wanted to improve the organizational methods I used in my own classes, in October I began posting questions in the Writers' Workshop Conference. Patricia Parrish of Mississippi inspired me with her practical advice from her experiences in organizing a writing workshop for one hundred eighth grade students. She counseled patience and continuing concern for the students' work:

> From an English teacher's standpoint, many students' writing skills seem poor. I'll tell you, though, when a student finds his or her voice, something he or she wants and needs to write about, that can and will change. Sometimes we can't tell when literacy is creeping into a student's subconscious. Keep having the students write for real purposes, to real audiences, and soon they should care about the quality of what they have chosen to write about.

Patricia explained that choice is a crucial factor in motivating students to write well, and that "peer response is critical . . . not just during drafting and revising, but afterward also."

I saw certain weaknesses in organizing my classroom as a reading-writing workshop. The workshop, as pioneered by Nancie Atwell and Linda Rief, allows students to select their own reading materials and respond with their own observations and with stories, poems, and essays that flow from their literary experiences. Mechanics, grammar, and style are taught through mini-lessons and peer editing while individual conferences guide the students in their reading choices and writing procedures.

I felt that my students needed more concrete direction at first. The workshop model flows most naturally from Whole Language classrooms that have developed students' familiarity with a variety of writing styles, peer critiques, and reading selections. My students came from very rigid, teacher-centered classes. The majority of them did not enjoy writing, and they had never had the freedom to pick their own books. I wanted to find ways to move toward a workshop format that all of us would find comfortable.

During the fall, I continued to ask questions of the Writers' Workshop conference. I began to understand how to adapt this approach for my students. Along with classroom management, I learned about which kinds of mini-lessons had been successful for others, tips on organizing student portfolios, and unique ways to use a reading log. Above all I gained hope and confidence. As Patricia said, "If something doesn't work, try something else, but you have to give students time to grow, to write, to read, to learn."

Talk to Your Friends; Reach Out to Your Family

As we planned our BLRTN conferences, Bread Loaf Director Jim Maddox reminded us, "You can choose your friends, but your family is your support system." Our friends lived across the United States or around the world. Our family consisted of members of the South Carolina Bread Loaf community and other teachers in our state who made networking a part of their classroom techniques.

At Bread Loaf one summer, we began with a series of planning meetings to design our on-line project. In choosing a focus for our state conference, we considered our professional goals and the unique qualities of our students. Professionally, we wanted a challenge, to experience a body of literature from a fresh standpoint, so that we could read, write, and reflect as learners with our students. Considering our students, we noted that rural students live close to the land, and that it would be interesting for them to reflect on their connections to it. We decided to read nature writers like Annie Dillard, and to have our students observe, research, and write about the endangered wetland regions near them. Our students would then share their work with students across our state.

Before we devised our strategies, we identified several professional needs and concerns:

• We were all English teachers; many of us knew little about scientific observation techniques, so we hiked with an environmentalist who helped us plan topics and taught us journal writing techniques to use with our students.

• Nature writing combines scientific terminology with poetic imagery. We decided to learn more about the genre and to select readings that would be appropriate for many reading levels and age groups, so we arranged a workshop with John Elder of Middlebury College, editor of *The Norton Anthology of Nature Writing*, who responded to our many questions about style and approach.

• We had not done nature writing ourselves, so we began our conference by writing about our own wetland areas.

I was unprepared for the moving, emotional tone of much of the writing. I had begun my own piece in a detached, scientific voice, but in other pieces, I began to see how nature writing can combine observation and emotion, merging the two with the reflective quality of memoir. Ginny DuBose, a high school teacher from the Georgetown area of South Carolina, wrote about the barren, abandoned rice fields near her home:

> The rice fields are flat and treeless, as all the cypresses were felled in order to harvest the rice. Here and there through the acres of sweetgrass and marsh grass there may be a solitary bare tree today. The grass grows two to three feet high and in the winter is a golden brown. At intervals there are narrow strips of water which have regained their "normal" channels. Plough mud lines the bottom, but I don't get too close because there are still gators lurking around.

Janet Atkins, another low country teacher, wrote about her river:

> The water was what we call black water, and this particular river, the Salkehatchie, is the headwaters of the Combahee. On a recent visit there, I noted how the water swirled in eddies as it headed toward the ocean. A turtle just under the water's surface snapped at bugs floating above it, and I noted with a certain pleasure that the old cypress tree now reaches at least halfway across the run.
>
> One of the trees on the opposite side of the run once had a rope swing on it. I would dare to swim out into the middle because I could usually touch the rock bottom when the current was slow to moderate, but I never dared cross

to the other side and swing from the rope. The water was so cold! Even when I was younger, I can remember people refusing to get in on a hot July day because they could not stand the cold temperature. Many times I silently thanked the Lord for not making me a Primitive Baptist since they came to our river several times a year to hold baptisms.

Janet had a unique way of relating her broad knowledge of literature to her environmental observations. She compared her river memories to a poem by George Herbert that begins, "As kingfishers catch fire, dragon-flies draw flame. . . ." The Herbert poem then goes on to speak of the calling that each of us has to be true to ourselves. For Janet, this meant "having an alert attentiveness to whatever is there in the present moment. I like to think of that turtle waiting for just the right moment when the water spider is poised on the surface and then 'splash' as he has his din-ner." Janet's moments on the riverbank have a magical quality that helped me appreciate the mysteries in my upcountry wetlands.

Their pieces later served as models for me in the late fall when I wrote a letter on-line to my students after we took a boat trip on Lake Robinson:

> Dear Students,
> Just as I want you to share your thoughts about the wetland experience with me, I also want to share mine with you. These are random thoughts, not an essay or a formal piece of writing at present. Of the comments I make, what sticks with you? What feelings do you share? What questions do you have? Let's write each other on-line, so that when we read our pieces, we will see them first on the screen, as we will see the writing of so many others this year.
> Your teacher, Mrs. Hardin

Around Lake Robinson and Its Wetlands

A gray sky looms around our small boats as we set off across the lake. Lake warden Chuck Barnes, bearded and intense, drives one boat, while his assistant, a laid-back, down-home fellow, pilots another. The air is moist, threatening rain, and we huddle inside our coats as the boats move toward the dam. Josh sits at the edge of the boat, leaning into the wind. "See any fish?" he calls back to Chuck.

Looking at the depth finder, Chuck shakes his head. "Nope. Noth-ing running today," he says.

Forty feet of water beneath us. The lake waters, propelled by the South Tyger River currents, rushing 65 feet down the concrete face of the dam to meander toward Lake Cunningham and the filtration plant.

This source provides the drinking water for the majority of the Blue Ridge and Greer communities. When we turn on the tap at school, when we stop at the water fountain, when we guzzle iced tea in the lunchroom, we are drinking Lake Robinson.

Yet, it is more than a source of drinking water. There is a spirit existing out here that is absent inside buildings. Perhaps it is the same spirit that spoke to the Cherokees when they roamed this place in the times before white settlers arrived. They called the mountains "The Great Blue Hills of God." Today the mountains seem to hover above the lake, misty blue. The water is gray, brown, swirling with silt and sediment stirred from the bottom by the rains and the cooling temperature.

Chuck says that warm water, like warm air, rises. That way, the entire lake turns upside down in a kind of thermal reversal. As the surface cools, the warmer bottom water rises to the top. The heating and cooling and the endless turning of the water, in tune with the seasons.

On my way to school in the mornings, I drive across a lake shrouded by mist, as though some giant bubbling fire beneath the ground were boiling all the water away from the earth's crust. The witch's cauldron of the earth.

So many signs of fall out here on the water—the leaves in an endless mosaic of gold, russet, and amber, purple and brown, green underneath, mirrored in the lake. Our boat went gliding, sliding into watery leaves which rippled out of our way and then were torn apart into gushing foam as we sped away.

Working in groups over a week's time, the students wrote responses to my letter, referring frequently to the observation logs that they each had kept during the boat trip. One student put each group's work on-line. Josh, who looked for fish throughout our trip, wrote a special note at the bottom of his group's response to explain how he felt about composing on the computer for the first time:

> Mrs. Hardin, this is weird. Writing on the computer doesn't feel permanent. Words fly through the air, stop for a minute on the screen, and then disappear, then come back again, like a magic spell. Weird. Josh.

Elizabeth wanted to express her concerns about the environment. She responded with an essay she wrote on her own:

> Turn on your tap so that cool, refreshing water can flow. Now, take a long swallow of that good old Blue Ridge Mountain water. One taste has the flavor of the mountain streams that wind their way through the gently rolling hills and around the grassy meadows of the Carolina Piedmont. Glassy and Hogback Mountains, the source of the water supply, stand like monuments behind the trees. From a trickling spring, the water flows into a wandering river, then

into a man-made lake, surrounded by pines and filled with life invisible to all but the watchful eye.

Her writing reflected what she had learned from the boat trip, as well as her observations of wildlife:

The marshes that filled with silt after the river was dammed up act as a sponge to cleanse the water before it reaches the watershed. Here small islands, patches of land daubed randomly among wide pools, protect muskrats and kingfishers. A blue heron swoops over the water, watching for fish that swim darkly beneath the surface. His great wing curves over his head as he pushes forward, soaring through the air. Above, dark rain clouds hang low and heavy, ready to replenish the lake below.

Elizabeth returned to this piece many times. "I've never written like this," she said in a writing conference and in her self-evaluation. "I've never thought about each word. I keep reading it again and again, changing a little something each time."

Barrett and his group tried to tell a humorous story exactly as they heard it from the lake warden:

"There was this old guy over here," said Chuck with a laugh, "who bought some lake property and thought he would plant lots of flowering trees, dogwoods, you know. He must've spent $200 on trees, and he planted them around his land, down to the lake, up his driveway. Next day, he come roaring up to our office just a' yelling. 'Somebody done cut down all my trees,' he yelled. I hated to tell him that somebody weighed about forty pounds and had a lot of brown fur. Those beavers just love sweet little dogwoods. I reckon he better plant scrub pines if he wants to keep trees on his lot. All them dogwoods are now part of that beaver dam over there.

"We wanted to use his words," Barrett noted later. "We wanted it to sound like him talking."

My students were eager to send their environmental stories to kids in other states. They had to learn, however, that computer conferences can move only as fast as the hands that type the stories. When New Mexico students responded weeks later with questions and poems, my students immediately began to compose answers. Nancie Atwell has described the perfect classroom reading response discussions as good dinnertable conversation. My students and I found that BLRTN on-line conversation is indeed homey and personal at times, like the chatter of good friends or family at the evening meal.

During the winter months, my students continued telling stories and recording interviews of local residents in their journals. One group wrote accompanying text for a photography book about their Lake Robinson trip; another exchanged postcard poems with ninth grade students in New Mexico, explaining their relationship to the Blue Ridge area, as in this poem by David Willard:

Blue Ridge Afternoon

Brown fall grasses stick out
Like cowlicked hair;
The birds are not singing;
They pout on fences
Like black notes on a music scale;
The bark on the pecan tree is old,
And wrinkled,
Its leaves fall and are blown by the wind
Like an old man losing his hair,
Not dead; just used up;
But the sun is warm against my face,
And I am full of life.

Kenneth Lane, a New Mexico student, responded:

The waves crash on the rocks,
And he sits on the shore.
As the stars and the moon looked down upon the earth,
They saw one lonely boy,
Dreading the next day.
So guilty yet so innocent,
Who cares what people say!
They laugh, and make fun of him.
Some people are so dumb.
But lonely is he, that sits by the sea,
Waiting for the sunlight to come . . .

Keeping It Close to Home

One option we had not tried was working on-line with another local school that wanted to share science activities and field trips. At a county networking conference in February, I met Johnnie Parker, a science teacher from an urban middle school about thirty miles away. Johnnie complained that her students were studying local water pollution but couldn't find a stream's source in downtown Greenville. "Not another word," I warned. "We should do all of our planning on-line, just to see how reliable our e-mail is."

After exchanging e-mail addresses, we began networking the next day. I had already planned a hike along the course of a stream for my students. Her seventh graders would join us, bringing along their water testing equipment. One of our parent volunteers, Rich Quemere, would lead the hike, helping students trace the path of the stream into the watershed. Johnnie and I spent six weeks working on-line, from our initial planning sessions to the final trip and evaluation.

To help the two classes get to know each other, we asked each student to compose a short autobiography in the shape of a name poem. Students drew a partner's name from a hat, and sent the poems via e-mail. The autobiographical poems had to reveal the authors' personalities, interests, and relationships with nature. After our trip, the students would evaluate each other's poetic accuracy. Lindsey Drake felt her poem really summed her up well:

> Lover of horses,
> Implicated in all family crimes by her wicked sister,
> Needs companionship,
> Detests goody-goodies;
> Savors chunky fudge ice cream to the last bite;
> Envious of straight-A students,
> Your friend, if you are willing to be mine.

Before the trip, Johnnie and I exchanged daily messages about experiments, designed student observation logs, and planned follow-up questions. After the hike, students compared response logs, traded the results of their pollution tests, and evaluated the name poems. Lindsey discovered that she and her partner both have access to America Online, and they started to correspond via e-mail.

Reflecting on the trip, I see that using telecommunications had several benefits for us and our students. In phone conversations, Johnnie and I tended to ramble, gossiping about acquaintances or debating needless points. Writing out our plans and sending them as e-mail focused us on the necessary details. For instance, we anticipated that every student would need a map of the trail to annotate and, since her students did not keep journals, a personal response log.

The students were eager to see how well their partners' name poems matched reality. Much of the nervousness common to seventh graders turned into instant collaboration. While we hiked, several Blue Ridge boys told local ghost stories. Johnnie's students had more experience with soil and water testing, and they demonstrated exactly how to take a reliable sample. The entire group worked together on gathering accurate data for their response logs. By the end of the hike, all of the students were planning a reunion at the local mall.

As an evaluation, Johnnie and I listed the elements of our on-line work that were most successful. First, we had limited the number of participating students. I used two small groups of five students each; Johnnie had one group. The chosen students were from a broad range of ability levels, but all were emotional about environmental issues. Next, we carefully planned the number and kinds of on-line exchanges, and we agreed on deadline dates for the students' work to be posted. Last, we provided a variety of activities. I directed the writing response portions; Johnnie took charge of the data gathering. Next time, we hope the students will be able to create charts, graphs, and community surveys based on their observations. We would also like the project to include a public presentation so that the groups can exhibit their collaborative efforts.

Inhabiting the Consequences of Our Work

In our state meetings, BLRTN Coordinator Dixie Goswami encouraged us to help our students use writing to benefit our communities by composing or revising various documents. Community-based writing projects allow students to improve their communication skills as well as to make a difference in their world. Students have rewritten brochures to appeal to young people, published community histories, or researched the benefits of class scheduling changes for their schools.

My students liked reading about other community-based projects on BreadNet and had many ideas about how they could share our wetlands project on-line. One group supplemented their own ideas for a writing project with suggestions from a wetlands forum sponsored by CNN and available on the Internet. As they conversed on-line with "environmentally aware" middle schoolers across the country, the group kept double entry logs. On one side they listed details from the forum that they knew already; on the other, they noted new ideas, organizations, or methods of protecting wetlands areas. Dail Wilson's log contained the following list:

Did Know
1. Adopt a Highway
2. Recycle
3. Make better building laws to keep silt and chemicals from wetlands
4. Make good rules about fishing and swimming near wildlife habitats

Didn't Know
1. There is an Adopt-a-Stream Program in Georgia; we could do this too.
2. We can get brochures from Water Conservancy.
3. Kids in Wisconsin made a film about their wetlands; I would like this project.
4. Some kids in Colorado did a duck race on their river to raise money for a wetland project.

Dail's group finally chose to publish a brochure. They began to collect data from every available resource. They debated over which facts to include. The entire group wanted to include a brief historical section about the Blue Ridge community along with some examples of area wildlife and methods of protecting the watershed, but some members were specifically interested in the region's Indian heritage; others thought people would like to learn the origins of place names like Blind Tiger Road. They finally decided that a brochure about Lake Robinson itself would help community members to appreciate the unique features of the lake, and to understand what they must do to preserve it. "We could put our brochures at the Lake Warden's office," suggested Stefan Bachman. "That way lots of people will see them when they get fishing licenses."

To illustrate the brochure, Dail's group obtained old-fashioned drawings of animals from public-domain graphics files on the Internet and an excellent map of South Carolina from the Smithsonian, and scanned one of their own photographs. They e-mailed the text to their mentor, a copy editor at an advertising agency in downtown Greenville, 25 miles away, who had agreed to help with the brochure's publication. After testing their brochure on parents, the copy editor, and the lake warden, the students used a desktop publishing program to assemble graphics and text and gave the completed files to the printer on several disks. By the middle of May, their brochures were available in five community centers.

Using the computer to compose, revise, and communicate encourages students to increase the amount of writing they do and their willingness to revise, but it also increases their expectation of immediate response. My students placed their brochures at the lake warden's office, local stores, and community gathering places, but they had to wait for people to notice and respond to their work. They treasured the few phone calls from area residents, a letter of congratulation from the state legislature, and requests to print additional copies for civic groups.

My students felt they had made a difference in the attitudes of Blue Ridge residents, but for me the greatest change occurred in my students' attitudes about writing for the public. They brought in dozens of brochures published by local groups and read them with critical eyes, evaluating visual appeal and word choice. They also thought of the writers who created the brochures. Whenever they found an e-mail address, they sent the brochure publishers a message of congratulations. "People need to write back to the authors when they like a brochure," said Josh.

Virtual Conversations

By sixth period every day, I have circled my room dozens of times, talked to individuals and groups, stacked folders of papers to check on my desk, and quieted the noisy or encouraged the quiet. The computer terminals are still busy until the last bus is called, with students sending a note or looking up some unusual fact. While I sit alone at my desk, a few die-hards cruise the Internet, looking for new video games. I begin to write responses for journals, check tests, enter weekly grades, and brush up the remains of the day while the janitor walks the hall, sweeping, the clanking of her cart stopping and starting like my hand above the paper.

At 5:00 P.M., I give it up, chase the Myst fans out the door, and turn everything off. I take home a few journals, a book to read for next week, and head out to my van. The sun is just turning the lake waters glistening red, and the wind from Glassy Mountain is fresh and clean. Back toward town, I cross the watershed going home. Canada geese are making test flights over the lake, and a heron curves low over Few's Bridge.

I settle into my evening routines: dinner, a walk with my son, bedtime stories, some time at the computer, a mystery novel, a restless sleep.

By 4:00, I'm awake again. I reflect that the grind of school dulls me emotionally, and sometimes I feel that I have little left for the others in my life. At 4:30, I lie down again, but the voices echoing in my head are too loud for sleep.

I give up on sleep and get up. Sitting in front of my computer, I log on to America Online, checking the news and imagining a trip to England. Then I log on to BreadNet, to check my e-mail. I bet that no one is on-line at this hour, but decide to check anyway. Surprise. Scott Christian from Alaska is on. His class is editing a book of writing from BLRTN students all over the United States. Just seeing his name gives me a lift.

As I read and respond to my students' articles and colleagues' suggestions and comments on BreadNet each evening, I talk to myself about the work I am doing this year. I review my own writing, my experiments with style, my attempts to model good prose for my students. I learn from others' questions. They tell me what they are thinking. When I speak out loud, I may speak without full consideration, but the computer screen focuses me on my words. "Do I mean that?" I ask. "How was my experience similar?" I have time to push the cursor back through the sentences— to delete, to rephrase.

With telecommunications, I have broken out of my isolated classroom. Now my colleagues can visit me daily if they wish. We can plan research; we can draft and rewrite and publish; we can make presentations of our ideas; we can share workshop or convention experiences. Though we are only scribbling on electronic paper, I feel the presence of the friends and family of our on-line community.

As a teacher, I am learning to be true to myself, to my writing, to my instincts, to my students. I'm still learning Janet Atkins's "alert attentiveness" to the present moment. Too often, the moments have flowed past me, rushing over the dam before I made meaning from them. The network allows me to save the artifacts of my classroom and to look at them again when the house is quiet and thoughts ease out, moving rhythmically or swirling murkily like a low country river.

Robin Lambert

The Kentucky Authors Project

Authors and Students in On-line Partnerships

THE KENTUCKY AUTHORS PROJECT was a one-year experiment de-signed to explore ways to bring students and published authors together in on-line writing partnerships. It involved fourth through eleventh graders and seven teachers at five Kentucky schools, and eight published authors.* The project had two main goals: first, for students to go through a process of writing and revising their own work, with an author's help, to produce a polished final piece for their portfolios; and second, for students to engage authors about the authors' writing processes, their lifestyles, and works the authors had published or were drafting.

About the Project

The five schools involved in the project were located in demographically diverse communities scattered across the state. The schools had partici-pated the previous two years in the Kentucky Telecommunications Writing Project (KTWP). Through KTWP, students were experienced in sending and responding to "notes" posted on electronic bulletin boards in several dozen topical conferences. They had also exchanged personal notes, read and discussed books in "lit groups," and participated in several shared curriculum projects designed by the teachers.

I joined KTWP as coordinator in August of its third and final year. Early in the fall, KTWP's supervisor asked participating teachers to de-velop a project involving authors and students in on-line partnerships. The request was accompanied by a $10,000 grant from the State Writing Program for authors' fees and on-line expenses. The KTWP teachers were excited but apprehensive, as they would be charting unknown waters.

---

* The eight authors were John Cech, Artie Ann Bates, Jenny Davis, Gurney Norman, Jenny Galloway Collins, Jim Wayne Miller, Kate Larken, and George Ella Lyon. The five schools were McNabb Elementary in Paducah, Holmes Jr. High in Covington, The Brown School in Louisville, Saints Peter and Paul School in Lexington, and South Floyd High School in Hi Hat.

The teachers decided to develop a general structure for the project before asking authors to participate. It started with a conference call involving me, the teachers, and our project researcher. Our basic plan paired each author with a group of students for the duration of the project. We decided to create an on-line "conference" for each group. Students would post drafts; authors would respond with comments, suggestions, and examples of their own work; and students could post their revisions. The conferences would be open so anyone in KTWP could browse and read the exchanges. (We agreed that interactions unsuitable for public perusal could be posted in the private on-line mailboxes of teachers and authors.) The teachers also decided that each student should try to complete at least one polished piece of writing in collaboration with his or her author. We left genre and topic open to negotiation between author and student. Once the project began, the individual teachers would work out the daily details directly with the authors with whom they were working.

We also wanted students to read their author's work and to post direct queries to him or her about his or her writing process, life, and work. We created no specific structure for this. Rather, we chose to see how these interactions might develop naturally in conjunction with the writing conferences.

The teachers suggested authors and asked me to make the contacts and arrange the pairings. Our pool of authors included writers whose work teachers admired, those who were known to work with school groups, and authors who were listed with the State Arts Council. Most lived in Kentucky.

We contacted nine authors, and all but one agreed to participate. As only one of the eight had experience with telecommunications, KTWP agreed to provide technical training and support. Most of the authors already had some computer equipment. KTWP borrowed or purchased the additional components each author needed for a functional telecommunications system.

We agreed to have the project begin with students and authors posting a personal introduction. We asked the eight authors to tell something of their lives and their approach to writing. We asked the students, after introducing themselves, to suggest areas of writing with which they wanted help. After these introductory exchanges, students posted pieces of writing. Some were continuations of their personal introductions; others were stories, poems, or essays, in greater or lesser states of completion. The authors responded to these posts, and the students came back with enthusiastic revisions, new pieces, or questions. This interaction continued through the school year.

What We Learned

Through the seven months of the Kentucky Authors Project, we learned a great deal that might be helpful to others interested in on-line partnerships between students and authors.

1. Teachers and authors should plan the project together. The plan should address specific needs and goals. Here are some important questions to ask: Are you looking for polished final drafts? Do you want students to concentrate on one piece or produce a number of pieces? Are there specific genres you want the students to work in? Are there aspects of writing you wish to emphasize—voice, for example? How will responsibilities be split between teacher and author? Will the teacher read every piece before it is posted? Will students post first drafts? Do the author and the teacher agree on the writing process and how it is taught? Will there be a final product, such as a class collection of stories and poems? How will the on-line partnership fit with the ongoing curriculum? While both teachers and authors should be somewhat flexible, they should decide how they will approach each of these issues before the project begins. At the project's end, everyone agreed that planning and training should take place in the summer, so that the partnership can be integrated with the ongoing curriculum from the beginning of the school year.

In addition, the author should discuss what kind of feedback he or she is most comfortable providing, and the teacher should indicate what he or she feels students need. Deadlines should be established for how often students post and how quickly authors respond. Teachers and authors should plan a regular process for "checking in" with each other to reflect on the work and make necessary changes. It doesn't matter whether the planning takes place in person, over the phone, or on-line.

Participants in the Kentucky Authors Project learned some of this the hard way. In the structure we developed, we failed to build in a process for teachers and authors to plan together once they were paired. Rather, we said it *should* happen and left it up to teachers to initiate. The conferences in which teachers and authors followed up with a specific plan were more successful and satisfying to all involved.

2. Conferences work best when authors combine personal "talk" about themselves with direct, specific responses to individual student writing.

As mentioned above, each conference began with personal introductions. Students talked mostly about their families, hobbies, and favorite books. Authors talked about their childhoods, their personal lives, and their writing. (Interestingly, most apologized to the students for their lack of technical skill with telecommunications.) The exchange of introductions drew students into the project and opened up topics for discussion. The following is an excerpt of author Artie Ann Bates introducing herself to a group of fourth graders:

> Dear Students:
> I'm looking forward to working with you on this writing project. This is the first time I have done anything like this, and it has been slow getting the kinks out of the modem. I think we will all have fun sharing our writing, and I shall put a map of Kentucky by the computer so I can see Paducah when I read your notes.
>
> You have been so nice to tell me about yourselves, and now I would like to return the favor. My name is Artie Ann Bates and I am 41 years old. My husband's name is John Cleveland, and our twelve-year-old son is Davy Cleveland. I have been a medical doctor in eastern Kentucky for seven years.
>
> My family and I live in the mountains of Kentucky, in a holler. In case you have never heard of a holler, it is a narrow valley between two mountains which a small creek has hollowed over thousands of years. We live in a century-old log house that was once my great-grandparents'. Their youngest daughter, Artie, was my grandmother and she was married in this house. There is much family history here, and a place with history is a gold mine to a writer.
>
> John, Davy, and I have quite a few animals; twenty-one, to be exact. We love animals and during the five years we have lived here, they have accumulated. There are four dogs, three cats, eight chickens, two ducks, one bunny rabbit, a horse, a pot-bellied pig, and an iguana. Everyone lives outside except the iguana, who is cold-blooded and must have the heat of the house to keep him warm. In time, I will tell you a little about each one of these pets, for each has a distinct personality. They are so different that if I described one of them, without saying the name, to either Davy or John, they could surely figure out the one of which I spoke. Perhaps there is one of these creatures that you would like to get to know first; if so please let me know.
>
> I am glad we are getting to know each other. Perhaps someday we can meet in person, but for now we will correspond via computer. Thank you. . . .

The authors' introductions prompted many questions from students, many of them personal, some of them about writing:

> Hello Ms. Larkin,
> . . . I really don't like writing because it takes a long time sometimes. I sometimes get writer's block. . . . If you have any positive suggestions to help me in some way please feel free. Thank you!

... I like to write but I have trouble getting endings. How do you make your stories end?

Dear Jenny,
What were your dreams when you were my age? Did you have any at all? Sometimes I think I have too many views on issues. Write me back.

Dear John Cech:
What kind of books have you written? I would like to be just like you. I think I will like your books when I get them. I like fiction books myself! I like very funny stories that are fiction books such as *Fudge-a-Mania*! I don't really have any experience with writing to famous people so if I make a mistake I am sorry if it is not proficient or distinguished! And I am a little nervous about writing. I hope I can get over it. Were you nervous when you started? Well I have to go sorry I have to but I do!

For some, a group response just wouldn't do. One ninth grader boldly expressed what was on her mind:

Dear Jenny,
Although you did send information on your background and history as a writer it did not come out very clear. Some of it was cut off. I can't send my pieces to someone I know so little about. If you would please, send me some more personal information. Answer for me these questions: How did you first decide to become a writer? Does it pay good? What are the advantages and disadvantages? Is it time-consuming? Do you work from your home? Was this always your dream? Are you rich? For now that is all I would like to know unless you just want to add some more information about yourself, your family. I would appreciate all of these to be answered, and in the meantime I'll be thinking of more!

Most students have a hard time imagining authors as real people and an even harder time imagining themselves as authors. The personal side of the author-student interaction often engaged students more deeply with their writing or encouraged them to reveal something important about themselves. After one author mentioned caring for a stepson with severe cerebral palsy, an eighth grader wrote back and revealed her own battle with the disease, which she had never before mentioned at school. In response the author said,

I understand why you try to keep your history with CP to yourself. People don't always understand and it's hard to feel different. I think though that probably your experiences, even though they are hard to endure, will make you a better writer in the long run because you have had to feel more than most people. Hang in there, and don't be afraid to be yourself.

3. On-line writing projects work best when they are an integral part of the curriculum. Most students participated well in the personal introductions and questions. Most also sent a draft for their author to respond to. In all cases, the authors responded to both the personal questions and writing samples. Fewer students revised and re-posted. Some wrote back more personal questions; some posted a second, unrelated, piece of writing; some dropped off the network altogether.

In schools where the Authors Project was an "add-on" component to the regular classroom curriculum, the conferences tended to lose focus and energy. They were more likely to fall through the cracks of the school day, and both students and authors expressed confusion and frustration. Without direct classroom support, most students lacked the motivation, time, or confidence to do the revisions required for a polished piece of writing, and the authors on the other end of the modem couldn't do much about it beyond offering encouragement. One author described her conference as "parallel writing," meaning that she would post something and students would write, but their writing would seem unrelated to her post.

4. Telecommunications makes possible long-term interactions and lends itself best to the earlier stages of the writing process. All the participants noted that the medium of telecommunications is particularly good at supporting the conceptual work of writing. Author John Cech described it as "great for seeding ideas." This was especially true when the conferences were well-coordinated between teacher and author, or when individual students took an exceptional interest. Jim Wayne Miller, an author who had a particularly productive relationship with one prolific young writer, described the process this way: "It's turning up things much like you would turn up an arrowhead while ploughing a field."

The opportunity to work over an extended period of time was cited by authors and teachers alike as a great advantage over traditional short-term writing workshops. Every author remarked that it was personally gratifying to see a work mature, to learn an individual student's voice. One said it felt like a "mentorship." The medium of telecommunications encourages frequent and ongoing exchanges and makes students more comfortable with writing; for instance, it makes it easy for students to post works-in-progress. A teacher of rather reluctant writers said this ease reassured and motivated her students, who would have been intimidated by having to produce a lengthy piece before receiving feedback. Authors commented that being able to post frequent, short responses helped them give specific suggestions without the worry of overwhelming students. It also allowed them to catch problems early and redirect students before a piece went way off track.

While telecommunications works very well for drafting and revising, everyone in our project agreed that a bulletin board service does not work for the final editing stage of the writing process. Technically, it is difficult to mark on a piece of writing directly. Our network had nothing approximating a red pen. Participants agreed that editing is best accomplished when teacher and student sit side-by-side and work out correct grammar and punctuation.

5. General exercises and advice were less effective than personal responses to student work. In order to encourage students to put up new pieces or to revise, several authors posted "mini-lessons" in their conferences. Generally these were short instructional posts having to do with elements of good writing. Several authors suggested exercises for students to complete. By and large, these met with stony on-line silence. One teacher told me privately that the mini-lessons "went right over my students' heads." The younger students particularly found it difficult to abstract from general posts to their own writing. In some cases, the sophisticated tone of the students' personal introductions may have misled authors:

> I enjoy writing poetry more than anything else and right now I am trying to concentrate on rhyme, structure, and rhythm. My poetry has always been very abstract. . . .

Some students simply viewed their writing as personal and didn't want to be told what to do. "I guess that you could say that I enjoy writing but only when I can come up with my own ideas. I absolutely hate it when a teacher says, 'Here, write a story about such and such,'" one said.

At the project's end, teachers said that for *them* the authors' instructional posts had been great. They learned from the mini-lessons and gained many ideas for future activities. But everyone agreed that mini-lessons are of little use to students unless they are coordinated with the teacher's activities, and are accompanied by opportunities to write and get a response. As author Jim Wayne Miller put it,

> Authors doing this kind of work shouldn't be concerned with uploading materials students haven't asked for. They should be more centered on student work. If an "essay-ette" is done, it should be drawn out of student work and posted as an epilogue or comment on student work.

Some Considerations for Working with Authors On-line

1. Select and pair authors carefully. When I first contacted the authors, I explained the program, and asked if they would like to participate in some way. I asked a number of questions to aid me in pairing them with specific groups of students: What age students do you prefer to work with? About how much time could you devote to the project each week? About how many students do you anticipate being able to work with in that time? What kind of computer equipment do you have access to? What kind of experiences have you had with on-line communication? This information enabled me to make pairings that were satisfying to both authors and students. It also enabled me to determine the number of authors we would need.

2. Authors should be paid. Several authors confessed a frustration with the frequency with which they are approached by schools to work for free. The Kentucky Authors Project was designed to pay authors. We based the pay scale for the project on roughly two-thirds the fee normally paid for writers-in-residence programs in Kentucky schools. The stipends were calculated on the number of hours each author estimated he or she would devote to the project. It was paid in two lump sums: one-half at the beginning of the project and one-half at its completion. The authors expressed satisfaction with this arrangement and felt it was fair since they were able to work at home, on their own time, without having to travel to the schools.

3. Allow plenty of time and support for technical training. While all of the authors had worked in schools, mostly in one-day workshops or short-term residencies, only one was familiar with telecommunications. Several needed training in word processing and in using a modem. While the authors were all willing to participate in pioneering something new, some expressed apprehension and sometimes deep skepticism. If they ran into technical difficulties early in the project, this skepticism was intensified.

And they did run into problems, many of which are common to most telecommunications projects. Every author used a different word processing and communications package. One had noise problems on her home phone line. Another had to learn to disable most of the features of her modem to connect with our bulletin board.

Because the authors were scattered across the state (and two lived out of state), training was difficult. We assigned each author a "buddy" who lived nearby and could offer technical support and training. Every author stressed this need for technical support. Several said they would have quit the program in the beginning had it not been for the immediate and personal support they received.

It took two full months to train the authors. Because the authors were not interested in the technology for its own sake and were anxious to get on with writing, this training period required support and encouragement. However, by the project's end all of the authors were enthusiastic about the new possibilities the technology offered.

The Advantages of Telecommunications

The authors also identified several advantages of telecommunications over traditional classroom writing workshops and residencies. These included:

• *The opportunity to reflect before responding.* Several authors said that because they did not have to provide an immediate response to student work, but could read and reflect at their leisure, they were able to provide more serious and considered suggestions. (They also noted that when a student note seemed urgent, they could respond immediately.) They repeatedly cited the opportunity to provide frequent short responses to student work as a distinct advantage.

• *Attention to language.* The authors noted that the fact that they don't see students and can't rely on the visual and aural clues of conversation forces them to pay extra careful attention to written language—both students' and their own.

• *Opportunities to work with students in faraway places.* Telecommunications helps overcome the constraints of time and distance. The authors felt that the opportunity to work simultaneously with students in different locales sharpened their own cultural perspectives and brought new and varied meaning to their work and reflections on it.

• *More opportunity to get feedback from young people.* Several authors in the project write for children and young adults. They posted pieces of their own work and invited students to respond. The flattered students responded eagerly and seriously, as in:

Dear Gurney [Norman],
After watching the Appalshop production of "Fat Monroe" and reading the story [in *Kinfolks*] I still have a few questions to ask. First off, were you involved at all in the production of the film? After reading the story I was really taken aback by how close the movie was to the story, there's almost no difference, which is something very rare. The story does have a few sentences which make a change that makes you feel much more at home in the story. I

think that in the film you really feel out of touch, like you're walking into the middle of something, it's really sort of awkward.

I know you spent a lot of time on this story, and did you ever consider adding more to the end? The story leaves you in a very high emotional state, but still with a lot of questions. Did you ever try tacking on a few sentences at the end as sort of an explanation of Wilgus's feelings? Not enough to take down the emotion, but to take away a couple of questions.

I'd also like to know a little about how you write. Revising and working on a piece for ten years is just unthinkable to me. Do you think that you could still work on it more, or did you finally get it right?

... Thank you for taking the time to correspond with us. I enjoyed your short story immensely. I thought that it made a very good point about how we learn lessons in our life, or at least how we should.

Sincerely,
Shaun Alvey

The authors appreciated such seriousness, and found the feedback valuable.

• *The opportunity to work at home on one's own schedule.* All the authors appreciated how telecommunications allowed them to set their own schedules. All were conscientious about making prompt responses, but were glad for the freedom from specific obligations as to time and place.

• *Opportunities to talk with other authors and teachers about the work.* The Kentucky Author Project provided two vehicles for project-wide communication between the authors and teachers. The first was a conference open to adults only, called "Author Talk." Designed to address issues of philosophy, approach, and process, the conference was for the teachers and authors to communicate with each other as formally or informally as they wished. While "Author Talk" did not receive heavy traffic, the authors felt it offered them an unusual opportunity to share their teaching ideas with others. A number expressed regret that they did not make better use of the conference. The second vehicle was a newsletter for public distribution describing activities in KTWP, among them the Kentucky Authors Project. All participants liked the newsletter and the sense of connection it provided with others in the project, and to KTWP as a whole.

New Questions the Kentucky Authors Project Raised

Telecommunications creates new problems as well as new opportunities. It is not as private as personal mail. It's not exactly one-to-one communication. It's more like one-to-many communication; but, unlike broadcast communications, it is interactive. It is not as formal as print publishing, but is a kind of publishing. It can be both chatty and serious. As Jim

Wayne Miller observed, "For a long time communication in much of the world has been oral. Then there was print, and oral and print communications went along together. This is a hybrid . . . It may be that the medium may alter the message sometimes." The forms and meanings of telecommunications are being created as those of us involved go along.

Several issues related to the newness of this form of communication emerged in the project. One had to do with manners. Some students seemed to feel less accountable than in a face-to-face situation. On one occasion a student made a particularly rude remark to an author. The comment prompted a discussion of the content and style of appropriate and useful criticism. Sometimes students seemed rather inattentive to what they posted. One author who worked with elementary students noted that the medium could foster a potentially counterproductive "casualness" in student writing.

Finally, telecommunications can blur the distinction between process and product. Its natural potential for supporting the early stages of the writing process may need to be balanced by emphasis on completing individual pieces. Participants should decide if they want to culminate their work on-line by publishing a collection of finished pieces. This issue of when to emphasize process or product needs to be negotiated by teachers and authors before the project begins, and then re-assessed during the project.

In any good project, all the participants must feel ownership for it to be successful. But we learned that *a sense* of ownership is not sufficient. Because telecommunications writing projects are new and few participants will have experience in charting a project's course, careful ongoing planning is necessary to keep them from drifting. Despite—and maybe because of—some of our difficulties, we count the Kentucky Authors Project a success. We all learned—about writing, about technology, and about the ever-changing process of communicating. Now, every one of us is looking for opportunities to undertake a similar effort in the future.

Beverly Paeth

Dear Jenny

IT WAS AN extraordinary opportunity for my junior high students. A published author whose books they could hold in their hands was willing to participate with them in an on-line writing workshop. My eighth grade Chapter 1 students at Holmes Junior High in Covington, Kentucky, were using telecommunications to create an on-line community of writers with four other schools in Kentucky. After two years of working and writing together on-line, we (the Kentucky Telecommunications Writing Program) decided to expand our program with a five-month writing workshop that would involve eight Kentucky authors. Each author would be paired up with a KTWP classroom.

The author I selected for my students was Jenny Davis, a writer and teacher from Lexington, Kentucky, about eighty miles south of Covington. I had met Ms. Davis several years earlier on a perfect fall day at an authors' fair celebrating Kentucky writers. I slowly strolled among the authors' displays, perusing their books in hopes of discovering young adult books for my classroom library. I purchased several books that day, including one by Ms. Davis, *Good-bye and Keep Cold*. I spent a few minutes talking to her while she autographed the inside cover. I remembered her as being friendly, a free spirit, warm, and approachable. Sometime during that school year I sat down to read *Good-bye and Keep Cold,* a beautifully written story about a young family in an eastern Kentucky coal mining town who face tragedy and learn how to get on with their lives.

When we were planning the Kentucky Authors Project for our on-line community, each of the teachers and administrators in our project was asked to select an author he or she wanted to work with. I immediately thought of Jenny Davis. I knew Jenny's books would touch my students because they were about the issues that interest teenagers: love, caring for others, family, tragedy, and friendships. The administrator of our project contacted Jenny and she agreed to work with my students.

Jenny's busy schedule allowed her to work with only eight students. I selected eight girls for the project because Jenny's main characters are girls about the same age as my students. I was hoping that my at-risk students would make an instant "connection" with her books. When selecting students for the project, I asked for two things from them: a commitment to participate until the project was over, and a willingness to read Jenny's books beforehand. The students varied greatly in writing ability: two I considered to be the best writers in my class; four were average; and two were novice. Because I taught five classes, I also tried to select at least one student from each class so that all my students were involved—indirectly or directly—in the project.

The selection process completed, the project began with the eight girls reading Jenny's books. At the time the project started, Ms. Davis had three published books: *Checking on the Moon, Good-bye and Keep Cold,* and *Sex Education.* (As you might have guessed, *Sex Education* was the one book everyone wanted to read.) Some girls read all three books, some only one. Then each girl first wrote a short introductory note to Jenny. In their notes, the students introduced themselves with short narratives, sometimes commenting on Jenny's books.

> Hi, my name is Titus Warrington and I go to Holmes Jr. High. . . . I'm 14 years old, in the eighth grade, like to read, like to use the computer and have my friends by my side.
>
> I'm reading your book *Good-bye and Keep Cold.* I really like your book. I was thinking of writing my own book but I don't have any ideas but one. That idea is about Howell Street Boys. They are a bunch of boys who live on Howell Street and hang out together.
>
> I am glad that we chose you. I'm pretty sure this year will be progress if we keep in touch. I am really easy to get along with I think. . . .
>
> If you think L.A. is bad you should see Covington. We have people begging for money, living on the river, afraid of work, and we have a lot of criminals.
>
> I have 2 brothers (Brian 18—alive and Phillip 17—died) and I have 2 sisters (Betty Jo 20—alive and Angel—died).
>
> Hello, my name is Rachael England. I'm an eighth grader at Holmes Jr. High. . . .
>
> Covington is not all that bad. People say it is worse than it really is. There is not a lot of crime here. It is actually kind of nice.
>
> . . . I like mystery and love stories. I am reading one of your books as we speak. I am reading *Sex Education.* I think it is pretty good. . . .
>
> I like to write stories and poems. When I write my stories I base them on dreams that I have. I can't really write poems unless I am sad or angry. I usually write my feelings. Half the time, I end up crying because I guess I kind of think what I write is the truth.

Hello Jenny. My name is Melissa Swafford. I am fifteen years old. I think it is pretty fun to be able to write a real author. I am starting the book named *Checking on the Moon*. So far I think it's very good. What are some of the other books that you have written?

. . . I like the kind of books that when you pick them up you don't want to put them down. A lot of suspense. I like to play pool with my friends. My brother gets mad when all of his friends pay attention to me. He doesn't want me to have a boyfriend and that gets me mad. I hope to hear from you soon.
Your friend,
Melissa

Hello, my name is Heather Price. I read two of your books, I think they are really good. I think you have good ideas writing the books. The one that really got to me was *Sex Education*. Mainly the part where David died. They went through all that trouble and then something happens.

My favorite hobbies are reading, writing, learning new things, making friends, playing basketball. I also like to hang out at school with my friends. My favorite classes are reading, math, science, and English.

In reading class I get thirty minutes to read then I get to do some writing. My reading teacher showed me the two books that you wrote, if she wouldn't of showed me them I would never understand about love.

The two books I read were about how to care for someone and how to go on with life besides sticking with something that really bothers you. It seems like you know how I feel sometimes. Your books are great, I could re-read them over again and again.

In her response, Jenny answered the students by giving some background about who she is, and her life as a mother, wife, teacher, and writer, and noting her inexperience with telecommunications: "This will be the first time I've ever used Internet or e-mail or whatever this is, so I'm going to be learning some stuff along with you." She introduced herself on-line to my students as:

. . . 41 years old, married, very recently, the mother of two children, and two step-children, a teacher, and, and. . . . How easy it is to sum up and how empty it all really is when you read it. I guess I forgot to mention the obvious—that I am a writer. This is probably because lately I've been so busy and my life has been so full that I've had very little time to sit down and write. . . .

The first problem the student writers encountered was coming up with ideas and subjects for their stories. Together, the teachers in the project (I was one of six) decided that students would work on either a personal narrative or piece of fiction, since both were required of all fourth, eighth, and twelfth graders for the state writing portfolios. I had a conference with each of my eight students and tried to help them with story ideas. A few wrote to Jenny asking for help. Stephanie, a quiet student and the best writer in the class even though she was repeating eighth grade, wrote to Jenny describing her struggles in hopes that Jenny would have an instant solution:

Hi!! It's Stephanie again. I tried to think of something to write about, but I couldn't come up with anything. I'm not good at coming up with things to write about. My stories are not that good or anything. But I don't think you're expecting a masterpiece.

I was wondering how you come up with the ideas for your books. I can't come up with ideas for almost anything that involves writing and using my brain. I was sorta hoping you could help me come up with some ideas for a fiction story. I would write a personal narrative but I've had a boring life so far. . . .

But before I go I would like to say that it's great that you've taken the time to help us kids out.

Sincerely,
Stephanie Edmundson

Jenny didn't tell Stephanie what to write about, but she did emphasize the importance of writing about what you care about:

Thanks for writing me. I hope this gets to you. I'm still not sure I trust the computer. I understand you want me to help you come up with ideas to write about. I'm probably not going to be able to help you with that. The truth is, we each have to write our own stories. My best advice to you would be to imagine yourself sitting down to read a really good book or story, one you don't want to put down. Now, what is it about? Who are the characters and what are their problems? Write the story you would want to read. If you like scary stuff, start there. If you like family stories or romance, give it a shot. You are the writer. The truth is, if you don't like what you're working on, you probably won't want to keep going, so it's important to satisfy yourself.

The only other "trick" I know is to get really quiet and see what comes into your head. Sometimes, for me, if I do that, I get bits of dialogue that eventually develop into something.

Good luck and let me see what you're doing.
Jenny

I relayed Jenny's advice to each of my other struggling student writers, and it helped them all come up with topics for their stories. After reading Jenny's note to Stephanie, the girls realized that common everyday experiences can be the basis for good stories. Rachael, another good writer, decided to write about her recent breakup with her boyfriend. Titus wrote about a group of kids who hung out together in her neighborhood on Howell Street. Nicole's best friend had had a tragic accident a few months earlier when she fell from a bridge. Genia wrote a fiction piece based on her sister's pregnancy. The rest of the girls—Stephanie, Heather, Marian, and Melissa—wrote scary fiction pieces because they were all big mystery fans.

I gave the students—who became known in our classroom as the Jenny Davis writers—time to work on their pieces. Of course, we had some days when this was impossible because of state testing, assemblies, and the other interruptions that occur in every school. The eight students worked independently on their own writing, asking for very little help from me. I wanted the students to feel that Jenny was their "teacher" for this project, not me. Jenny and I decided that I would handle editing for punctuation and spelling since it would be too hard and time-consuming for her to do it on-line. She would work with questions of content and revision.

We wanted to involve Jenny early on in the process and to encourage the kids to e-mail her frequently. They began to send first drafts to Jenny and to ask questions: they wanted to know if they needed more details, if they used too much dialogue, if their beginnings captured the reader's attention.

Titus wrote:

Dear Jenny,
Hi, it's Titus! This is the first chapter of the Howell Street Boys book. I just wanted to ask you a question so I can work on this book to get it done. Do you think I should have a prologue in the beginning and then start Chapter One with "One hot summer day?" Sorry it took so long to get this thing started. Please let me know where you think I can add more details or improve my writing.

Jenny responded:

Dear Titus,
Well, you've made a good start on the Howell Street Boys book, although since it's also about the girls on Howell Street, you might want to rethink the title. I do think a prologue would work here. In fact, your first paragraph is like a prologue and you might consider expanding it. You say the Howell Street kids fight every day. Do you know why? What do they fight about? Have you ever read a book called *The Outsiders* by S. E. Hinton? If not, I recommend it. It's also about gangs and I think you might really like it.

One thing you might try to do is develop Cliff's character a little more. What does he like? What does he look like? What do he and Stephanie talk about? Mostly, I'd say, keep going. You've got a good idea. I'll be looking forward to reading more.

Jenny's prompt responses always started off with positive comments. "I really like the way you started your story, Heather. I like the way you use dialogue to pull your reader into the story." "Nicole, your story about Angie's fall and recovery literally took my breath away."

Jenny answered the students' questions and then gave specific advice. When Genia asked her whether she used too much dialogue, Jenny answered, "I like your dialogue and on the whole it works just fine." Jenny followed this with a question she had about one character's actions. She never overwhelmed the writers with more than they could handle. She carefully developed a good rapport with each student even though these conferences took place in cyberspace.

> Dear Genia,
> I really like the way you started your story. I could imagine how Missy felt, scared, alone, and pretty confused when she found out she was pregnant. I also think the conversations between Missy and Todd were pretty realistic. He at first felt trapped, but then he wanted to take responsibility. Her parents are really upset and don't know how to give her any help. Genia, since Missy is telling the story, she would refer to Mrs. Swafford as Mom, not Mrs. Swafford. I liked your dialogue and on the whole I think it works just fine. One thing I didn't understand was when Missy says she has proof that the baby is Todd's, and she says her proof is her cousin Cheri and Many Barge, the Wolf Lady. You probably need to explain that. I'll be waiting to see how this ends up. Thanks for sharing.

As the students and Jenny corresponded, a mutual trust was established. Because Jenny writes honestly about teens and their emotions, my students felt they could write with the same kind of candor. (For example, in her book *Sex Education* a teenage couple struggles with the question about whether to have sex.) My students wrote honestly about issues like teen pregnancy, their relationships with boys, and gangs, often revealing bits and pieces about themselves. Jenny was never judgmental or shocked. Unlike Jenny, I was with the students day-to-day, and was sometimes stunned by what my students revealed in their writing. I wasn't always sure that they kept in mind that sending writing across a network (even though these were rough drafts, not polished pieces) was a type of publishing. Their stories were being read by everyone on our network, not just Jenny.

I soon began to see that the students took this project very seriously. They put a tremendous amount of effort and time into their writing. They took their stories home, asking their parents and family members to read them. In class, they asked other students to read their pieces because they wanted the reaction and advice of peers. When Jenny gave suggestions or asked questions, the students immediately set to revising. Revision has always been very difficult for my Chapter 1 students—once a draft was done, they felt they had completed their "assignment." But these writers kept going and their pieces became longer and longer and better and better over the course of five months. Marian, who used a two-page story that she wrote in October as her Jenny Davis piece, wound up with an eleven-page story complete with a title page, table of contents, and chapter titles. The girls all told me that they wanted their pieces to be good because they were working with a "real" author and they didn't want to disappoint her.

About two months into the project, three of my students (Marian Marshall, Genia Petty, and Heather Price) and I got to meet with Jenny at a state technology conference in Lexington, where we were showcasing our telecommunications project, the Authors Project. We invited Jenny to join us in our booth, and she agreed to meet with us after she was done teaching for the day. The Student Showcase was held in a huge hall that was bustling with activity. Students from across the state staffed booths displaying school projects involving technology. Teachers walked down aisles asking questions about the projects and gathering handouts. Heather, Genia, and Marian, anxiously awaiting Jenny's arrival, kept busy distributing handouts and explaining our project. They chatted among themselves, speculating about how they thought she would look, what she would be wearing, and if they would be able to pick her out from the hundreds of teachers walking by. Suddenly, a woman rushed up to our booth wearing what my students described as a Mary Poppins hat and granny glasses. They knew. It was Jenny. The girls shyly introduced themselves, and Jenny immediately knew who they were. The girls asked Jenny questions about her books, especially *Sex Education*. They all wanted to know where the idea for that story came from and were enthralled by Jenny's story. Genia had been sitting at a computer in our booth working on her story about a pregnant teen, so Jenny sat down and worked with her for about thirty minutes. She didn't disappoint. My students were impressed.

Even though meeting face-to-face with someone that you have been corresponding with on-line isn't always feasible, it was an added bonus. However, this project was successful because of the relationship that was established on-line through writing.

Marian had written some poems that she showed me but no one else. After meeting Jenny, Marian gave me permission to send her poetry to

Jenny by "personal mail" so no one but Jenny could read it. She trusted Jenny.

Jenny read the poems and thanked Marian for them:

Dear Marian,
Thank you for sharing your poems with me. I think it's hard to let someone else read the inside of your soul, which is what poetry is. I like your poems very much. . . . One thing I like best about your work is that you put your feelings right out there. It makes it very personal and I feel connected to you. I understand that line about wondering if you start over if you'd get everything right. It's a great thought, one a lot of people have. I imagine we'd make, if not the same mistakes, different ones if we did have a chance to start over because making mistakes and learning from them seems to be a big part of what life is about. Your poem "The Light" is a real celebration of life and love. I hope you keep writing. Thanks again for sharing.

Marian was encouraged by Jenny's response and continued to work on her poetry as well as her story "A Trip to the Graveyard." After school was out for the summer, she wrote about her participation in the project:

When I was first told about this project I was very excited. The thought of me writing an author really excited me, although I did not know anything about the author, Jenny Davis. To tell the truth, I had never heard of her before. When my teacher gave me one of her books, *Checking on the Moon*, I took it home and read it. After reading that book and Jenny's other two books, I had a better impression of what she was like, the books gave me an idea of how Jenny wrote and thought.

I had started a scary story earlier in the year for an assignment at school, but it was a *short* story. I took that story "A Trip to the Graveyard," and used it for this project. The reason I did that was because I felt that since I was writing to someone who had already written three books, she could help me make this story into a good story. I sent Jenny what I thought was my completed two-page story but I still needed a good ending. I asked Jenny for some ideas. In her response she told me a lot of good things about my story that encouraged me to want to write more.

When I revised my piece I went over it once by myself, other times with my friends, and sometimes with teachers. I had to go over it a lot of times before I could send it off to Jenny again. No matter how many times I went over it, I still had fun.

When I was finished I was surprised that my two-page story turned into an eleven-page story. I sent my final copy to Jenny and she wrote me back and said how proud she was of me. She said, "I can't believe how much work you've done on your story. It's amazing when I look back and see what you had just a few months ago. This story is great." When I read that, I felt I did great. It was the best thing that anyone has ever said to me.

I did get to meet Jenny in person at a technology conference with my teacher and some of my classmates. When I met Jenny, she was what I expected, very pretty and very kind. After meeting her I felt she was very trust-worthy, so I decided to send her some of my poems that I did not show anyone except my teacher. Jenny's response gave me the courage to share them with others.

The project was more than writing and getting help with it. It was also about friendship and finding someone you can trust, someone like Jenny. She now has a fan for life.

I was amazed by the time and commitment of my "Jenny Davis writers." I learned that because my students were keenly aware of their audience—a published author—they put more effort into their pieces than when the audience was their peers or a classroom teacher. These girls worked on one piece of writing for a five-month period, something none of my other reading and writing students had done. We had other classroom projects going on at the same time and students sometimes took time off from their Jenny Davis pieces, but they always returned to them. Some pieces turned out to be quite long, over ten typed pages. Some students wrote their stories in chapters. Heather, who plans to write a sequel to her story "The Missing Grave," wrote at the end, "Want to find out what Amy means—read the next story, called *Is It Okay to Walk Back to the Cemetery?*" Heather also documented her involvement in this project with a short narrative:

> When I was in the eighth grade I did a lot of writing during the year. In fact, all the eighth graders in Kentucky had to complete a writing portfolio. The most fun and the hardest writing I did all year was a telecommunications writing project with Jenny Davis, an author and a teacher. I had never written so much or put as much effort into anything as I did this project.
>
> The story I decided to write for my project with Jenny was called "The Missing Grave." I like to read mystery stories that have something to do with friends. I am a big R. L. Stine reader. His *Fear Street* books are mysteries that always involve teenage friends. I wanted to see if I could write a story like that. I wrote a few pages and sent them to Jenny. Then she wrote back and told me that she liked my "use of dialogue that pulled the reader into the story." But she said she was confused by one part, and that it would be a good idea to add more details and that I should try to develop the characters a little. I went back to my story and put more details in and I worked on describing my characters. I felt good that she inspired me to work harder and keep going with my story.
>
> Each time I added something in one part, I had to go back and revise other parts of it for it to all make sense. With all the classwork on top of that, I thought that my story would never get done. I even took my story home to work on it. I wanted to put all of my best effort into it so it could be the best piece I wrote. I wanted it to be my best piece so that I would have something to look back on and to remember that I do have a talent for writing.

I was the last student to finish my story and the last to send it to Jenny. But when she gave me the response, "Wow! Your story is really good. It was impossible for me to quit reading because you built up so much suspense, I just couldn't stop . . . ," I felt good about myself because I wrote a story that somebody would like to read. When Jenny added, "R. L. Stine better watch out!," I knew I could write.

My one regret was that we did not start the Authors Project earlier in the year. Time simply ran out. My eight students worked until the very last week of school trying to finish their stories. Some of them needed more time to revise again but could not. And unfortunately, because we did this project the second half of the school year, most pieces were not finished in time to use in the eighth grade writing portfolios that are used in the state-wide assessment (these are scored in March).

I know my "Jenny Davis writers" received incredible benefits from their five months on-line with her. As the project started to wind down and my students began to think about summer vacation, a few of the girls sent Jenny some final comments:

Dear Jenny,
. . . I was reading some of the stories that some of the girls in the project did and they have a very good story. I and the others appreciate you helping us in writing and good luck. I hope you write another book because you write some good books.
Sincerely,
Titus

Dear Jenny,
Hello! How are things going? Just fine here, I just finished my story. It's pretty long but I hope you like it and enjoy reading it. I am going to work on Part Two this summer. I want to thank you for all your help and meeting me in Lexington. I had fun this year, you helped me improve the writer that I am. Have a nice summer and thank you for all the help.
Your friend,
Heather

In her final note to her eight writers, Jenny made it clear that learning and friendship had occurred in Lexington as well as Covington.

Dear All,
It's hard to believe that the school year is over, but it is. I have really learned a lot working with you all this year and I've enjoyed it. I printed copies of everyone's stories and I will hold on to them. As a class, you are a powerful group of young women with tremendous energy and honesty. Thank you one and all for sharing your writing with me.

Please take care of yourselves this summer. You know as well as I do how many opportunities there are during the summer for getting in trouble, or doing things you might regret later. Think twice, and remember you are each important to me. I want you all safe, sound, and not pregnant come September! Whatever happens, I'll be thinking of you and would love to hear from you.

My home address is _____. If you want to get in touch, feel free. Thanks again for a great experience this year. Keep writing.

Best wishes,
Jenny

Jenny Davis

Being "Dear Jenny"

WHEN I WAS FIRST asked to participate in a technology project I thought it was a joke. I've barely mastered the telephone, still can't use a bank machine, and get cranky at the sound of velcro. I'm a person who loves the smell of a freshly sharpened pencil, who has been known to hug a notebook, and who can happily spend hours debating which color ink to put into my fountain pen. I was hardly a logical choice to teach writing via computer to kids in another city.

However, I am not only a writer, I am a teacher as well, and one of my professional development goals for that year (mandated by my school) was to make it at least into the twentieth century, if not leap ahead to the twenty-first. My students know much more than I about mouses (mice?), modems, and memory. It was time, apparently, to take the step. I was also intrigued by the notion of being able to work at home. I had recently married and acquired a full-time stepson who is confined to a wheelchair. Our range of motion is much more limited than it used to be, and it was important to find ways to make our home both a comfortable and productive place.

The most important reason I decided to give it a try was a mixture of guilt and defiance. I had recently turned down an opportunity to be a writing mentor to a high school senior in my own community. Although the chance to nurture a young writer is exhilarating, it's also extremely time-consuming, and I was panicking, with the start of school and my new life as the full-time mother of three and wife of one, that I wouldn't have time for extras. However, once I'd finally and firmly said no to the mentoring job, I felt bad about not giving back to a world which has given me so much. Hence the guilt. The defiance came in the form of the fatal fantasy besetting so many women today: I can do it all!

In fact our project *was* beset with technical difficulties from the first. The computer I had was an Apple IIC, one which I had used to write my books, and which I was comfortable with to the extent I will ever be comfortable with a machine. Nonetheless it was apparently hopelessly outdated when it came to the world of the Internet. The project provided me with a modem and with a lovely, incredibly patient, helpful woman

147

named Kathy Rey-Barreau who was to be my technical advisor. We strung cords from the phone in the kitchen to the library, an awkward setup that snarled household traffic, but had the benefit of forewarning everyone that I was trying to use the *!#* modem and set to work . . . or tried to.

After several attempts to connect me to the Internet, even Kathy was getting frustrated. Apparently, my computer was having trouble obeying orders. (Secretly, I was proud of it for being so out of date and dim about the world of technology. We were truly a team!) Finally, and this took several weeks, during which time I began to despair of ever actually teaching writing to anyone, I was able to make contact with the girls at Holmes.

We began with introductions, a logical step. All of the girls had read one or more of my books and they were full of questions and comments. I told them some about myself, my family, my writing process, and my background. I teach fifth and sixth graders on a daily basis, and it was a change for me to be communicating with older kids. These girls soon revealed themselves to be street smart and almost world-weary, except they also exuded an excitement about this project that was both endearing and a bit daunting. I had no idea if I would really be able to live up to their expectations. Somehow, the idea that I was a real, live author was extremely exciting and important to them. Having always been plagued by the notion that I'm not really an author, just a person who has managed to write a few books, this struck at my insecurities.

Still, the important thing was the work, and when we finally got down to it I found myself quite comfortable giving feedback. The main challenge was to limit my responses so that they would be useful. How well I know how an editor can overwhelm a writer with insight. I used the same technique I use with my students in class. I found something I was honestly excited or moved by and commented first on that, and then asked some questions, no more than two or three, usually about characters, sometimes about plot or setting, but real questions that I wanted to know the answer to. This strategy is as effective as it is simple. It's a genuine response to work, tempered only by the knowledge that no matter how ragged a piece may look to me, it may in fact represent the very best a person has to offer . . . at least so far.

I imagine that my own experiences with writing and being edited have made me sensitive to the pain a thoughtless comment can cause. Writing is so hard, not just finding the words, but finding the strength to say them, to commit them to paper, and share them with someone else. I try to be gentle in all my dealings with other people's writing. Also, I'm really not much of a critic. The truth is I find it very easy to discover something fresh, funny, beautiful, or engaging. One of my good points as a teacher is that I'm easily entertained!

I was astounded with the energy and excitement the girls exuded. Their writing was all over the place in terms of style, subject, and proficiency, but the central fact was they cared about their work and it showed. It also motivated me to be careful and caring in my responses.

Perhaps what strikes me most about this whole experience was that I *had* to focus on the writing, there were no distractions. In the classroom, I am well aware of which student looks tired, who is hyper today, whose parents are going through a divorce or are away on a trip. I know when my sixth grade can't take in anything I'm saying because they're worried about the big science text next period, and like all teachers, I'm acutely aware of the behavioral consequences of a drop or rise in the barometer. These are concerns classroom teachers deal with daily. On-line, we had none of that. Only the words in front of us, and because of that, those words became more important than ever. They had to count, because their meaning couldn't be expanded with a grin or a grimace, there was no eye contact to help me determine whether my meaning was clear or confusing. In some ways it seems astonishing for a writer to admit what a challenge dealing only in writing can be, but there it is. Of course when I submit a manuscript of a book or a story, I realize the words must stand on their own, but these weren't finished pieces, these were conversations with real children, and I was often afraid of being misunderstood.

In fact, that happened very little. I was really impressed with the diligence with which these girls worked and reworked their stories. They also seemed comfortable asking me questions to clarify comments they didn't understand. I credit their teacher, Bev Paeth, with providing them time, encouragement, and confidence. She is truly a gifted teacher and I felt honored to be sharing the project with her. It was a treat to be able to meet some of the girls at the technology conference here in Lexington. I was able to put faces to some of the names, and they were able to do the same with me. In fact though, the real work was done in our hearts and minds and on the screen, word for word.

I suppose it is just as well that it never occurred to me that my conversations with the girls were being read by anyone other than them and their teacher. In preparing this article I've become acutely and embarrassingly aware that *of course* other people were following it. I've wondered if I would have been as spontaneous and free with my comments had I been aware of a larger audience. At any rate, none of my words or theirs can be taken back, so we'll let them stand. I loved getting to know those girls, having a chance to be with them in their ever-evolving process of writing and growing up. I'm a little less afraid of the computer now, and would welcome another chance to interface on the Internet.

Trevor Owen

An Odd Pleasure

Canada's Writers In Electronic Residence Program

A GROUP OF STUDENTS gathered at the school where I was teaching, Riverdale Collegiate Institute in Toronto, Ontario, during the first year of the Writers In Electronic Residence (WIER) program. The group had worked on-line with a writer, poet Lionel Kearns from Vancouver, and with a group of students from Cariboo Hill Secondary in Burnaby, a Vancouver suburb, for several months. They were making a special phone call to the Cariboo class. We were all excited, and the students were particularly anxious to have a live discussion about their experiences over the term.

The call turned out well. The students got along easily, read and listened to one another's works, and waited politely as one student, who had written under the pseudonym "helga," took some time to think through her answer to the question of how she felt about her experience in WIER.

"It was an odd pleasure," she said, "to be taken so seriously."

The elegance and truth of her answer, seen first in the nods that went around the room that day, have taken on new meaning in the years since then. It has become a kind of mantra to our happy little program, alerting us to the privilege of our purpose, and guiding us to consider the gravity of that privilege.

This essay is an invitation to consider the WIER program, for which I serve as Program Director, in the context of helga's "odd pleasure." If you're like me, it will be a pleasure, certainly, but a pleasure tinged with irony, some sadness—even anger—and, most importantly for teachers and writers who work in classrooms, surprise.

What Is WIER?

The WIER program brings writers into classrooms in "electronic residencies," undertaken in the textual environment of a computer conference. The project uses the Internet to connect students across Canada with writers, teachers, and one another in an often animated exchange of original writing and commentary. The writers, who are all well-known

Canadian authors, read the students' work, offer reactions and ideas, and guide discussions between the students.

I first had the idea for WEIR in 1984 when I heard about a then-new Canadian writers' network, *SwiftCurrent*, which provided authors access to one another in a national professional dialogue, and gave subscribers access to authors' recent works in an "electronic literary magazine." I thought it was a great idea, and that a similar network linking writers with students would make a useful contribution to learning. However, while the organizers of *SwiftCurrent* were generally supportive of the idea, they saw it as beyond the scope of their network. They were kind enough to permit a few e-mail-based exchanges between writers on their system and the students in my class, but I didn't manage to get WEIR off the ground until four years later.

At that time, I proposed operating a simple e-mail-based project between one writer and my class, and several *SwiftCurrent* authors expressed interest. One of these, Vancouver-based poet Lionel Kearns, took an active interest in the idea, and introduced me to Gerri Sinclair at the Faculty of Education at Simon Fraser University (SFU), also in Vancouver. Thanks to their efforts, SFU offered to mount the project on its computer systems, and Lionel served as the first "writer in electronic residence."

Novelist Katherine Govier joined in for part of WIER's second year. Katherine was quite taken by the project and participated in WIER for several years. As chair of The Writers' Development Trust (WDT), a national organization dedicated to Canadian writers and writing, she saw an opportunity to promote WIER and, in the process, generate more work for writers. In 1990, she guided the WDT to adopt WIER as its educational initiative, and to provide fundraising support.

In the spring of 1992, the Faculty of Education at York University in Toronto assumed responsibility for pedagogical development and technical support for WIER. York opened its first WIER writing conferences in January, 1993. This initiative came thanks to the faculty's dean, Dr. Stan Shapson.

Today, WIER is a partnership of the Writers' Development Trust and York's Faculty of Education, working with corporate and government sponsors throughout Canada. We use a FirstClass® conferencing system, which offers both a graphical-user interface (GUI) and a command line user interface (CLUI), located at York. WIER is accessible over the Internet.

WIER is a fully national program, operating in schools from coast to coast to coast, involving hundreds of teachers, thousands of students, and a fine and growing coterie of writers who are interested in the new type of work that WIER has created. There are programs for students at elementary through college levels. We also work with teacher education programs, in which student teachers undertake practice teaching placements on-line we have called the "virtual practicum."[1] The student teachers respond to the students' writing, and work on-line with experienced sponsor teachers to develop an understanding about the impact of WIER on classroom learning and teaching practice. Writers and teachers who have experience with WIER serve as on-line moderators in each conference.

While the WIER program serves as a clear example of how technology can have an impact on classroom life, from the outset our primary purpose has had little to do with the technology that sustains it. Rather, WIER has always been rooted in a strong sense of purpose—to link students and their teachers with Canada's authors in an exchange of original writing and commentary.

How It Works
Students work off-line before working on-line; in fact, most of the students first encounter WIER in print, reading the works of other participants in classroom binders or library files. They use word processors to compose their own works and responses to the work of others. Then, when the students are ready, they send their work to WIER's on-line conferences.

Most of the original writing is poetry and short fiction. WIER encourages students to submit works they consider to be in draft stages— "writing they care enough about to want to work on more," as WIER author Kathy Stinson put it—in order to promote the value of their interactions with writers and others on the system. These on-line interactions also encourage writing in other forms, especially in response to particular issues or concerns raised on-line.

These textual discussions become part of normal classroom activity, as students and teachers read the writing and commentary, and consider the impact of on-line experiences in their own classrooms. WEIR has come to regard this process as central to the program's success, bringing a "local shape" to the on-line experience.[2] Put another way, it is the idea that on-line learning happens partly on-line, but mostly in the classroom that allows WIER to advance an understanding of the "electronic residency" as a community of interaction.[3] This community involves participants in the life of the classroom *and* the on-line conferences, rather than using WIER as a kind of "service" that can be delivered by technology. In short, it is the involvement with WIER's on-line writing community that matters.[4]

We have come to understand that on-line learning experiences are experiences of language through interaction and reflection more than experiences of technology through access to information and the immediacy of its delivery.[5] WIER's pedagogy emphasizes the use of technology as a catalyst for learning rather than as a "tool" of production.

A Reflective Community

Throughout Canada, WIER teachers report that they have "changed their teaching" after seeing professional writers interact with their students. The teachers remark especially on how the writers focus on an individual piece of student writing, rather than on that student's overall performance—how *not knowing* the student can actually be advantageous. The teachers often express how they have altered their practices in order to spend more time responding to student writing—with the students—and less time "giving marks" or "marking kids" in isolation.

As one might expect, students, teachers, writers and, in some cases, parents, report how writing "improves." But more important, I think, are the reports of how students demonstrate a greater investment in their own learning through participation within—and identification with—a community of writers.

The following example is an excerpt from the discussion that evolved in response to "Snowflakes," a poem by Katie Schuele, an eleventh grade student at ECS School in Montreal:

Snowflakes

Cold
Wet
Dizzy
A draft in my throat
Each flake
tastes good. Like
Pickles
Chocolate
Pizza.
Broccoli
that one was too small.
The bigger ones taste better.
They melt like butter
they disappear. I must
eat them before

the ground does or our
boots soil them.

   —*Katie Schuele*

Dear Katie,
Snowflakes taste like pickles out there in Québec, eh? Out here in Ontario
they taste like marshmallows, like candy floss, like . . . whipping cream.
What might they be in B.C.?

   My favourite line is "a draft in my throat." I thought, yes, that's what
cold snowflakes are like as they go down. A terrific line.

   Maybe you have two poems here. One about tastes, and one about eating cold snow. If you want to use food metaphors, you might think about
foods which in some way resemble snowflakes. Ask your friends at lunch
what snowflakes taste like to them. Ask them how they taste like whatever
they name. Do any of the foods mentioned look like snowflake shapes, do
they feel like flakes, are they white? I think you already know this because
you write that they melt like butter. That food metaphor is perfect. A pickle,
on the other hand, doesn't melt. I almost feel as if I gag on it. Do you see the
difference? Well, have fun considering all sorts of food. Let me know the
menu.

   —*Cornelia Hoogland, author, London, Ontario*

Dear Katie,
I love the idea of snowflakes tasting like pickles, etc. Cornelia asks what they
taste like in B.C. I'm from B.C. We don't get snow much (on the coast) so I'm
not a connoisseur of snow. Rain, yes. I can tell you the Thousand and One
Tastes of Rain sometime. . . .

   I'm wondering about the way your poem ends. The last image seems to
get a little bit away from the food idea you've got working all the way
through. I like "I must / eat them before / the ground does" as a last line, but
when you bring the idea of the boots into the poem it takes us off in a new
direction almost. Does this make sense to you? How do you feel about making revisions when you finish a poem? One of my last poems went through
96 drafts, and then, even when it was published in a book, I felt there were
some things I still wanted to change! But I also get "given" some poems.
They come to me, I write them down, type them out, and never change a
word. These are the poems I often love best, because they go on seeming
fresh to me in a way—innocent, as if they've just been born.

   —*Susan Musgrave, author, Victoria, B.C.*

Katie,
I must be honest. As an eighteen-year-old girl in Toronto, I don't usually like
poetry. When I was younger, it seemed that everyone around me was writing
teenaged depression poetry (I call it TDP). This poem is so far from TDP, it's
amazing.

I especially liked your use of words like "dizzy" to describe snowflakes. Because of your poem, I can now look at snowflakes in a new light. Snow-flakes as pickles, chocolate, and pizza! I also liked the way you had them "melt like butter" and disappear.

—*Meredith, student, Toronto*

What Happens Next?

You can see how these responses focus on the writing. The authors and students respond to Katie's work—writer to writer. Rather than focusing on "evaluating" the "quality" of writing, the responses convey specific ideas about the work itself, and directions Katie might consider.

It's worth pausing for a moment on this point, because what happens next is important. I can report, from personal observation in classrooms across Canada as well as from the testimony of numerous teachers and students, that these responses from writers and others on-line have an impact in the classroom. You can imagine, I'm sure, what it must be like to be in school and receive a response to your work from a published author—especially from an author whose book you may be reading at the time.

The result is that students consider the comments and make decisions about what they want to do with their writing. They may comment on the responses, disagree with some of them, and engage in an on-line dis-cussion about their piece. They may decide to retain the version they origi-nally posted on-line. In any case, the students learn more about the decisions they make when writing—and, most important, I think, that the decisions they make are their own.

WIER actively encourages students to bring a sense of closure to the on-line discussions. The impact may be evident more in classroom discus-sions than on-line, and in some cases a student may simply move on to other things without returning to the on-line forum. In this case, Katie considered the comments, revised her work, and offered some comments of her own.

Snowflakes (revision)

Cold
Wet
Dizzy
A draft in my throat
Each flake
tastes good. Like
Popcorn

Chocolate
Whipped cream.
Broccoli
that one was too small.
The bigger ones taste better.
They melt like butter
they disappear. I must
eat them before
the ground does.

To Cornelia Hoogland,
Here's the menu (see revision) . . . , I took your advice and I changed the foods that make people gag. You were right, I like it better this way. I thank you for your advice and time. I hope you like what I've done to it.

To Susan Musgrave,
Thank you for the response and the pointers. I got a lot of feedback from my poem and most told me about the same things that you did. I agree. Snow should be represented as things that melt in your mouth. I kept one of the lines as broccoli because the small ones aren't as tasty. I have taken away the line about the boots. Thank you very much for everything. I hope you like what I've done with it.

To Meredith Dault,
I can't thank you enough for the encouragement. I was so happy to hear that someone else finds TDP sort of annoying. Don't get me wrong, I don't think that I am God's gift to poetry. I only wish that I had the talent to write about more mature things such as love or something, but I remain writing about snowflakes and things of that nature.

I did get some advice from other people who told me to change a few things, which I did. Mostly, I changed the food I used to describe the taste of snowflakes. I changed it to things that melt a little more than pickles or pizza. I hope you still like it.

Thanks all,
Katie

Writing and Writing For School

Teacher David Beckstead also found the investment that students feel in WIER really matters. His case study of one WIER school found that students identified two types of writing. One was known simply as "writing," a form they saw generally as purposeful and personal, undertaken in response to things that mattered to student writers. They described the second as "writing for school," a necessary component of things to be endured in student life; something produced for grades. The students were *quite* clear that these two types of writing were distinct from one another. What they saw as "writing" was something they saw as having value— and not likely to appear in school.

David described this experience in an article called "Not Knowing Is When You Actually Get The Truth," from which the following excerpts were taken:

Over the winter of '92, I had the opportunity to speak with four student writers who had participated in the high school portion of WIER. These interviews formed the data for an ethnographic study I was doing concerning students' views on WIER in the context of their English classroom. . . . Student comments are shown in italics.

Not knowing [who the author is] is when you actually get the truth.

Wait a second here, you mean that student writing, perhaps with a name attached and handed in, is not, in essence, truthful?

If a student is able to write freely without the teacher saying anything, they [the teacher] would be getting something totally different.

But how can putting a name to the work affect things?

They [teachers] will mark you on who you are rather than what the poem is about.

A lot of times you're marked for who you are . . . before you hand it in they've [the teachers] already marked you.

So classroom writing has this stigma attached to it, of something not real, done just for marks? Could, then, the pseudonymous nature of WIER along with the nature of textual communications actually work in favor of students, and in favor of their writing?

I think that's the greatest thing about the program that she [the professional writer commenting on the work] doesn't have to know you. Your writing describes pretty much who you are.

But what about inflection, seeing the author as a physical presence, human contact, etc., etc.?

Our writing reflects who we are.

In other words, not knowing is when you actually get the truth!!!

Hmmmmmm.

What if the director had chosen to quote one of these students instead of the wise old sage? Would a room full of teachers see the relevance of the student voice?

Perhaps knowing who to listen to is when you get the truth!

Getting at Truth

Getting at "the truth," as David saw it, is as important for teachers as it is for students. Barb Stevenson, a teacher at the Viscount Bennett Centre, an adult education program in Calgary, saw it too. In the following excerpt, Barb offers a fascinating glimpse into how WIER can build new approaches to learning.[6] Barb's remarks make clear that, unlike the changing pressures of work, evaluation, and curricula, the technology was something she *could* control.

> Teachers often comment that they are successful the third time they try a new teaching approach. As we begin round three of the WIER program, we can look back at the process of implementation and determine whether we can claim success.
>
> We have over 3,500 students at Viscount Bennett Centre returning to upgrade their high school qualifications. Our students, ages 19 to 69, attend for reasons that vary, from the need to improve their marks to the desire to improve a life dependent on social assistance. We have several good writers, many passionate writers, and a wealth of personal experiences to write about.
>
> We are fortunate to have a well-equipped setting and people to support the technology. The Learning Resources Centre, a renovation of the library in the center of the school, consists of a traditional quiet work area on the lower level and an upper level with a computer lab, plus several stations with differing technology available. Students are free to pursue independent learning or to work in groups. One corner of the Centre is devoted to the concept of a Writers' Corner. It is a place for writers and a place for tutorial help with writing across the curriculum. Four months after opening, WIER became a part of this corner with the simple addition of a telephone line and modem to one computer station.
>
> We do have some unusual difficulties to work around. Our teachers are all part-time, making communication with them a challenge. Our students have busy lives; many have work and young children to care for outside of class. Like the teachers, the students are not at school every day.
>
> As the project teacher in the Learning Resources Centre, I signed on to WIER for the first round and attempted to have the other teachers buy into the concept. A few of their students came with writing, which I sent on-line. I also captured and printed out all pieces of writing and stored them in binders in the Resources Centre. I sent copies to the teachers of particularly informative critiques by the authors participating in the project. It seemed as though we had expanded our teaching force by the number of authors in the WIER project. Some teachers brought their classes into the Centre to read the writing in the binders, and they wrote responses to some of the writing. We were invited to do a "show and tell" to senior administration.
>
> It all sounded wonderful, as many innovations do, but we were failing to attract all but the few teachers who already had a comfort level with word processing. We needed to get others involved. Very little writing by other students was being read. Students were thrilled to get responses to their work,

but they never continued the dialogue with the writer on-line. They sent and got their reply—period. It was the same as handing back a paper with red circles—it went no further. We wanted the students to see their writing as a process. That was not happening.

The following fall, two teachers decided to try to offer the experience of telecommunications to their classes. We identified a project already planned on another service where schools were gathering information across the country for a geography assignment. Our two classes would answer their questions and, in return, they would respond to questions sent by our students on topics related to conflict resolution. The students wrote and sent via telecommunications a series of interview questions to three people: a local student, a member of the community, and a student from a school in another part of the country. Students had several writing assignments within the project, which culminated in a videotaped "Oprah"-style talk show. For the show, the students assumed the persona of one of the people they had interviewed and answered the interviewer's questions. It was a special experience for the class. We learned the value of making telecommunications more than just a personal experience. However, next term the two teachers did not want to do it again. For them, it had taken too much class time.

In the winter semester our school signed onto WIER for the second time. Interested teachers selected some keen students to send and capture student work using a Macintosh and a modem in our "Writers' Corner." While the students involved enjoyed it, the activity was still outside of the classroom and WIER was seen by most teachers as valuable, but extra. None of our senior level classes participated, due to a perceived lack of time and the pressure to prepare students for the diploma exam. After all, passing the exam is what the students paid for! The adult students tended to view activities like WIER as extra, and some even felt the teacher was shirking her duty when time was spent on activities not directly tied to the topic being taught.

Then WIER offered a special reading workshop project. This allowed us to lure the teachers who were teaching reading strategies. Although the timing did not allow direct on-line activity, we still found that the captured material formed wonderful resources for further teaching of reading and strategies. Now we could use WIER even when we were not on-line. Our pool of interested teachers was growing and we had a pool of students with some experience with telecommunications. We were moving to a "critical mass" that would make the project viable. We are ready for round three to be the best yet.

While this process has been evolving, the Resource Centre itself has also evolved. We are involving more people in a wider variety of ways. The Writers' Corner has grown to include peer tutors for writers and noon-hour workshops by teachers on selected topics. Students this term can take a series of workshops on "editing on the computer." In addition, we have added a new course in reading strategies. Writing, captured on-line from WIER, will be the reading material used to learn strategies for improving comprehension. As more teachers take ownership of WIER, we get closer to our goal of having telecommunications fully integrated with classroom activity.

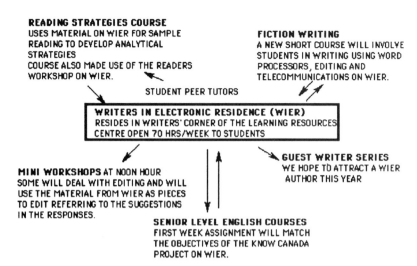

Fig. 1. *The operation of WIER at Viscount Bennett*

Discovery and Surprise

What makes WIER work at Viscount is, I think, Barb's discovery of the on-line writing's value as *reading* material and a willingness to accept her discovery as, in effect, theory that can guide and inform new practice. This is the "surprise" I mentioned at the beginning of this essay. Part of Barb's re-conceptualization of her teaching was her realization that WIER could be a kind of "teaching partner." In no way is WIER a "service" she needs to deliver. A visit to "Writers' Corner" in the library at Viscount Bennett, with its file drawers of student writing, author biographies, and displays of books by the authors they work with on-line, reveals how such a partnership can blossom.

Another part of this re-conceptualization has to do with how people regard the presence and use of technology in learning. When something new enters something known, we tend to emphasize the new thing, so when we talk about "information technology," we are understood to be talking about the technology rather than the information. This produces a "technology frame" for understanding information technology. In this frame, we become concerned about being "computer literate."

The trouble I have with this kind of "literacy" is that so many see it as a kind of technological grammar in which technology becomes a "tool" of production rather than a catalyst for learning, and we teach "how to use the word processor" rather than create, in effect, a field trip into new experience.

Interaction Technology

As it happens, the kind of work that students, teachers, and writers do in WIER is often taken for information technology. What I'd like to do here is consider another way of framing on-line activity and its impact on writing. What would happen if information technology was seen instead as *interaction technology*? How might our understandings change?

The use of telecommunications in writing classrooms suggests many possibilities. In WIER, for instance, "distance" becomes more experiential than geographical. When students and writers actually have the opportunity to interact freely with one another and to control their own participation in the meaningful exchange of ideas, the impact of distance, along with our understanding of it, changes shape and tone. Constituencies that were once "distant" from each other—in this case, writers, students, and teachers—begin to learn more about each other through considered, written interactions. In doing so, they learn more about themselves.

Talking or Writing

On-line writing embraces both the asynchronous nature of telecommunications and the considered nature of writing to nurture reflective interaction among students. Most of this reflective interaction, however, does not happen on-line. As you saw in Barb Stevenson's discussion, WIER students capture or download new submissions and responses frequently, print them up, and work with them as part of in-class reading programs. Students then have the opportunity to consider their thoughts during class, to compose them at a word processor, and to save them as files. When they are ready, they send their files to the on-line conference. In this way, computer conferencing has much more to do with writing than with technology.

I want to consider how this differs distinctly from the "technological frame" I mentioned earlier. Many telecommunications projects are wrapped in a technological embrace. I believe that this stems from the almost instantaneous transfer of information the technology allows. This ability has an impact on how people use the medium because it encourages immediate response in on-line exchanges. This kind of exchange has a language. It is the language of talk, or immediate response, rather than writing.

Given the communicative possibilities of e-mail and computer conferencing, I believe there is a progression in which an embrace of the medium as "immediate" instills, and even develops, notions of how the medium will be used.

Electronic mail is a good example of how computer communication operates as talk within the technology frame. In electronic mail, it is common to find so-called "one-to-one," or even "one-to-many" messages and responses that, while written, are tapped out on the keyboard as if one were carrying on a verbal conversation.[7] Notes are often short to enable reading on-screen, and have the effect of encouraging participants to respond immediately—while on-line—in the familiar "call and answer" style of face-to-face discussions.[8] E-mail users tend to accept notes in the same ways that people in face-to-face interactions accept conversation—without too much concern for grammatical structure, or small errors. This is not to say that one *must* use e-mail in this manner, or even that there is a kind of prescription for this kind of use. But this is how most people think of electronic mail.

Computer conferencing differs from e-mail in its ability to sustain opportunities for "many-to-many" communication.[9] There is a greater opportunity to engage in what I have called "considered response," or what might now also be called reflection through writing.

So, while student responses in WIER and other on-line projects are often conversational in tone, they are *considered* responses. Generally, they have been composed, off-line, in response to other students' writing. The responses have also been read off-line, usually in print. The students' on-line interactions reveal a reflective process, one that engages students in selecting and making decisions about their own language.

This kind of exchange also has a language, and it is the language of writing. As WIER has developed, it has become ever-clearer that reflection through written interaction is well-suited to computer conferencing: both are dependent on the opportunity to reflect as a component of response.

The Writing Frame and the Electronic Residency

In WIER, participants begin to see the on-line experience as a community of students, writers, and teachers more than as a technology that delivers information. Distance and time become experiential resources in this community, allowing participants to see the things they know—and want to write about—in new ways, building a framework for learning about writing through their interactions, both on-line and in the local classroom. Here are some key ideas in the WIER writing frame:

• Promote writing rather than technology.

• Focus on the writing an individual student sends on-line, not on his or her character or overall performance.

• Encourage response to on-line experiences.

• Embrace distance as a resource for learning, rather than as a barrier to experience.

• Make the classroom a place for students to expand upon their on-line work.

• Understand computer technology as a catalyst for learning rather than as a tool of production.

• Emphasize on-line writing programs as reading programs.

• Promote a sense of equity; seek to identify any differences between those who have a voice on-line and in the class.

• Strive to make students' experiences as reflective and responsive as possible.

I noted earlier that the centerpiece of WIER is the electronic residency, an interactive forum in which all participants engage in a common task—learning—with one another. Two major elements distinguish the WIER electronic residency from many other on-line programs. The first is that the "residency" *includes* the local classroom. In WIER, it is the classroom, not the on-line conference, that serves as the forum of response and reflection for students and teachers. The second is that WIER is for all participants. As a program, WIER actively seeks to address issues of importance to each individual group it serves, creating:

• New learning opportunities for students;
• New work opportunities for writers;
• New approaches to teaching for educators.

WEIR also seeks to address issues of importance to the new group they comprise, taken together—the opportunity to engage in mentorship that, like literature, allows all of us to see ourselves reflected in the experiences of others.

Publish and Perish

Most teachers are familiar with the "writing process" approach. In this approach, as John Willinsky describes, writing is directional, a process that "had to come from something, had to be worked, and had to be going somewhere."[10] This approach begins with some form of investigation of ideas ("pre-writing"), moves through drafting and "revision," and ends with "publication."

While I have no argument with the development of this continuum *per se*, it does concern me when students think it is the only direction in which writing can reasonably travel. The "somewhere" to which writing is headed in WIER can—and often does—lead to the "improved" or "finished" work. But it has become clear in WIER that this direction carries with it the danger of the "writing for school" problem that David Beckstead found. What's important here, then, is that the direction in which writing is traveling in WIER is not toward publication, but toward a responsive forum. Choices can be made in this forum—choices that the students begin to see as properly guided by themselves. This understanding is important to WIER's success.

The Odd Truth

"It was an odd pleasure to be taken so seriously."—helga

At the beginning of this essay, I suggested that WIER developed its pedagogy for on-line learning by focusing on its purpose, rather than the technology that sustains it. I noted that this thinking was based on an understanding of the on-line interaction as an experience of language rather than an experience of technology, a forum in which the expertise of all participants is what engages them in learning together. I believe that this understanding alters the direction in which the teaching of writing is headed in many schools, because its direction is toward change and involvement rather than production and publication.

I say these things on the strength of having learned something from them myself, and the fact that I learned them through the kind of involvement I have written about here. It was "helga" who guided me to see the value of these thoughts at the end of WIER's first year. But I have to admit, as happy as her comment made me then, and as grateful as I am for having had the benefit of her insight, I have been increasingly saddened by its truth in the years since.

It's that word *odd*.

Why would "being taken seriously" be an "odd" pleasure for anyone in school?

Like you, I'm sure, I can think of no reason at all.

Postscript

After leaving high school, "helga" explored other interests. She graduated with a B.A. in Philosophy from the University of Toronto in April, 1996, and began a Bachelor of Social Work at York University that May.

Notes

1. Trevor Owen, "Computer-mediated Writing and the Writer in Electronic Residence," in R. Mason and A. Kaye, eds., *Mindweave: Communication, Computers and Distance Education* (Oxford: Pergamon Press, 1989).

2. Ibid.

3. Trevor Owen, "On-line Learning Links are Language Learning Links." *ECOO Output,* 12(1) (1991).

4. See also Linda Harasim, Starr Roxanne Hiltz, Lucio Teles, and Murray Turoff, *Learning Networks* (Cambridge, Mass.: MIT Press, 1995).

5. Trevor Owen, "Poems That Change the World: Canada's Wired Writer." *English Journal,* (84)6 (1995).

6. Barb Stevenson, "Implementing WIER in an Adult High School: Round Three." *Telecommunications in Education News,* (5)1.

7. Linda Harasim, "On-line Education: A New Domain," in R. Mason and A. Kaye, eds., *Mindweave: Communication, Computers, and Distance Education* (Oxford: Pergamon Press, 1989).

8. L. Davie, "Facilitation Techniques for the On-line Tutor," in in R. Mason and A. Kaye, eds., *Mindweave: Communication, Computers and Distance Education* (Oxford: Pergamon Press, 1989).

9. Linda Harasim, "On-line education: An environment for collaboration & intellectual amplification." in Harasim, L., ed., *On-line Education: Perspectives on a New Environment* (New York: Praeger, 1990), pp. 39–66.

10. John Willinsky, *The New Literacy* (New York: Routledge, 1990), p. 38.

Bibliography

Beckstead, David. "I Detest School, but I Love to Learn." *Wired Writers and Their Views on Writing, Teachers and the Writers in Electronic Residence Program.* M. Ed. thesis, Kingston: Queen's University, 1992.

Harasim, Linda. "On-line education: An environment for collaboration & intellectual amplification." in Harasim, L., ed., *On-line Education: Perspectives on a New Environment.* New York: Praeger, 1990.

Harasim, Linda, Starr Roxanne Hiltz, Lucio Teles, and Murray Turoff. *Learning Networks.* Cambridge, Mass.: MIT Press, 1995.

Owen, Trevor. "Computer-mediated Writing and the Writer in Electronic Residence," in R. Mason and A. Kaye, eds., *Mindweave: Communication, Computers and Distance Education.* Oxford: Pergamon Press, 1989.

———. "Waiting to Connect: the Writer in Electronic Residence," *The Computing Teacher,* (17)5 (1990).

———. "On-line Learning Links are Language Learning Links." *ECOO Output,* 12(1) (1991).

———. "The Writers in Electronic Residence Program," in *Literacy in Classrooms.* Ottawa: Canadian Teachers' Federation/Hilroy Foundation, 1991.

————. *Computer Conferencing: the Last Word*. Victoria, B.C.: Beach Holme, 1992.

————. "Poems That Change the World: Canada's Wired Writer." *English Journal,* (84)6 (1995).

Owen, Trevor, Ron Owston, and Charyl Dickie. *The Learning Highway: A Student's Guide to Using the Internet in High School and College*. Toronto: Key Porter Books, 1995. Website: www.edu.yorku.ca/Learning_Highway.

Stevenson, Barb. "Implementing WIER in an Adult High School: Round Three." *Telecommunications in Education News*, (5)1.

Teles, Lucio and Nancy Duxbury. *The Networked Classroom: An Assessment of the Southern Interior Telecommunications Project (SITP)*. Burnaby, B.C.: Simon Fraser University, 1991.

Willinsky, John. *The New Literacy*. New York: Routledge, 1990.

Acknowledgments

Portions of this paper were developed under the auspices of the Canadian Teachers' Federation/Hilroy Foundation "Teacher Research on Literacy" program (1990) and have been reported in their publication "Literacy in Classrooms," as well as in *ECOO Output*, the publication of the Educational Computing Organization of Ontario.

Portions were developed from material that appeared in "Wired writing: the writer in electronic residence" in *Computer Conferencing: The Last Word* (reference above). I refer readers who may be interested in the historical development of WIER to that article, and to Lionel and Gerri's chapter in the same book, "From Text to Multimedia: CMC in the 80s and 90s."

Copyright for the poem "Snowflakes" remains with its author, Katie Schuele.

The teacher vignettes were developed under the auspices of the "Minor Research Grants" program at the Faculty of Education, York University. The excerpts from the "Snowflakes" discussion were selected by April Hall, WIER's coordinator. Their assistance is gratefully acknowledged.

The Writers In Electronic Residence program is administered by The Writers' Development Trust in partnership with the Faculty of Education at York University in Toronto. For more information, contact:

> Writers In Electronic Residence
> 24 Ryerson Avenue
> Suite 207
> Toronto, Ontario
> Canada, M5T 2P3
> Phone: 416-504-4490.
> Fax: 416-504-9090.
> E-mail: wier@edu.yorku.ca
> World Wide Web: www.wier.yorku.ca/WIERhome

Claire Bateman

Other Voices Other Rooms

WHEN I WAS INVITED by a colleague to participate in a computer conference on poetry with students and other teachers in the Bread Loaf Rural Teachers Network, I was intrigued by the idea of exchanging responses to poems with others but intimidated about working with sophisticated computer technology. After all, I thought to myself, I'm a spacey, rightbrained poet. Surely there's no place for me in the technocratic universe. Why, I wondered privately, can't we just send postcards? And so at first I asked my colleague Chris Benson to print out the students' messages on hard copy for me, and just went down to his office to send my responses, which I'd composed beforehand on my familiar yellow legal pad. Then Chris told me that he thought I should read the messages online. "It would give you a better sense of the conference as a whole," he explained, euphemistic speech, I believe, for "Come on, Claire, don't be such a wimp!" Always one to rise to a challenge, I procrastinated as long as I could, then complied.

Yes, I made and continue to make many mistakes, but I have to confess that I found the on-line world to be quite magical, like a coral reef that grows by self-accretion, or like Gaston Bachelard's realm of childhood, the kingdom of miniature to which there is no end, where every room is bigger on the inside than it is from without, and mysterious boxes (or in this case, specific conferences) open to disclose still more boxes, a micro-universe filled with doorways that open into other conversations, an extended series of chambers one might visit in a dream. How different this is from the physical structure of the classroom, where no matter how anti-hierarchical I try to be, the room itself constrains the process, confining us in the uncomfortable chairs within the four straight lines of the walls.

Who was it that said "The quality of the imagination is to flow rather than freeze"? The imagination flows more freely in spaces where there is some element of mystery and privacy than in spaces that are wholly defined as public, and where the physical arrangement proclaims that everything is about grades—about product, not process. Architecture never lies. And so we rearrange our desks into a circle, or we meet outside in a grassy spot on campus, and yes, sometimes the imagination has some breathing room, but I can't help but believe that it thrives best in a setting where it is possible—even likely—for one to get lost for a while. It's easy to get lost on-line, to wander for a time. It's clearly much more difficult to get lost in the classroom!

In fact, I believe that the on-line process is mimetically related to the action of the poet's mind in which there is, practically speaking, no center, no beginning, middle, or end—or rather, perhaps, the center is everywhere, and the process is more simultaneous, multiphrenic, and multivocal than it is orderly, linear, and conclusive. On-line, for example, we saw Dixie Goswami demonstrate the fluidity of the imagination when she pointed out that by shifting and reassembling the students' phrases on the screen, many become poems as you watch! Dixie "found" this humorous poem in Jeremy Dow's prose response to Alice Walker's poem "Women":

My Great-Aunt

People always told me how sweet
and well-behaved she was.
But I knew her when
she was an old woman.
And she was totally different!
    She cussed and
    argued and
    chewed tobacco
Until she died.

Indeed, when I log off, I have the sensation of coming from a pleasantly noisy party where I encountered many voices. So perhaps my real reason for initially fearing the computer was not, as I'd assumed, that it is too much of the world of science for me, but actually that it partakes of the world of magic—and the human animal has always had a deep-seated fear of magic! But in this computer conference, as on Prospero's island, the voices are present to "give delight and hurt not." As the author H. L. Goodall has said, the only answer to life's strangeness is further and deeper strangeness, not simplification and clarification. Certainly this is true of both poetry and the increasingly complex technical world.

R. W. Burniske

Great Expectations
Electronic Novellas in the Making

WHEN TEACHERS envision telecommunications projects, they usually imagine exotic keypal links between schools in Des Moines and Damascus or Peoria and Pretoria. While I've organized such endeavors, and enjoyed success with them, I'd caution educators not to overlook the potential for telecommunications within their own communities. The project I'm about to describe grew out of prescribed coursework, involved students in one location, and integrated traditional pedagogy with electronic communication.

The Setting

Kuala Lumpur, Malaysia. For the uninitiated, the name conjures exotic images, but the Kuala Lumpur of today cares more about development than exotica. Like many a metropolis, it aspires to be "the city which never sleeps." As I write, construction crews literally compete to finish building the two highest towers in the world. Sunsets, when the ubiquitous shroud of air pollution allows, reveal a skyline punctuated with hydraulic cranes; condominium complexes and shopping malls sprout like mushrooms after an early morning rain.

The International School of Kuala Lumpur (ISKL), located in the former tin mining town of Ampang, reflects the frenetic growth of the greater metropolitan area. In the past decade, Kuala Lumpur's development has transformed ISKL from a country day to suburban and soon-to-be urban school. Comprised of a student body representing fifty nations, ISKL has responded to these developments by doubling its enrollment (from 840 to 1680), building a new elementary school campus in the suburb of Melawati (six miles away), and adding a new wing to its Ampang campus. The entire school is now connected—from offices to classrooms, libraries to lounges—by a state-of-the-art computer network.

Although exciting, this "progress" is equivocal. A school cannot undergo such rapid change without altering its "ethos." ISKL has forfeited its small-school intimacy for large-school competitiveness; the introduction of an electronic bulletin board service (BBS) has made the workplace more efficient, but less human. What's more, the school celebrates what it terms "co-curricular activities" at the expense of academic rigor. When asked where they go to read during "free periods," students reply: "You can't read on this campus. There are way too many distractions." Within this environment it is often difficult to give intellectual matters serious, sustained attention. The culture of the mall displaces the culture of the library, a point symbolically punctuated by the construction of music department rehearsal rooms beneath the school library.

To exacerbate matters, students and faculty are frequently excused from classes for school-sponsored activities, such as athletic competitions with international schools in Southeast Asia. Consequently, there's a loss of continuity in the classroom, and forfeiture of the time required for thoughtful reading, writing and reflection. How does the classroom teacher celebrate the "life of the mind" in a culture enamored with the "cult of the body?" How do we integrate telecommunications and the curriculum without neglecting critical thinking and the humanities?

The Art of (Reading) the Novel

During my four-year stint at ISKL I taught the International Baccalaureate's Higher Level English course, a two-year program culminating in oral and written examinations. While similar to the Advanced Placement (AP) program, the "IB" is more prescriptive, and students do not always enroll of their own volition. Since many European universities do not recognize international school diplomas as official transcripts, but demand the IB diploma instead, students planning to matriculate at those institutions have little choice. For those enrolled in the IB Higher Level English course, there are four requirements: World Literature (which includes two essays for external assessment); Detailed Study (the focus of a formal oral examination); School's Free Choice (used for internal assessment); and Groups of Works (the study of a particular genre/theme for written examinations).

To fulfill the Groups of Works requirement, ISKL selected "The Art of the Novel," creating an eclectic mix of *Great Expectations, The Portrait of a Lady, Heart of Darkness, Kiss of the Spider Woman* and *The Handmaid's Tale.* To season this diet of prose and make it palatable for students, I decided to experiment with "reading styles," allowing the structure of the texts to shape our approaches to them. Students wrote weekly journal entries, concentrating on the demands of each novel—the way, for instance,

Manuel Puig's footnotes forced them to consider a "parallel" narrative while trying to follow the challenging pastiche of "dream narratives" and dialogues. I also asked them to document their own "reading style." Some had never thought about this before, though they could describe habitual reading environments: in bed, on the school bus, et cetera. This led to a discussion of how reading practices influence the understanding and appreciation of a text. Do we "hear" the words during a silent reading, or simply see them? Should one pause in the midst of a paragraph to reach for a dictionary, or wait until the end of the passage? Several students noted that, for the first time, they were cognizant of *how* they were reading as well as *what* they were reading. This would prove critical, months later, to our discussion of telecommunications and electronic publishing.

Throughout the year, the linchpin of our discussions was *Great Expectations*. The most appropriate strategy for the study of this novel was the one which its original publication demanded: weekly installments. Thus, each week we indulged in "read-aloud" sessions, gathering in a circle, taking turns reading one paragraph aloud, regardless of length, before the next in the circle took a turn. We paused after paragraphs—to discuss, re-read or laugh—and continued in this fashion until we reached an asterisk denoting the end of Dickens's original 1861 installment.

When March arrived, and found us mid-way through the novel, I distributed copies and asked my students to finish reading it in modern fashion: two weeks' time. I also asked them to write journal entries, comparing the "read-aloud" experience with their private, silent readings. Most of them preferred the former, recalling how characters sprung to life when we "enacted" the text (when Pip attended Miss Havisham's birthday celebration, for instance, we read the installment gathered in a tight circle on the floor, lights off, passing a candle from one reader to the next). Others observed how the passage of time in their own lives led to a more authentic—albeit vicarious—experience of Pip's maturation in the text. Where we previously needed a month to read four installments, describing, say, two years in Pip's life, the readers suddenly "covered" the same interval in one evening. Our discussion of time and reading styles made us wonder if accelerating changes in modern society, so noticeable in Kuala Lumpur, and the attendant distractions, so prevalent within the school environment, endangered the novel as a "species" of literature. Happily, this exercise helped us return to oral traditions, recalling intimate, childhood encounters with literature while inspiring our imaginations. As one student later wrote:

We forget how important reading aloud was to the original audiences of books like *Great Expectations*. Reading aloud is for children (or so we think). We adults (and adult wannabes) zip through a text speedily and silently, with perhaps a little chuckle at the jokes and a supressed sniffle at the deathbed scenes. Reading aloud in class allowed us to more fully appreciate the humor and make the emotional scenes more poignant. You can't rush through the boring or uncomfortable bits when someone's reading aloud. You're forced to listen, and I think you pay more attention. You also realize, as perhaps you wouldn't when laboring through Chapter 12 at three in the morning, that Dickens aims to entertain. I appreciate the way we stopped the reading for discussion or speculation about impending plot-twists, because otherwise I may not have thought about the book until I had finished it. I have a tendency to pick up a book and just plow through to the end, then stop and take a breath and wonder what it was all about. It's easier to complain about Dickens's unlikely plots and maddening coincidences once you've finished the book. Midway, there are all sorts of choices he could make, and the direction of the story isn't always obvious.

—*Mulaika Hijjas*

It would be misleading to claim universal approval for the read-aloud sessions. There were thoughtful criticisms, to be sure. Quick readers felt impatient when it was a slow reader's turn, while certain daydreamers admitted they had missed parts. Others found it difficult to read a novel over many months' time, and wondered how anyone could have done this habitually. We discussed attention spans, pondered reader-response theories, and considered the impact of modern society—from television to computer technology—upon a "community of readers." Several students felt obliged to reread segments because they weren't "comfortable" with their understanding of them. Most significant, however, was the alteration of classroom dynamics and reading experiences, which compelled students to think about their "relationship" with a text. The following, from a student reflecting on the experience, speaks to some fundamental issues:

Until last year, I only remember reading aloud in school as a young child. Once I mastered the skill of reading silently, I preferred the faster, internal method of reading and comprehending. I assumed that since the words and the ideas were the same, so were the experiences. My perspective on reading aloud changed last year. . . . First, reading aloud uncovered the humor in Dickens's characters and writing. Often, we stopped in the middle of a passage and laughed. I found the image of Mr. Pocket pulling himself up by his hair particularly funny. If I had read that passage silently, I would have missed the absurdity of that image. Secondly, although reading silently would have been faster, reading aloud gave us the opportunity to react and discuss the text as we read. Too often, our discussions about a piece of literature are removed from the text. Finding passages can be tedious, so we make generalizations instead. However, when reading aloud, initial reactions and comments about a passage can lead to interesting discussions. Our discussions about Pip's attitude toward Joe stemmed from our reactions to specific passages.

—*Natalie Audage*

Looking for a Latter-day Dickens

What, you may ask, does any of this have to do with telecommunications? Well, discussions of reading and publishing practices of the past naturally invite questions about those practices in the future. What's more, with the arrival of March I confronted a typical IB/AP teacher's conundrum: how can one simultaneously complete the course material, achieving some sense of closure, and begin review for external examinations? Like many teachers, I wished my students had greater appreciation for "The Art of the Novel." Yes, we had read and discussed the prescribed texts, investigated the background of respective authors, and written journal entries and essays, but something was still lacking. Somehow, I wanted to "show" my students what I had been "telling" them about novels. I wanted them to dive beneath the surface of the texts—beneath the experience of active readers even—to a place of knowledge and understanding reserved for practitioners of the art. I thought about Dickens's serial publication once more, marveling at both his fertile imagination and personal stamina. I asked the students if they thought such a feat could be accomplished in this era. One of them, a budding "cyberpunk," said he not only thought it could, but that he imagined it was already happening somewhere on the Internet.

Perhaps it was, but I couldn't find any evidence of it while surfing the "Net" at my home in Ampang. So I began designing a project, one that would turn each of my students into a latter-day Charles Dickens. I decided to use the school's electronic bulletin board service to publish weekly installments of my students' own, original novellas, which sophomores in my other classes would then read and critique. Meanwhile, anyone in the community who wished to read the installments could simply open the Great Expectations folder on the BBS and download the files. To attract an audience, and publicize these electronic manuscripts, I adopted the persona of Mr. Jaggers, the infamous attorney of Dickens's novel, and sent his missives to the BBS periodically. The following was the first of those efforts:

Dear Reader:
Curious, aren't you? Bit of a BBS voyeur? You'd like to know what this new folder with the auspicious title is all about? Well, indulge me for a moment, and I'll tell you a brief tale. . . .

Once upon a time there were some talented students in English 12 classes studying Charles Dickens's novel, *Great Expectations*. They experienced much of the novel like its first readers—in weekly installments. Then one day, just after they'd finished their reading, they were challenged by their tutor, a tall, bearded fellow with penetrating eyes, who usually haunted their days and nights with questions, questions, questions, but this time only smiled and said, "It's time to emulate not only the readers, but also the writer."
They started in horror, eyes wide, mouths agape.
One poor lad cried out, "You don't mean. . . ."
But the tutor's sinister chuckle, and the sight of his cursed syllabus, silenced them all. Here is what their tormentor presented that day:

*Announcing: "Great Expectations—Electronic Novellas in the Making."

*"The Art of the Novel"—What better way to conclude our discussion of the novel as a literary form than by writing one?

*Publishing—To strengthen one's appreciation of Charles Dickens, Henry James, and other practitioners of the novel-by-installment, we will publish work on a weekly basis. Impossible, you say? Welcome to the world of electronic publishing!

*The Installments—Your reading public's demands are simple: provide them with thoughtful, clever, and entertaining weekly installments of 1000–1500 words. The choice of setting, viewpoint, style, etc. is up to you, but it's probably wise to think of the narrative as a "person in a place with a problem," and of the story as an expression of how that individual would work through the problems while becoming initiated to the world and self.

*Allusions: To make it more challenging, and "show" you how great writers work, each installment must include one literary allusion.

*Deadlines—Now you'll get to see what Dickens felt like—from December 1860 to August 1861. Here's our publication schedule:

March 15th—1st installment
March 22—2nd installment
March 29—SPRING BREAK
April 5th—3rd installment

In May, following the IB/AP exams, you will be expected to write two more installments . . . we'll discuss that later. For now, start thinking of a person in a place with a problem—and what you'll need to do as a writer to keep a reader's attention.

What does all of this mean for you, dear Reader? As of 5 o'clock in the afternoon, on the dates indicated, thirty budding novelists will submit their work to the BBS for your enjoyment. Don't miss the first installments! Please note: initially, the respective class folders will be reserved for authors' submissions only. Eventually, we hope to accommodate reader responses, but for the time being, please understand. For now, know that we're trying to limit confusion and help you, dear Reader, in your pursuit of reading pleasure. Thank you for your attention. We hope you'll join us March 15th, to see how a modern-day Dickens would launch *Great Expectations*.

Yr hmble srvt,
Mr. Jaggers

The Plot: Installment #1

Jaggers sent another note the following week, just before publishing the first installments; then came the initiation of thirty young writers to the wizardry of electronic publishing. For the majority, it was their first encounter with e-mail. In two brief sessions they learned how to log on to the school's BBS through a shared account and post their submissions in the "Great Expectations" folder. The following, submitted on March 15, attracted readers within minutes:

A Real Dream

I used to come here with my brother all the time. I'd make him go to the counter and order because I'd told him the old lady behind it scared me. He'd order two "sticky buns" for us and four meat pies for the family, while I crawled under the counter to get to the back of the shop. From there I could see the baker, a big old man, as he prepared the bread, pies and cakes for the next day. I'd drink in the smells that lingered from that day's baking. After a while I'd go back outside. David didn't seem to mind how long I took; I guess older brothers are like that. I'd find him at the window of the newsagent next door, eating his bun and looking up at the model aeroplanes that hung above the advertised books and stationery. He really wanted to fly. It always took him a few minutes to notice me, then we'd turn and walk home. I loved those days.

Today it's Mike who orders for me. The shop remains the same, except the old lady and baker are long gone. When we have our order Mike and I take our spoils to a small corner table away from the door, through which a draft of cold winter air seeps. We talk.

"So how's school?" he asks, mouth full of pie, little pieces of flaky pastry caught at the corners of his mouth.

"'s O.K." I say.

"Are you sure you understand all that stuff?" he asks, pointing at my school bag, whose weight I've dumped at my feet.

"Yeah. It's not really hard. It just takes a lot of time."

"When're your exams?"

"November."

"That's tough."

"No, not really. I've been through worse." This unexpected statement leaves the conversation dead. But he knows what I mean. Mike looks up from his food to see my face. I am glad that my hair, its dark strands fallen from the ponytail I scrape up every morning, covers my eyes. Even without seeing my eyes, or the expression of emotion within them, Mike reaches over and takes my hand. He's never done that before, but it seems right. The warmth of his hand is like recognition of a fire inside me. My own private furnace of thoughts and dreams, and pain. Since David's death at the beginning of last summer holidays, when he and Dad had so enthusiastically taken to the skies, I haven't been able to find a way to put the fire out, to bring myself back into the real world. The unexpected action makes me quiet; Mike is quiet too. We sit. The remains of our meal cool in the centre of the table. I see the table, with the cans of drink, plates and cutlery spread out on the red checkered cloth. I see our hands too, and I consider how it is that our hands could mean so many things other than what they do. And yet they don't. They have changed roles since they first met, like the shops of our town, moving from one location to another, closing and reopening in new locations though they stay the same shops. I suppose that that should be comforting, when reality remains basically the same. But it isn't. And I decide then to take some action to change some little thing at least. I get up, Mike's hand still in mine, and we walk home. I want to tell him that I dread going into my home. But I think that this would be wrong. I can change my mind later.

"Let's get an ice cream, or something."

"It's winter, silly." He looks at me out of the corner of his eye.

"I know that. Come on let's do something! Please." I hear the force in my voice and understand that I have gone too far. Too far to turn back that is. He keeps my hand in his, though I would let go. And waits until I decide. So I do. I offer to make him something at home. And though we've just eaten, he accepts. We turn the corner to my house.

There is no mistaking the anger with which my father slams the car door, nor the screech of tires as he drives out onto the road. He didn't even check for traffic, and floored the accelerator before the car was even pointed in the right direction. The car slams to a halt when an approaching car makes its presence felt by blasting its horn, over and over again.

I want to ignore this, but I can't. There would be no joy in that. I am glad in a way, that my point has been illustrated, without word or action on my part. Mike can see the way it is. There is no need to look inside. To see the mess of possessions that symbolise the ruin of my family. The mess that I had long ago given up as permanent. At least this is what I think. Mike thinks otherwise. Acts otherwise. He pulls me, and I follow. Up the front steps we go, and into the hall. He stops. If I'd told him, he wouldn't have believed me. Now he can see. It's not that the house is dirty, but that it is unkempt. Old newspapers line the hall. That they ever got put there in the first place is a miracle. No, not a miracle. Me. There are spiders on the ceiling. In one place, a spiderwoman's eggs hang. Where she was once busy, they now lie in wait. Caught in the web that fate has spun for them. Rather like this house. Except in this house the web is internal. Spun from guilt and accusations.

It was your fault.

No it was not.

How could you have done that?

I didn't mean to, Christ woman, can't you see that.

No. You've taken my son. Our son. He's gone forever. I told you he was too young.

He was 19 for godssake!

Too young.

He knew what he was doing.

You shouldn't have let him up there in the first place.

He could have done it without me. But he didn't.

We find my mother sitting alone in the kitchen, her radio playing quietly as she sips from her wine glass, pretending that nothing had happened.

—*Amanda Jessup*

The Readers: A Problem of Response

How does a teacher respond to thirty students writing 1000-word novella installments every week? How might the teacher disseminate copies of this work without causing a meltdown in the school's photocopying room? This is where electronic publishing proves itself an ally. After initiating the twelfth grade authors to the school's BBS through shared accounts, I set up three more accounts for their critics, tenth grade students in my "Introduction to Literary Analysis" (ILA) course.

The ILA scholars were conducting their own study of the novel, devoting the spring term to *Tess of the D'Urbervilles*. Thus, they were a well-primed audience for "novellas-in-progress." Each tenth grade student drew one twelfth grade author's name from a hat, and had the choice of a second author on their own. This guaranteed every twelfth grade author at least one reader; popular reaction to the novellas would dictate how many additional responses an author received. The critics were free to change their second choices—provided they did not critique a subsequent installment unless they had read all of its predecessors. The critics were then required to write a full-page critique for both authors, analyzing the prose as well as plot, character, and theme. These letters were to be handwritten and submitted for my perusal—and assessment—before their delivery to the authors.

In this fashion, we mixed old and new forms of written communication. While the authors employed twentieth-century telecommunications for serial publication, the critics emulated nineteenth-century correspondents, handwriting their critiques and sealing them with wax or playful postage stamps. I instructed the critics to encourage their authors while voicing aesthetic concerns, aiming for a mutually rewarding experience.

The authors had an appreciative, though critical, audience to help them develop their novellas and writing; the critics learned vicariously about the challenges of imaginative writing, while gaining practical experience in literary criticism. The following critique reveals how satisfying some critics found this arrangement, especially as sophomores unaccustomed to seniors' attention—or respect!

Dear Steffen Jacobsen,
Once again, you have managed to totally capture my attention, and transported me into another world. This time, to a world with scenery.

You included so much scenery, that I got a feeling that I was actually there. Whole paragraphs that describe a single room, versus your previous odd word or sentence. It is so relieving, to know that someone out there is actually listening to what I suggest. Detailed scenery opens up the author's mind, and allows the reader to see what's inside. You included plenty of sensory detail. This helped me a lot. One of my favorite bits was: "spittle splattered my face and I closed my eyes, drawing my sleeve across." I fully imagine the way a small Indian boy would do that. It brought me sheer joy.

One thing that really bothers me is Avih's speech patterns. In the beginning, he spoke very simply, with three- or four-word sentences, like: "He loved her," "He never loved me," and "I was the third son." In this entry (#3), his speech is getting more like regular speech, with extensive sentences, like: "I had a small room above the parlor, to which I retired every day at ten, two hours after the sun had set," and "Chipped paint from the ceiling continuously peeled off and fell upon me as I slept." Maybe you are doing this on purpose, but it confuses me, and perhaps some of your other readers. Another speech problem is when the fat man says, "Hey, boy! Yah you." I can't quite see an Indian man saying "Yah you." Once again, your American English experience makes its mark on your work.

Another bothersome thing is the obviousness of the plot. I know some foreshadowing is good, but this is pushing it. When the fat man drank the tea, you said: "He downed the contents in one gulp." I find it real hard to down a cup of hot tea in one gulp. When he wanted another cup, it was just too obvious that you were trying to poison him. Maybe you should have taken a more subtle approach, like having him slowly sip two cups of tea, and then having him die.

Other than that, I think that the story is great, and I can't wait to find out what that dirty boy has to do with that man's death.
Sincerely,
Joe Rahim

The Symbiosis: Writers (and Readers) in Electronic Residence
From the outset, several authors wished to reply to their critics. I stymied this, however, because I wanted the authors to "answer" their critics through their fiction, not an appendix to each installment. Nevertheless,

the hiatus between installments #3 and #4, for IB and AP examinations, invited a departure from our routine. Before the authors responded, however, I admonished them not to "tell" too much, but to question the critic, offer a word of thanks, or seek more specific criticism. In the following letter, written after the fourth installments, the author concedes some fundamental errors while sharing a significant lesson with his critic:

> Hey Akshay (Sateesh)—Thanks a lot for reading my installments, I just want to say that I take your comments very seriously.
>
> To be frank with you, I encountered many problems writing these installments. I think it has got to do with a good first installment to lay the groundwork. I made several mistakes in the first installment. For example, I hate the name "Dean." I don't know why I put down that name in the first place. The name, Dean, really did not reflect a Malaysian schoolboy. Secondly, the age is supposed to be 16 or 17 years old and not 11 or 12 years old.
>
> Along with several other mistakes, by the time I got to the 2nd installment, I hated my story. I almost completely lost interest. This "loss" of interest was largely because of the fact that I was afraid to choose the path of the story. I was uncertain here, uncertain there, till the story could not get anywhere. I don't think I spent insufficient time. I spent enough time all right, but too much worrying!
>
> Next time, when I have another chance to write installments, I will begin my story with my character clearly defined. I don't mean knowing exactly the whole story from the beginning but knowing what I'm coming up against (the main character). Secondly, I'll relax and be sure of myself. No good worrying!
>
> Thanks again.
> Nasrul Bakar

The Concluding Episode: Narrative Closure

As the fifth and final installment approached, Mr. Jaggers made one last appearance on the ISKL electronic bulletin board. This time, he was uncharacteristically deferential. Perhaps even a curmudgeon like Jaggers was awed by "paperless publication" and its empowerment of these fledgling novelists:

> Dear Reader:
> While we know you have "great expectations" for the conclusion of your favorite electronic novellas, we also know this to be a chaotic time for our young authors. They're a bit preoccupied with endings just now: the end of a school year, the end of a high school career, and, yes, the end of a novella.
>
> Some are better with endings than others, of course, and will undoubtedly submit their final installment today, May 24th, to the BBS. Others? Well . . . they're a temperamental lot these artists, but they've promised to make

their submissions available for faithful readers no later than Friday, May 26, just in time for your weekend leisure.

We of Jaggers Publishing wish to thank you all for your interest and support throughout this endeavor. We'd say more, but we've learned to not only recite Longfellow, but to live by his wisdom, at such moments:

"Great is the art of beginning, but greater the
    art is of ending;
Many a poem is marred by a superfluous
    verse."

Sincerely yours,
Mr. Jaggers

The fifth, and final, installments were posted one week before final exams. The authors were exhausted; many had recently completed their IB/AP examinations. Nonetheless, they were determined to write the final installment, perhaps to satisfy loyal readers or, just perhaps, to satisfy themselves. By now the narrative "voices" were well established, and so were the relationships between authors and readers, as the following critique demonstrates:

Dear Mike (Ackhurst)—How do I love your story? Let me count the ways. . . . Sorry, couldn't help it. This has to be my favorite installment; not many authors can get their readers to FEEL something when the story is finished— congratulations! This installment helped me realize that people's lives are unique to themselves and the facts don't need to be known to anyone except that person for their life to be special.

The funny thing was that I didn't feel "hollow" after reading this. I felt like I had gained something and I'd like to thank you for that.

Just one minor detail: Gordon's mother sits down beside him twice, but there is no mention that she got up in between. I just thought I'd mention that small oversight.

I do have one question: if in installment #4, Gordon was so mad at whoever stole some kid's bike and threw it into the dam, then why does he steal one himself? Is there a hidden message here? I like the fact that you left a little bit of "space" to imagine what happens to Gord and what happened with Baiba. Leave the reader wanting more: you've definitely mastered that.

Well, Mike, what can I say? Critiquing isn't exactly easy, so I guess I'll leave it at that. Good luck in the future with all of that "cheese wisdom." Maybe I'll see you in Canada sometime!
Sincerely,
Alexa Giorgi

P.S.—Thank you for teaching me what I really needed to know: "The cardinal sin of any lifetime is to try and rewrite it the way it should have happened. A temptation to us all, and a first degree tragic flaw." You've shown me what I've been doing wrong. I'm going to keep this in mind.

The Postscript: Young Authors' Reflections

Among the greatest surprises of this project was the way in which the authors, high school seniors in their penultimate weeks, responded to their critics. Their anxiety before receiving the first critiques was nearly palpable. With each successive critique, however, they grew more comfortable with the symbiotic relationship between reader and writer. As an advisor to various school publications I've witnessed the disappointment of student writers who wonder if anyone is reading their work. In this instance, however, there was no question. Someone was definitely reading, and responding, sometimes in an encouraging way, sometimes not.

This "guaranteed" audience, and the immediacy of its responses, highlights a significant feature of on-line writing: its authenticity. The creation of electronic novellas enabled students to engage in more authentic reader-writer relationships. This was especially meaningful to the authors; much of the student writing for an IB course, after all, is destined for an examiner's eyes only—whether it be a World Literature paper, "Extended Essay," or written examinations. As a result, students often feel like their writing is tossed into a void. Writing workshops in class allow for peer response and help fill that void, but over a two-year period they lose impact and efficacy. The publication of their writing in electronic form, however, re-invigorated these students for a variety of reasons, most of which relate to this "authenticity."

For one, there's the thrill of response from relative strangers, people who—unlike classmates—come to know the writer primarily through their writing. While dreading harsh criticism, the authors also learned that the adulation of an admiring fan could flatter and worry a creator, simultaneously empowering and humbling. Secondly, as the works evolved, the authors grew more attached to their creations, which they most definitely gave "serious, and sustained, attention." In spite of myriad distractions, these authors focused on their work and defended it against the abuses of weak readers. They experienced the bewilderment of the writer wondering if a reader's misunderstanding stems from poor writing or reading. Finally, the intimacy of this endeavor led to a genuine desire to "communicate"; the authors' vehicle was serialized fiction, the critics' was handwritten epistles, but the mutual aim was understanding.

Much to my surprise and delight, the project has became a "moveable feast." I learned that many of the Great Expectations authors transported their electronic novellas to college, where they've already found uses for them. This added benefit of telecommunications—the creation of a portfolio, a collection of works-in-progress that students can take from secondary school to university—allows further development of one's work, and help with a difficult transition in life. I received the following e-mail letter from a student who made good use of this "electronic portfolio" while shifting from a high school in Southeast Asia to a university in North America:

> Saturday, September 23, 1995
> Message From: hijjas@husc.harvard.edu, Internet
> Subject: I continue to procrastinate
> To: Buddy Burniske
>
> I am especially pleased today because I found out that I got into a Creative Writing class (Fiction), which is apparently extremely rare for a first-year student. Naturally (because it's the only thing I have!) I used my novella for my submission. . . .
>   . . . Publishing our novellas on the BBS was perhaps the best use of them. One wants to get some recognition for one's landmark artistic achievement, but not too much! The BBS provides a fairly gentle testing ground. The ILA students who reviewed my work were very respectful. (The most strident comment I got was scrawled in crayon by a fifth grader: "Get rid of the frog"). It was gratifying that people were following the story and had some interest in where it might go. The ILA reviewers helped my writing because they could tell me what aspects of my story were utterly confusing to everyone except me. They gave me a sense of which passages were over-written and which were underdone.
>
> —*Mulaika Hijjas*

I wish every author reaped such benefits from this project, or that the electronic publishing had been flawless. However, because the school had only two telephone lines dedicated to the BBS, and thirty students needed to submit their installments via two shared accounts, there was a considerable queue at computer terminals on deadline days. This begs one of the more popular questions which skeptics of telecommunications projects ask: "What about computer novices—aren't they spending more time thinking about technology than their writing?" To address this in practical terms, we should ask how inexperienced students overcome limited "computer literacy" and its anxieties. The following e-mail letter reveals one student's initiation:

> Friday, September 22, 1995
> Message From: smw5x@virginia.edu, Internet
> Subject: Re: "Expectations Great & Small."
> To: Buddy Burniske

E-mail, Internet access . . . benign words, yes, in today's accelerated age. However, tell a student who has never "netted" before that their final project includes writing on-line, and we plead, "No, please leave us alone!" [. . .]

Wednesday at 3:45, I complete Chapter One. With confidence I walk into the computer lab only to see eight classmates waiting for our one on-line computer. The word "deadline" starts to sink in. Finally, it's 4:40 and there's only one person ahead of me; access is fast, but not immediate. Then it's my turn.

Did Mr. Burniske say "cut" then "copy" then "paste"? Trembling, I pray I didn't delete three days' work, but the words "transfer completed" ease me. Since I don't trust this new technology, I close and re-open my file, reading my entire installment. Only then do I notice two typos, now indelible, exposed to all. Chalk it up to learning.

—*Sarah Wolf*

What about those at the other end of the "computer literacy" spectrum, those already initiated to e-mail, hypertext, and all the rest? I'm wary of generalizations, but the following e-mail message, from a student designing home pages on the World Wide Web at the time of this project, demonstrates how effective electronic publishing can be in showing a writer the significance of the human element in telecommunications:

Monday, September 25, 1995
Message From: namele@mail.wm.edu, Internet
Subject: "Expectations"
To: budjack@tropics.pc.my

The critiques of the ILA students were, for me, one of the best parts of the entire project. It was fascinating to see how someone else entered the world I created, and to see what they thought of it. I began to see distinct novellas: the one I wanted to create; the one I was creating; and the one someone else was reading. Perhaps many writers know exactly what they are communicating to their readers; I sure didn't! With the responses I received I was able to re-focus, and try again to show what I saw in my mind's eye to the reader. . . . I knew where the reader was, and I knew where I wanted the reader to be, and this helped me immensely while writing each successive assignment. Publishing [by installment] was another thing that affected my writing. Once I put my installment on the BBS, that was it. Anybody could read it, and there was nothing I could change. Somehow this was difficult for me; it was unlike any writing I had ever done. The act of making my story available to the public and putting it forth to them as a "novella" in installments forced me to write in such a way as to lure the reader back. I had an audience I needed to please, and the desire to write something that would please or at least interest that audience drove me more than anything else has ever driven my writing. An audience is a terrible thing to waste.

—*Nick Mele*

The Publisher's Farewell

Every class is a work in progress. The Great Expectations project was a good illustration, though, of what a teacher can achieve when his or her own "voice" is allowed to find expression within the "text" of a course. This is what I find demoralizing about the carnivalesque atmosphere of schools: it demeans the "sacred text" of our classrooms. Extracurricular activities that pull students from the classroom dialogue tear the fabric of a "text," an intricate tapestry of language and thought that demands the collaborative effort of students and teachers. One cannot weave "in absentia," nor hide the flaws of an ill-woven cloth.

While it is by no means a panacea for our problems, I do believe telecommunications will help language arts teachers mitigate them. In a very short time, telecommunications enabled me to show my students the importance of self-discipline in writing—as well as how demanding, fickle, and frustrating readers can be. This, in turn, fostered questions of meaning, intention, and reader response, which compelled the authors to ask questions, take greater pains with the "voice" of their narratives, and strive for consistency in style and tone. Ultimately, they learned what it means to weave their words and dreams, their visions and intentions, while listening to the queries of a critical reader and the demands of a narrative seeking a life of its own.

The problems? The ease of electronic publishing, initially a blessing, can quickly become a curse. How, for example, can anyone read and respond to all the words scrolling up the screen? How can we make sure young writers pause to reflect, gaining the critical detachment necessary for thoughtful revision, rather than becoming preoccupied with superficial concerns like font styles? How do we make sure the efficiency of e-mail transactions doesn't destroy the humanity of the relationships they nurture? In many ways, it was fortunate that we never did find a way for readers to send e-mail responses to the "Great Expectations" folder. As ISKL's computer network evolves it may provide e-mail accounts for every student. Until that time, however, the use of shared accounts makes e-mail critiques problematic. Why? The "Great Expectations" authors were essentially working in the "public domain"; the critics were not. After all, think how embarrassing it would've been for authors to receive "honest," though uncharitable, criticism that the entire community could read on the BBS.

While the creation of private e-mail accounts might resolve this, it could also breed hydra-headed problems. For instance, with more e-mail accounts, and greater "ease" of publication and response, there comes an exponential growth in writing. This places remarkable strains upon the language arts teacher, compelling one to adopt new methods of instruction, response, and assessment. New questions would inevitably arise: Can—or should—a teacher peruse his students' e-mail correspondence? After the first few installments, I felt like Big Brother eavesdropping on intimate conversations; so I stopped reading the handwritten letters and simply checked to make sure the critics had done their work. How does one grade a "letter to an author" anyway? Given the collaborative nature of this endeavor, would it be fair to fault one party for the other's failure to reciprocate? What if the reader had a mediocre author? What if the author had a negligent reader?

Finally, every telecommunications project I've been involved with has raised the issue of sensitivity in some way. In a telecommunications project I designed for international schools, "The Media Matter," I asked students to examine how they "read" the medium itself—newspapers, magazines, radio, television, and the Internet—to discuss how the sources of information shape perceptions of news stories. Students from Europe, Africa, North America and Asia shared their perceptions via listserv and questioned their counterparts' findings. Predictably, one group took exception to another's critique, prompting their faculty sponsor to share these thoughts:

> I don't know why it is that this medium seems to pump up the emotional pitch so much in the transmission. Or is it that we write more when our feelings about something are spiked? In any event, my comments about your kids' messages were not a criticism, but an inquiry. Your suggestion that we examine this with our kids is just what I am intending to do today. Why did this come across to me in this way? Is it a language problem? Was it intentional? Was it intended to be highly confrontational? Did those students intend to be rude and patronizing or did we misinterpret their tone?
>
> —Lowell Monke

Tone. Just another four-letter word? Yes, and we must handle it carefully. Telecommunications, at least in its present form, is about people learning how to *read* each other, how to understand the nuances of another's language, thought, and tone. While it accelerates the pace at which we exchange information, it does not necessarily improve communication. The danger, in fact, is that it will just help us miscommunicate more rapidly. We of an older generation learned this from another medium: the LP. Playing a 33 and 1/3 album at 78 rpm seldom helped one understand the song's lyrics, or appreciate its tone. The same applies to e-mail. Just because I've "processed" more words, more quickly, doesn't mean I'm making more sense. Nor does it mean a reader will apprehend my meaning or tone.

Communication, whether through verbal or written media, print or electronic, remains a challenge. If, as some believe, electronic mail signals a renaissance of the letter, we would do well to remember the wisdom of Joe Gargery, who offered wise counsel when the ambitious young Pip abused his listeners' ears one night: "If you can't get to be oncommon through going straight," he observed, "you'll never get to do it through going crooked." Despite his limitations, Dickens's illiterate blacksmith knew how much patience and vigilance are required for "communication," and how much integrity is necessary for one to realize Great Expectations.

Bibliography

Audage, Natalie. "Expectations great and small." Available e-mail: budjack@tropics.pc.my. from ncaudage@phoenix.Princeton.EDU. Sept. 21, 1995.

Dickens, Charles. *Great Expectations*. London: Penguin Books, 1965.

Eisner, Elliot. *The Educational Imagination*. New York: Macmillan, 1985.

Hijjas, Mulaika. "I continue to procrastinate." Available e-mail: buddyb@iskl.po.my from hijjas@husc.harvard.edu. Sept. 23, 1995.

Jessup, Amanda. "A Real Dream." Available e-mail: Great Expectations@iskl.po.my. March 1995.

Mele, Nick. "Expectations." Available e-mail: budjack@tropics.pc.my from namele@mail.wm.edu. Sept. 25, 1995.

Monke, Lowell. "Re: Curmudgeon." Available e-mail: budjack@tropics.pc.my from lm7846s@acad.drake.edu. Sept. 21, 1995.

Wolf, Sarah. "Re: Expectations Great & Small." Available e-mail: buddyb@iskl.po.my from smw5x@virginia.edu. Sept. 22, 1995.

Acknowledgments

I wish to thank: Joe Rahim, Nasrul Bakar, and Alexa Giorgi for permission to publish their letters; Dan LoCascio, the ISKL computer guru, for logistical support and private tutorials; Mary Rideout, Ampang librarian, and her staff, for patience with authors and critics at library computer terminals; and Jackie, Justin, and Kiki, for "all the larks."

Janice M. Stuhlmann

Calling All Characters!

Telecommunications and Children's Literature

Dear Harold X.,
Well, how are you?
Have you got your shot yet? Well, if you did, did it hurt?
I hope not. Because it doesn't hurt me when I get a shot.
Only when they get that long, sharp, big needle it hurts.
LOVE,
Jessica, Grade 3

In this letter, Jessica used telecommunications to ask Harold the Dog, a character in *Bunnicula: A Rabbit Tale of Mystery* by James and Deborah Howe, about an event in the book and the dog's reaction to it. Ninth grade students in Jeradi Hochella's remedial reading class at Waynesboro High School in Waynesboro, Virginia, played the role of Harold the Dog. Jessica was in April Lloyd's third grade class at Burnley Moran Elementary School in Charlottesville (about forty miles away).

This article describes the cross-age Elementary Books Project. The project was developed by Lloyd and Hochella as a means to combine telecommunications and children's literature to create innovative new learning experiences for their students. The two teachers developed this project because they wanted to create integrated learning environments where students read for a variety of purposes and engage in different forms of writing (letters, exposition, narration). The two teachers also hoped to increase students' awareness of voice and audience.

The Elementary Books Project

April Lloyd uses children's literature to integrate the curriculum. Her third grade students began the school year by reading *Ramona Quimby, Age 8,* by Beverly Cleary.

She explained:

> To me, everything starts with a novel. If you are studying Ramona Quimby, you study Oregon because that's where Ramona lives. Ramona mentions the Oregon pioneers, and you get into a lot of different types of discussions based on the natural curiosity of kids.

Lloyd was an avid participant in electronic newsgroups and thought it would be fun and exciting if her students could correspond with "Ramona Quimby" using that format. She liked the idea of using electronic newsgroups because her students would read and write in new ways, and telecommunications is a good vehicle for getting questions answered almost as quickly as they are generated.

Lloyd initiated a newsgroup called Elementary Books on Virginia's Public Education Network (Virginia's PEN), a state-wide telecommunications network that links all of Virginia's public schools and universities. Her initial plan was to have the teachers and students in the Charlottesville City Schools write to Ramona Quimby at Lloyd's electronic mail address, and Lloyd would reply as Ramona. Her introductory letter follows:

> Dear Third Graders in Charlottesville,
>
> Hi! I'm Ramona 2-uimby (sic). Ha! Ha! I guess if you have read my book *Ramona Quimby, Age 8* you got that one. If not, I hope you will read it and write to me. I will try to write back to you as often as I can. Please tell me about yourself and your third grade classroom. I love hearing about other third grade teachers and the kids in your class. Are you doing any interesting experiments or starting any new fads? Have you read any good books or done any neat projects with them?
>
> Well, I'd better go. Willa Jean is getting wise to my letter writing on the computer. She wants me to play dress up . . . YUCK!
>
> Write soon!
> Love,
> Ramona

By using her own e-mail account to respond as Ramona, Lloyd created a problem she had not considered: her real name and address automatically appeared in the header at the top of each message. At first, Lloyd's students didn't notice, but a short time later she received a letter from another teacher that began "Dear Ramona/April." Lloyd and a student (Abby) were reading messages posted to the Elementary Books newsgroup at the time:

> The next posting (message) was addressed as "Dear Ramona/April." I hit "return" really quick, but the computer was slow and it took forever.

> Abby, who is very bright, asked, "Why did they write to you? Are you Ramona? You just write back to us at the end of the day, don't you? This doesn't go anywhere does it? This isn't anything."

Lloyd also discovered that her name and e-mail address appeared in the header on the newsgroup's menu:

Topic: Letters to Ramona

1 April Lloyd	Tue, 06 Oct 92 19:26:05 GMT
2 Carrie Miller	Wed, 07 Oct 92 14:16:59 GMT
3 April Lloyd	Wed, 14 Oct 92 15:34:13 GMT

To make the Elementary Books newsgroup work, Lloyd realized that she had to get the character's name to appear at the top of each message and on the newsgroup menu. After she discussed these problems with the systems operator for Virginia's PEN, he established an electronic account for Ramona Quimby.

As Lloyd anticipated, her students were thrilled to have the opportunity to correspond with Ramona, and soon her students and many others throughout Virginia were asking Ramona (Lloyd) about herself and offering advice on how to handle particular situations from the book. At this point, given the kids' enthusiasm, Lloyd decided to extend the project to another book: Roald Dahl's *Charlie and the Chocolate Factory*. The system's operator created an account for Willy Wonka and expanded the newsgroup by creating mini-conferences, called "strands." These strands represented individual titles and housed the correspondences for each character. This new organization allowed students to follow on-line discussions more easily. A parent of one of Lloyd's students was active participating in on-line newsgroups, and he agreed to "be" Willy Wonka.

In the meantime, Jeradi Hochella was struggling to motivate students in her ninth grade remedial reading classes. Although Hochella was a veteran teacher, she was new to her school and grade level. Early on in the school year, she realized that traditional ways of teaching had not worked for her students. According to Hochella, almost all had repeated at least one grade and for them, successful learning experiences had been rare: "Reading was hard for them, and they just weren't interested." She began to look for alternative methods and materials to increase interest, to promote achievement, and to help her survive the year.

Hochella, an active user of telecommunications, became aware of Lloyd's Elementary Books Project and thought it would be an excellent way for her students to read books at appropriate levels and increase their literacy skills. She contacted Lloyd and volunteered her students to portray Harold the Dog from *Bunnicula,* Mr. Popper from *Mr. Popper's Penguins* by Richard and Florence Atwater, and Nate Twitchell from *The Enormous Egg* by Oliver Butterworth.

Ninth Grade Students' Reactions

Hochella knew that her students would be reluctant to take part in the Elementary Books Project, so she decided to "sell" the idea as a community service project. "How can we use a computer to send messages to third graders forty miles away?" a student asked. Hochella explained that through phone lines, computers talked to other computers all the time. As Hochella logged on, she asked the students to listen carefully. "How many of you have been in a store buying something and heard this noise? [Static and crackle.] That's telecommunications."

Hochella's students read *Bunnicula* first and corresponded under the guise of Harold the Dog. Since Lloyd's third graders were already accustomed to writing to storybook characters, they zealously began to question Harold about the escapades and temperaments of the characters in the book. The ninth graders, however, were confused about how to respond, and Harold's initial responses were terse and lifeless.

To remedy the problem, Hochella and her students studied the letters written by Ramona Quimby and Willy Wonka. Although this helped, the writing style of many of her students continued to be stilted. They complained that it was nearly impossible to write letters to people they had not met. To overcome the impersonality, Lloyd sent pictures of her students to Hochella, which the ninth graders taped to their computers. This visualization technique helped them "see" the students at the other end; as a result, their letters became more lively and conversational:

Dear Harold,
My dog Spot have Black and wite Spots on his boby and he ate My two Cats. he Hide After he Did that.
I,m Righting and Drowing a Book about Tenage Muntain Ninja Turtles. NaTasha is my iLlistrder. She draws the pictures for the Book.
Bye
Richard

Dear Richard,
I'm always working on gathering ideas for new books. Writers do that. We keep our eyes and ears alert and ready for new ideas (and our noses ready for steaks). Maybe I could read one of your books sometime.
   What does your dog Spot look like? I am always interested in finding out about one of my fellow canines. Does your family treat Spot like the Monroes treat Chester and me?
   Well, I'm pretty tired so I think I'll go curl up on my rug. Hope to hear from you again.

Faithfully yours, ||
                             \ OO /
                            OoooO

Harold X.   oooooooo

The K-9 Correspondent   ooooo
                             ooo

After Hochella's students loosened up and wrote more, they began to concentrate on voice. They studied the idiosyncrasies of each character to match the character's voice and personality, and discussed characters' thoughts and actions. They also discovered that the third graders focused on minutiae rather than main ideas. Nonetheless, their questions covered a variety of topics. To respond, the ninth graders carefully reread sections of the book and worked in teams to write replies.

The ninth graders decided to develop a HyperCard stack for *Bunnicula*, as a reference tool for the third graders. They combined text, graphics, and sounds to provide information on six different topics: vampires; the Carpathian Mountains; the Cyrillic alphabet; Russian wolfhounds; other books to read; and information about the book's two authors.

Fig. 1. *The* Bunnicula *HyperCard stack created by the ninth grade students*

Users could navigate through the program by using the mouse to select topics they wanted to explore. The ninth grade students enhanced the program by adding sounds. For example, when the vampire was selected, he said, "Good evening. Welcome to Transylvania." Following the greeting, a screen containing information about vampires appeared. Developing this HyperCard stack encouraged the ninth graders to research different topics and to engage in expository writing. They also gained experience using different types of software programs, as they scanned in pictures, created their own illustrations, and incorporated text and graphics into a finished product.

As the ninth graders portrayed other characters, they developed other projects as well. For example, while portraying Nate Twitchell from *The Enormous Egg,* several students designed and built an "enormous egg" using a blueprint they developed. The egg opened, revealing a baby dinosaur.

Third Grade Students' Reactions

Lloyd's third grade students loved writing to storybook characters. Lloyd commented:

> It drives itself. They are the ones who want to get on the network, so they're on it all day. Constantly. They start at 8:30 in the morning and just rotate on and off.

Third graders really liked using the computer for writing. When asked how it was different from other writing, one student, Quinton, replied:

> It's real different from writing to other people, your friends and stuff, because if you write to them, then you have to mail it. Here, you type it in and it's gone. It's on the telephone. You hear it ring, and the telephone takes it. I think it's neat.

Another student, Daniel, liked using a computer to write to characters because he didn't consider it to be "schoolwork": "I think it's fun because we get a lot of time off from working. We got to use computers for half an hour, and we didn't have to do work." Daniel had used computers in the Writing to Read Program. He thought using a computer made a difference in his writing because he liked to type. He was less enthusiastic about using a pencil to write journals or other class assignments. "Using a computer just makes it seem less like work," he said.

The students experienced frustration as well: they were disappointed when they didn't have time to log on. They were also frustrated when someone was taking too long at the computer. Lloyd explained, "There is only the one computer station, and it takes some students a long time to type and post a response." Students also became annoyed when the line to the local node (network connection) was busy.

Benefits to Learning

Increases in Comprehension and Vocabulary. For the third grade students, reading comprehension increased because they read and reread for a purpose. Many times, the characters would ask the younger students to reread passages or to try to "figure out" answers based on what they already knew. For example, one student asked if Willy Wonka could give him the Golden Goose. Wonka asked the student to think about the book and figure out the answer for himself. "Where did the geese live?" Wonka asked. "And what is it that they do, and why can't I give you a golden goose?" Answers like these influenced the third graders to answer their own questions. Lloyd stated, "They feel like they have power, and it's not that the power comes from somewhere else and they get told answers. They figure out the answers and that's really the key to it."

For the third graders, vocabulary also became very important because students wanted to understand every word in the characters' responses. For example, in the letter from Harold the Dog to Richard, Harold asks, "What does your dog Spot look like? I am always interested in finding out about one of my fellow canines." Richard immediately asked, "What's a canine?" Lloyd commented:

> Students do the things that you want them to do when they read. They will reread if it doesn't make sense. They will stop, puzzle over something, and ask questions about the meaning of the text if they do not understand.

Responding to letters on an electronic newsgroup provided ninth grade students with opportunities to become involved in many different types of reading activities. It also increased their self-esteem and confidence. The project created a "risk-free" environment for ninth grade students to read materials at appropriate levels without ridicule from peers. They also asked their teacher for recommendations about books they might enjoy, and one day, a student's grandmother called to thank and chide Hochella. She stated that she was thrilled because her grandson was reading at home for the first time in his life, but that she was also dismayed because she couldn't make him stop to go to sleep.

Increases in Writing Skills. The use of telecommunications provided students with opportunities to write for real audiences, and Lloyd and Hochella found that this caused students to read and write with greater depth and accuracy. Spelling and punctuation were no longer contrived exercises in grammar books. Lloyd explains:

There's an awful lot of writing with a purpose, which drives them to spell correctly, to capitalize correctly, to do punctuation. All the things that teachers kill to get their kids to do, they want to do because they want Mr. Wonka to think they are smart. They want Ramona to think they are intelligent. They want Bunnicula to be impressed with the words they use.

Lloyd also noticed that students became more conscious of word choice. For example, James and Deborah Howe used homonyms throughout *Bunnicula*, and students did the same when corresponding with Harold. "Let's see if he notices that I put steak, instead of stake," one said.

Lloyd encouraged the students to write in pairs and collaborate on responses. She explained:

This taps social skills as well as communication skills, and provides students with opportunities to construct their own learning. First, they have to share ideas and decide what to write. Then, they have to write in plural form. Instead of "I," it becomes "we."

Hochella's ninth grade students enjoyed collaborating and working together in teams. For example, since a group of students was writing as one character, they realized that the character's voice had to be consistent. They analyzed characters' thoughts and actions, discussed nuances, argued over interpretations, and shared responses before posting them on the newsgroup. This co-authoring technique created more dynamic responses and changed students' attitudes about the writing process. One of Hochella's students commented, "My opinion changed when I started writing. It got better."

When asked how they liked working together to write responses, another student replied:

When we were writing by ourselves, I didn't like it. I liked it better when we did it in a group. I just got more ideas when we were doing it together, and I was helping, not just trying to do it by myself.

By engaging in different forms of writing (letters, exposition, narration), the ninth graders began to understand different styles of writing. Also, they learned to adjust to a particular audience. They had to concentrate on making the characters' responses and the information in the HyperCard stack interesting, and yet understandable, to younger students.

In addition, the ninth grade students were also more motivated to write well and to take pride in their work. But perhaps the greatest benefit was that learning was "sneaking up" on the students. As one high school student put it:

> At first I didn't know what it was all about. Then I started to understand when we started writing on the computers. I thought it was pretty fun. It beats doin' homework. You ain't gotta go home and write all the stuff up. You sit in class and read a book. The book was pretty funny. I liked it.

Lloyd and Hochella's Reactions

Lloyd was thrilled with the results, as was Hochella:

> It was great. I couldn't believe how interested my students were, and I was shocked with the spin-off projects. You should have seen them working on that HyperCard stack! Talk about reading and writing! And they were so proud of their "enormous egg." They created it from a blueprint they drew up on the computer. It even had a little dinosaur inside. It just goes to show what kids can do if they're motivated.

The students were not the only ones to change. Both Hochella and Lloyd could see themselves approaching the instruction of reading and writing differently and more effectively. They also felt they were creating a curriculum that was richer and more diverse. Through the use of group work, they felt that their classrooms had become more student-centered, leaving them with more time for individualized instruction.

Also, by collaborating on projects, students were learning from each other. Both teachers felt that participation in the Elementary Books Project changed the dynamics of their classrooms—from competitive to cooperative. They thought collaborative projects enhanced students' creativity, challenged them intellectually, and encouraged them to seek alternative solutions to problems. In addition, they thought that student assessment based on extended projects, progress, and effort reduced the social pressure associated with repeated failure, and encouraged students to succeed.

Developing a Similar Project

Virginia's Public Education Network (Virginia's PEN) enables teachers to send and receive electronic mail messages, share data and information, and tap into other state and national resources via the Internet. Other states (e.g., Texas, Massachusetts, Florida, Kentucky) also have state-wide educational telecommunications networks, and still others are in the planning stages. It may also be possible to establish a project such as this one on a commercial telecommunications network designed for educational use.

Initially, Lloyd wanted to use the resources on Virginia's PEN in her classroom, but found that most of the activities on them were resources for teachers only, and that many of the activities for students were not interesting, interactive, or meaningful to her students. In the beginning, the students used her personal e-mail account to correspond with characters. As discussed above, this had some serious limitations, and was a major reason why Lloyd established a special newsgroup for the Elementary Books Project. By doing this, she was able to adapt the network to meet her own curricular needs.

The system's operator at Virginia's PEN was instrumental in developing a working format for the newsgroup. He realized early on that navigation would be a problem, and that students would become frustrated if they didn't know where to look for a letter or where to post a response. The creation of mini-conferences ("strands") allowed all the letters and responses for any one character to be located in the same place, making navigation easier and reducing confusion. The following menu displays the strands in the Elementary Books newsgroup:

Newsgroup: va-pen.elem.books
1. Welcome!
2. Ramona Quimby is back!
3. WILLY WONKA—THAT'S ME!
4. Bunnicula and Friends!

A Few Words of Caution

First, recruit volunteers wisely. Portraying a character can be very time-consuming, and students become frustrated when characters are slow to respond, or don't respond at all. It is also important that the characters try to engage students in a dialogue and encourage them to answer their own questions.

The second caution involves moderating the newsgroup. The moderator (the person "in charge" of a newsgroup or a strand in a newsgroup) should be able to delete postings (messages) that are inappropriate or move them to another location. Even though the Elementary Books Project was divided into individual strands for each character, people still posted messages in the wrong place. This confused participants and detracted from discussions. To avoid this, Lloyd and Hochella established guidelines for posting, in a strand entitled "Welcome!" They also cleaned up the newsgroup on a regular basis by moving messages to the proper locations and deleting older ones.

The third caution involves literature selections. To remain sane, limit the character's discussion to only one book in a series. There are a number of Ramona and Bunnicula books and it would be very confusing to carry on a conversation about all of them at once. If students ask about other books, instruct the characters to return them gently to the book being discussed.

Also, the characters in the Elementary Books Project began to feel overwhelmed by the volume of letters. To remedy this, Hochella and Lloyd developed a schedule of dates for specific books. This method released characters from a year-round obligation and allowed teachers to plan accordingly. As the popularity of the Elementary Books Project increased, more books were added to the project and additional volunteers were recruited to portray characters. The following is a list of the titles and dates for the year:

1) *Charlie and the Chocolate Factory* (Sept.–June)
2) *The Stories Julian Tells* (Sept.–June)
3) *Ramona Quimby, Age 8* (Oct. 15–Feb. 1)
4) *Bunnicula* (Dec.–Feb.)
5) *Clifford* (Nov.–Dec.)
6) *Mr. Popper's Penguins* (Jan.–March)
7) *Viola Swamp* (Jan.–Feb.)
8) *Winnie-the-Pooh* (Feb.–March)
9) *Amelia Bedelia* (Feb.–March)
10) *Frog and Toad Together* (March–April)
11) *In the Year of the Boar and Jackie Robinson* (April–May)
12) *The Enormous Egg* (May–June)
13) *From the Mixed-Up Files of Mrs. Basil E. Frankweiler* (Dec.–Feb.)
14) Books by Dr. Seuss (Dec.–Feb.)

Conclusion

By integrating telecommunications and children's literature, Lloyd and Hochella created learning environments that extended beyond classroom walls and provided students with opportunities to become members of larger communities. The impressive immediacy of telecommunications influenced students to interact with text differently. They realized that peers would read and respond to their work, and this increased their desire to be understood; therefore, they read and wrote with greater depth and accuracy. They placed greater emphasis on spelling, punctuation, audience, voice, and style. The students became active learners and began to think of themselves as readers and writers. They gained confidence in their abilities as they tapped hidden talents and learned to work together.

Both teachers found that students were excited about the project and that students were reading and writing more enthusiastically. Throughout the project, the real identities of the characters remained anonymous, and many of the younger students actually thought they were writing to Harold the Dog. Some of the older students were skeptical, but some still hoped Harold the Dog really was sneaking into the Monroes' den at night to use the computer!

Bibliography

Allard, Harry. *Miss Nelson is Missing*. Boston: Houghton Mifflin, 1993.

Atwater, Richard, and Florence Atwater. *Mr. Popper's Penguins*. Boston: Little Brown, 1938.

Bridwell, Norman. *Clifford's Puppy Days*. New York: Scholastic, 1994.

Butterworth, Oliver. *The Enormous Egg*. Boston: Little Brown, 1956.

Cameron, Ann. *The Stories Julian Tells*. New York: Pantheon, 1981.

Cleary, Beverly. *Ramona Quimby, Age 8*. New York: Morrow, 1981.

Dahl, Roald. *Charlie and the Chocolate Factory*. New York: Knopf, 1964.

Geisel, Theodore Seuss. *The Cat in the Hat* . New York: Random House, 1957.

———. *The Cat in the Hat Comes Back*. New York: Random House Beginner Books, 1958.

Howe, Deborah, and J. Howe. *Bunnicula: A Rabbit Tale of Mystery*. New York: Atheneum, 1979.

Howe, James. *Rabbit Cadabra!* New York: Morrow, 1993.

Konigsburg, Elaine Lobl. *From the Mixed-Up Files of Mrs. Basil E. Frankweiler*. New York: Atheneum, 1967.

Lobel, Arnold. *Frog and Toad Together*. New York: Harper & Row, 1985.

Lord, Bette. *In the Year of the Boar and Jackie Robinson*. New York: Harper & Row, 1984).

Milne, A. A. *Winnie-the-Pooh*. New York: Dutton, 1954.

Parish, Peggy. *Amelia Bedelia*. New York: Harper & Row, 1963.

Acknowledgments

I would like to thank Jeradi Hochella and April Lloyd for the contributions they made to this article.

Scott Christian

Designs of the Mind and Heart

Creating an Anthology of Student Writing On-line

One who learns from one who is learning drinks from a running stream.
—Siletz Indians

NIKISKI, ALASKA, is a small rural community on the Kenai Peninsula. If you were to drive down the main road, it would appear that only a few hundred people live here, but the gravel roads that leave the highway create an intricate maze of homes on the many lakes nestled in the spruce forest that blankets the peninsula. About half of the homes are built from local spruce logs. Often a large gangly moose wanders through the yard. There is smoke curling from the chimney, five-foot snowdrifts against the side of the house: such is the stereotype of Alaska. But instead of making a living from a dog team and a trap line, the majority of people in Nikiski work in the petroleum, fishing, and tourism industries. Despite our healthy economy, we are about two hundred miles from the nearest major city, Anchorage. Unlike many Alaskan communities, we are connected to Anchorage by the "road system"; most are connected only by plane, ferries, and phone lines. In a place as large as a third of the continental United States, with less than seven hundred thousand people, there is a strong need for networking and sharing resources. For this reason, telecommunications is booming in "The Great Land."

Several years ago at the Bread Loaf Rural Teacher Network annual meeting, I saw the first edition of our newsletter, which featured writing by teachers in the network, and suggested that we think about creating a similar publication featuring student writing. Publishing has been an integral part of my classroom since I began teaching, because it provides a tangible purpose for kids to write. Now that my "classroom" had expanded through telecommunications to include other classrooms around the country, it seemed only logical that we would celebrate the learning and writing through a high-quality student publication. I should have known that by suggesting this, I was also volunteering myself and my students to complete the project. *Lesson number one: Never suggest something that you're not willing to volunteer for.*

The idea was greeted with much enthusiasm and placed on our master list of goals for the next school year. In the idealistic context of this meeting, where teachers from around the country were extolling the virtues of connectedness and support, this project seemed quite feasible. It was only later, during the tasks of gathering, sorting, revising, editing, and desktop publishing, that I found myself struggling for a whole new way of thinking to approach the project. Although there were some baffling and difficult obstacles to overcome, and the usual unexpected snags and delays, the finished publication is now in the hands of all of the contributing writers, teachers, and fellows of the Bread Loaf Rural Teacher Network (BLRTN). Here is a brief reflection on the process of creating this anthology, called *Designs of the Mind and Heart*.

Back in the reality of the classroom, I realized that my journalism class needed to finish our school yearbook before we could think about the BLRTN publication. As anyone who has ever been involved in the arduous and seemingly endless production of a yearbook can attest, the idea of asking the staff to take on yet another publication, given the necessity of meeting the rigid company-imposed deadlines, is beyond foolish. So, as our last deadline loomed near, in mid-February, we had a "friendship circle." This is the term my yearbook staff uses for the days when I put all of the chairs in the yearbook room into a circle and we talk about the yearbook, writing, photography, driver's licenses, and Screaming Yellow Zonkers. On this particular occasion, I asked them what they would like to do after the yearbook was finished. After the usual suggestions of flying to warm places, torturing the principal, and buying new wardrobes, I gave them three options. We could create a traditional school newspaper (as we had done the previous year), a local school-based literary anthology/magazine, or . . . a prestigious, high-quality literary anthology from students around the country using telecommunications. (I suppose they had some idea which option I favored, but I wanted there to be at least an appearance of democracy.) When the editor spoke in favor of the Big Telecommunications Book, it was only a matter of time before we had consensus. I did tell them that this would be a lot of work, possibly (ha!) requiring time after school, as well as serious thoughtful writing to other students. I mentioned that if we accepted this job, we would have a responsibility to see it through, and, most importantly, only ten weeks to pull it off. For some reason, perhaps due to the exorbitant number of journalistic crises that we have been through together, they—with no small amount of hubris and bravado—agreed to take this on.

To begin, I sent a few notes to the leaders of the network, teacher friends who might be interested, and my local administrator, regarding ideas for the call for submissions. Their suggestions resulted in the following message in the BLRTN conference on BreadNet, available to all of the members of the network. Since the students were still working on the yearbook, I took the lead and wrote it myself. It was posted March 1.

Dear Teachers,
I have a small group of journalism students who have volunteered to work on a BLRTN student writing publication this spring. We're not quite sure what the publication will look like yet. As the submissions come in, we'll develop a plan for the layout. Here are the guidelines for submission. Please read these over carefully with your students before sending writing or drawings. It is the teacher's responsibility to secure written permission to publish from each student whose work is submitted. We are looking for a title for this publication. Hopefully, one will arise from the writing. However, if you or your students have a suggestion, we'd love to hear it! Feel free to submit any high-quality piece of writing that has happened during the school year. It is not required that this writing be a part of a telecommunications project.

This publication, like the BLRTN Newsletter, will be posted on several Internet listservs as well.

1. Each teacher can submit no more than two student essays, stories, interviews, articles, poems, or drawings. After the deadline for submission, our editorial board will select the pieces to be published. Students will hear from the editors within two weeks regarding their pieces.

2. All writing must be submitted on-line. You can send the writing directly to my mailbox. If you send pieces as attached files, Microsoft Word and Microsoft Works are preferred. Handwritten submissions will not be accepted. Communication between the editors and writers will also occur on-line, with an occasional phone call if needed. Submitting students should be aware that our editors will be suggesting changes and revision when needed.

3. Drawings must be in black and white only, and no larger than 8 1/2 x11".

4. All writing to be considered must be received on-line no later than Monday, March 27th. Earlier is better!

We're looking forward to hearing from you!

After this message was posted, there was an eerie silence. With the exception of Sondra Porter, a teacher in Trapper Creek, Alaska, who sent two submissions almost immediately, very few submissions came in during the next few weeks. So, I posted several reminders about the looming deadline. Although Chris Benson, the editor of the BLRTN newsletter, remarked that the only people that care about deadlines are editors, I for one, as a somewhat authoritarian yearbook advisor, hoped otherwise. After a couple of weeks, I posted this note, followed by several more reminders.

> Dear Teachers,
> Just a reminder that the deadline for submitting student writing and draw-ings will be March 27th. If each teacher could send one or two top-notch pieces of writing, this could be a very special publication, celebrating our students' work. We will have a tight schedule to get this done, so keep in mind that this is a real deadline. We will not accept manuscripts after this date. I posted the guidelines in each of the state folders* recently. If you'd like another copy please ask.
> Best wishes to all,
> Scott

Then it happened. Within twenty-four hours of the deadline, approxi-mately eighty pages of text arrived in numerous files. As soon as I opened my mailbox, I realized several things. One, the vast majority of files had been labeled "Student Submissions" on the "subject" line, which left thirty files in my mailbox with identical tags. *Lesson number two: Tell all of the submitting teachers to send their files with* their own names *on the subject line.* That way, as the files are downloaded and saved on disk, the students working with the files can track them easily. And, when they respond to the authors, the student editors will know whom to send the messages to. In the call for submissions, number one clearly stated that teachers should send no more than two pieces of writing. The idea was that the teachers (and the students) would be discriminating, and do at least some of the selecting before they sent their work. Evidently, several teachers overlooked this, or perhaps felt that they were exceeding expec-tations by sending numerous files. *Lesson number three: Do all you can to make sure everyone follows the ground rules for submission.* When a teacher sends too many pieces of writing, send them back, and ask him or her to winnow the submissions to the very best work. We did this in a number of instances.

The next step was to get the writing from the files in my mailbox into a form in which my students could read it. I should point out that I have one Macintosh computer in my regular classroom, with a modem and phone line. This is where most of the telecommunicating took place, as

---

* Within BreadNet, each participating state—Alaska, Vermont, New Mexico, Arizona, Michigan, and South Carolina—has a folder where teachers from that state post and receive notices. Teachers check this folder regularly.

well as at my home, where I have a similar arrangement. In the yearbook room, where the class meets, there were two computers—neither connected to a modem. So, the files had to be saved on a floppy disk, printed out in hard copy, and transferred to computers upstairs. When you save a file from First Class, the telecommunications software BreadNet uses, it is saved as a Teach Text file, so I saved all the submissions that way first. Then I saved them again, with the teachers' names as the titles of files, in our word-processing program—keeping in mind that several student submissions were sometimes in each file. This was a time-consuming project. *Lesson number four: Ask a student to help you with every stage of the production, so that they can learn the technology, and save you time.* This is sometimes easier said than done. There are times when for the sake of expediency the teacher needs to step in and make an autocratic decision—or spend an evening transferring files, sorting files, making lists of things to do, etc. There has to be a balance between student ownership and getting the project done. Since this was my first time through a project like this, I think I led a bit more than was necessary. Next time, I will turn more of the decision-making over to the students.

It was with great anticipation that I walked into the room with several xeroxed copies of the student submissions. It was a big, heavy stack of paper and looked very impressive. To start, I read aloud a couple of the pieces that had caught my eye as they were coming in. After we discussed them briefly, the students asked if they could get into smaller groups to read and discuss them. As I listened in, I understood that they asked for this because they wanted to be honest, and at times critical, about the writing. They felt more comfortable doing this in small groups. The students continued to read and discuss the writing in small groups for two more periods, and I stayed out of the conversation because I wanted them to speak freely.

After a couple of days, we reconvened in the Friendship Circle. I divided the students into groups that I thought could work well together, and gave each group a section of the work submitted. I explained to the students that they needed to do three things: 1) Read each piece out loud and discuss whether it should be published or not; 2) If they felt that it should, to discuss ways the writing could be improved through revision; and 3) Draft responses to the authors whose work we were going to accept.

At the time this seemed perfectly reasonable, but by the end of the period, I realized that the kids had no criteria by which to evaluate the writing. The students had difficulty knowing what to say about a given piece, other than to comment on whether they liked it or not—or about the mechanics, spelling, punctuation, etc. The first message that was being typed on the computer began with "Your spelling is sound . . ." and ended, two sentences later, with "Your punctuation is very solid." Now, I should point out this was largely a new experience for them. In our yearbook class, spelling, grammar, and punctuation are our chief concerns. If we have the time, so that we can look at the meaning, the style, the voice of the writing, we do so, but because we have such a small staff, and fifty plus clubs, teams, and organizations to cover, we seldom have this luxury. So, in effect, talk about mechanics was often synonymous with talk about writing in the yearbook room.

Time to regroup. Over the weekend, I looked at the writing, and saw a wide diversity of content, style, voice, and quality. There were polished pieces that were clearly ready to be published and others that appeared to be first drafts. We needed to find a way to work with the authors on-line. It was at this point that I asked Rocky Gooch, the technical coordinator of BLRTN, to set up a folder for the responses and discussions about the writing. It would only be accessible on-line by those teachers on the network whose students had sent in work. We didn't want it to be completely public. As soon as the conference appeared, communication was greatly simplified, because we no longer had to rely on the mailboxes. I could post one note, send it to the Student Publication folder, and all of the participants could read it.

The next Monday we were back in the Friendship Circle. We took the entire week to read aloud and discuss several pieces in depth. After we read each piece, we talked not only about how it did or did not work, and how we could talk to the author about improving it. Our first question was "What is this piece about?" What is the central meaning being conveyed? What is the writer's purpose? After we came to some agreement on this, we moved on to the question of how effective the piece was in accomplishing its purpose. "Is the organization effective? Is there material that doesn't belong here, that gets in the way? Are there ideas or passages that need to be developed or clarified? Is there something missing?" Once we were comfortable with our answers to these questions, we would move into the line by line mode, and talk about specific phrasing, word choice, paragraphing, etc. Basically, we were hoping to move the writing towards clear, effective poetry and prose that moved the reader. We wanted to avoid the flowery fluff and clichés that often appear in student anthologies. We were looking for good, straightforward writing— "truth telling," as Ken Macrorie would say.

It was a very time-consuming process, but well worth it. We couldn't do this together with each piece, but after our discussion the students were able to continue this process in small groups. *Lesson number five: Help your students learn to talk to authors as editors, and help them develop a vocabulary to discuss the writing.*

The other task during these discussions, of course, was deciding which pieces we would accept for publication. Certainly we couldn't accept everything, nor did we want to. But we couldn't just arbitrarily say yes or no either. As part of the discussions, we agreed that we would not accept a piece if it seemed like there was a great deal of work to be done—if, in effect, it seemed like a first draft, because of our time constraints—or if we felt the piece was not consistent with the tone and flavor of the publication as a whole. By the time we finished this process, we only had a few pieces that we chose not to accept. It was then suggested, since we did not post any criteria when we called for submissions, that we give *all* writers the opportunity to revise. If an author accepted our suggestions and his or her piece was improved, we would accept it, regardless of the size of the final publication. We anticipated that many writers either would not agree to the changes, or would not respond at all, in which case we would make a decision whether to publish "as is" or to reject the writing. *Lesson number six: When you ask teachers to submit their students' writing, give them a notion of the criteria the work will be judged by. What are the qualities you, as editors, are looking for?*

During the next three weeks several things happened. First, we searched for a title for the book. We "mined" the pieces for phrases that looked like possibilities. We brainstormed themes and possible titles. With the usual insanity and dark humor of the staff, many were not repeatable. I've learned from this group of students that it's better to let them blow off some steam and have a little fun than to expect them to act like professional journalists all the time. Despite their goofiness, we did vote several times and finally narrowed it down to three possibilities. We then posted these on-line and asked the participating classes to vote as well. As the votes came in, I printed them out and showed them to the class. I realized then that the students had never "seen" the technology, only the documents that I printed from the conference. So we connected one of the Macs to a phone line, and I projected the screen using an overhead device. We then went live on-line, and had a chat with Rocky Gooch. The kids were thrilled. We then sent messages to a few of the classes who had responded to our query about titles, and waited for results. Although it wasn't my first choice, *Designs of the Mind and Heart* was the favorite among the students, both on-line and among my staff. The title came from a poem by Stephanie Blake from Sylvia Barlow's class in Chinle, Arizona: "Understanding the designs in the mind and heart only, never drawn, and / Got to finish by sundown—can't weave at night, can't leave a section undone, / Sold as rugs, but really an ageless art."

After we had a title for the anthology, we wrote the titles for all the accepted pieces on the board and tried to find some way to organize them. We decided to divide the book into sections by theme or genre. The purpose was two-fold. On the one hand, we wanted to divy up the work among the Nikiski staff in a way that made sense. On the other, we felt that the book would be more presentable, and more readable, if it were divided into sections. We brainstormed many themes, narrowed them down to four, and began to group the titles under the headings. It was quickly apparent that this wouldn't work—too many pieces fell easily into several categories. So we went to Plan B and decided simply to divide the book into Poetry and Prose. We then assigned all of the pieces into one of these categories, split the staff into two groups, and went back to the messy business of discussing the pieces and drafting responses to the writers.

Combined with the tasks of finding a title and deciding the book's format and layout, this process took more than three weeks. I was growing concerned about whether we would finish the project before the end of the year. As the Nikiski staff finished drafting a response, I offered suggestions, and they revised. Finally, the responses were printed, proofread, and sent to the writers, who responded in different ways. Some accepted our suggestions and agreed to make the changes:

Student: Ethan Duni
Title: And the River

Thank you for submitting your prose piece "And the River." It was a delight to read. The imagery was clear to us as we read. We felt that the piece flowed very nicely, with the exception of the first paragraph. It seems as though some of the words that you have chosen don't quite fit. For instance "intrusively" stands out and disrupts your opening line. We're not sure about how the blue can be intrusive. Our advice is to look closely at that first paragraph. Focus on the words in each sentence so that you can draw your reader into the scene smoothly. We are also assuming that "rymical" should be "rhythmical" and "deep down film" should be "deep brown film."

This is a very good piece of writing, and it deserves a close look. We thought the last line was just right! Nice work.

The Nikiski Journalism Staff, Prose Division

To the Nikiski Journalism Class, Prose Division:

Thanks for commenting on my piece of writing. Having been assigned the project during the preparation of my local Explorer Post for what-should-have-been-spring's rafting season, boating was on my mind. If I have one strong memory of boating, it's the take-out at the San Juan, the same described in my piece, and one I'm not likely to forget. I did change the first paragraph as you suggested:

"The clouds lazily drift their way across the nostalgically blue sky in vaguely the same direction as the river. The murky water they call the San Juan drags itself along the sandy shore, the scene lit like a movie set by the noontime sun."

By the way, it is "deep-down film of river filth" in the next to last paragraph. Thanks very much for your comments.

Ethan

One particularly pleasant and personal exchange concerned a poem submitted by Katie Morzinski, from Los Alamos. It shows how the students' voices come through not only in the poems and stories but also in their correspondence about the writing. Katie's poem was popular among the runners on our staff (including the advisor!):

Cross Country

Excitement still lingers,
A presence in my mind,
A reminder of the rush;

Of coming over that last hill,
Feet pounding on the pavement,
A cramp in my side, ignored.

Of rounding that last curve
And seeing the Finish,
People lined up along the ropes,
Each screaming louder than the one before.

Of lengthening my strides,
using my long legs
To pull past the girl in the red tank top
with the long swinging braid.
Finally dropping abruptly to a walk,
Gasping for air, water, relief.
Seeing Lauren finished already.
No jealousy. Not yet.
Just congratulations and a hug.

Of screaming the morning away,
Willing our faster friends,

To pass that girl, to beat that guy, to win,
A modified game of cards in the grass.
A hat with a six-inch brim.
Mrs. Powell everywhere with a camera,
Snapping remembrances of Lauren and me.

Title: Cross Country
Student: Katie Morzinski

Thank you for submitting your poem "Cross Country." It was a delight to read. We especially liked the image of the girl in the red top with the long swinging braid. The line about jealousy is right on too. It's such a big part of competitive sports. Cross country is big here. Our girls won state, with the runners placing first, second, third, fourth and sixth for our top five. It was the best score in the history of cross country in Alaska. Our top boy also won the boy's race. It was a great year! Our only suggestion is to re-work the line with "junior varsity and varsity."* We agreed that this disrupts the tone of the poem, which is largely personal, and gives it more of a journalistic feel. Could you think of another choice of words there? Other than that, we are anxious to publish your poem. Keep Running!

The Nikiski Journalism Class, Poetry Division

Title: Cross Country
Student: Katie Morzinski

You suggested that I change the line "junior varsity and varsity" in the last stanza. I did and it should read "Willing our faster friends." I hope that is okay. I wanted to tell you why I wrote "Cross Country." It is because I wanted to be able to remind myself of what cross country was like that season. That meet was a pretty typical one, except it was 3.5 miles (not the usual 3.1), and I didn't always pass the girl in the red tank top. Lauren Powell is my best friend, but she can also do everything better than me. Since CC increased my jealousy of her, I wanted to be able to see my feelings in writing so I could figure out how to not be jealous. Writing always helps me sort my thoughts out.

CC isn't really very popular here, but it is among my friends. Our girls won state too for the first time in a really long time. Boys got fourth. Thank you for commenting on my poem.

Katie

In other cases, the editors merely congratulated the students on a fine piece of writing, and the writers responded with a "thank you," as in this exchange with a student in Peoria, Arizona:

---

* This line was in an earlier version of the poem.

To: Jerry Roybal

Thank you for sending your poem, "My Grandfather."

It was really cute. We especially got a good laugh at his round belly that is so wonderful to put your arms around!

We think that your poem sounds really good as it is and we don't have any revision suggestions.

Thank you,
Laurel, Jennie,
Nina, and Michael

Dear Laurel, Jennie, Nina, and Michael (Nikiski Journalism Class: Poetry Division)—Thank you for selecting my poem about my grandfather for your publication. It will make my whole family so happy to see it in print. Thank you. Jerry Roybal, Peoria, Arizona

There were also students who read the response and wanted their writing to remain as it was submitted. Here, the editors asked for clarification and the student writer, R. P. Williams in Mississippi, responded this way:

To: Renee Moore
Poem: I Have Nothing
Student: R. P. Williams

Thank you for your submission. The rhythm was very good and the piece flowed along very well. It is a powerful poem. One of the suggestions that we have is the fact that the poem doesn't really connect with the title, and the last stanza doesn't flow as well as the rest of the poem. Could you address these suggestions in your next draft? Or, explain the connection with the title? Thanks again.

Willy, Sierra, Chrissy, and Jessica

To: Willy, Sierra, Chrissy, and Jessica
From: R. P. Williams
Poem: I Have Nothing

I appreciate you accepting my piece of writing for publishing. This poem was written during a time of sorrow. All the things in the poem are worth nothing if there's no use for them. As I asked myself these questions, "Nothing" was the repeating answer. I look highly upon the things I named in the poem. So, "I have nothing."

These exchanges were fairly typical of the correspondence. Almost half of the writers, however, did not respond. There were several reasons for this. One, many teachers assumed that their students' writing was going to be published as written, without revision. We received several messages from teachers who were surprised by our editorial responses, even though the original call for submissions clearly explained the process. *Lesson number seven: Make sure that all of the participants know not only the criteria for acceptance, but the process which leads to publication.* The second reason many writers did not respond was our own poor timing. By the time we put our responses on-line it was early May, and spring fever was sweeping the country. This leads to one of the critical lessons we learned from this first experiment. *Number eight: Begin the project early in the school year, with plenty of lead time for teachers to make good selections and for meaningful conversations to happen between the writers and editors.*

Those writers whom we did not hear from posed a dilemma. Would we publish their writing anyway? We took these on a case-by-case basis. Some we decided to publish without revision. With some we took the liberty of making very minor, often grammatical, changes. Others we did not publish. This was a difficult and uncomfortable process. None of us wanted the authors to feel disappointed or misled. We took solace in the fact that we had offered them the opportunity to revise, and this opportunity had been, for whatever reason, neglected.

As revised pieces came in, the Nikiski staff saved each piece as a word-processing file so the files could be placed into pages in the desktop publishing program. We used the authors' names as file names, saving the poetry on one disk and the prose on another. We also backed up each set on two hard drives. Because we were using computers that had been around quite a while, we were very careful to save regularly and to back-up often. Meanwhile, the poetry and prose divisions each created a table of contents, listing the title of the piece, the writer, the teacher, and the town they were from, in the order that they would appear. These tables of contents were then posted in the students' publication conference, where participating teachers were asked to check for typos and misspellings, and to make sure we hadn't lost any writing along the way. (We had!) One of our staff artists, Nina Kovac, created the artwork for the cover, and I asked one of my eighth grade students to draw the artwork for the section dividers. (We were disappointed but not surprised that we didn't receive any artwork from elsewhere on the network. We attributed this to the text-based nature of the on-line technology.)

It was a hectic time! We were under the gun to get the publication mailed off before the school year ended. With less than three full weeks of school left, we decided to move ahead with editing, proofreading, and layout even though we hadn't received all the revisions. Our policy was

that we wouldn't change anything in a piece of writing that would sub-
stantively change the content or voice of the piece. We mainly focused on
spelling, verb agreement, capitalization, and punctuation. Our thinking
was that we could add the revisions as they came in. During the next two
weeks, there were numerous times when students worked during their
lunch hours, before and after school, and occasionally during other
classes, when their other teachers generously would let them come over
to work. At one point I bribed four members of the staff with a Chinese
dinner for a particularly late night of work. Since we had only two computers, the production of the anthology was very time-consuming. There
were numerous cycles of placing the documents into the desktop publishing program (Aldus PageMaker 4.0), and then editing, proofreading,
printing, proofreading, printing, etc. The students were quite familiar
with the process from their experience laying out the yearbook. By the
time we printed the last time, on the *very* last day of school, each piece
had been read and edited at least four times. When we printed out hard
copy for the last time and xeroxed the final draft, there was a feeling of
delirious pandemonium.

In the end, sixty-three writers from twenty-four classrooms across
the country were published in *Designs of the Mind and Heart*.

* * * * *

In addition to the lessons I've mentioned in this article, I have a few other
recommendations for teachers attempting a project like this. First, I would
ask two students at the beginning of the project to work as researchers
throughout the creation of the publication, to observe closely the action as
it unfolds, to interview editors, writers, and teachers about their impressions of the process, to document specific problems and successes as they
arise, and most importantly to reflect back on the process and to draw
some tentative conclusions. This would provide a more complete document for others attempting a project like this, as well as some insight into
how students write and respond to each other's writing. Student researchers might have noticed early on that we received only one piece of artwork.
We were so focused on the writing that we neglected to encourage artwork,
which could have dramatically improved the final publication.

* * * * *

The day after school was out we sent the publication (hard copy and on
disk) to Chris Benson, the Publications Director for BLRTN. He, with
two others, read and proofread the anthology. I've learned that no matter

how many times you proofread and spell-check writing, someone will find errors. It was this final layer of proofreading and editing by an out-side team that took the publication to the next level of professionalism.

By the time I arrived at Bread Loaf in June, the book was ready for the printer. After some negotiation, we decided to print 300 copies. The printing was paid for through funding from the DeWitt Wallace-Reader's Digest Fund (sponsor of BLRTN) and the Clemson Writing in the Com-munity Programs. We printed enough copies for each author and partici-pating teacher to receive two copies, with a supply of extra copies to be distributed throughout the Bread Loaf network and friends. At the end of the summer session, we picked up the boxes from the printer. Six Bread Loaf teachers helped gather and prepare the publication for mailing. It was a very happy time. Each teacher involved in the project returned to his or her school in the fall to find copies of *Designs of the Mind and Heart* in their mailboxes. Here are a few of their responses:

From: Rosie Roppel
Subject: Book
To: Student Pub
      Scott Christian

Hi Scott, I just returned home and got my publications. WOWWWWW!!! What a great job. I'm thrilled and will show our school board and take my kids to dinner and present theirs to them. What a great deal you've done. Thanks so much. I know that will hardly put a dent in all the hard work you have done!
Rosie

From: Chad J. Graff
Subject: Designs of the Mind and Heart
To: Student Pub
      Scott Christian

Scott,
Let me add my voice to the chorus. The book is a beautiful achievement. My students' eyes lit up, "You mean my poem is in there?" It was a great way to start the year. Thanks Scott and thank your students too.
Chad

From: Patricia Parrish
Subject: re: book
To: Student Pub
      Scott Christian

Scott,
Let me add my thanks and congratulations to you and your students for producing such a wonderful book. Is there any chance my student Erica

Sherrill could buy an extra one? She'd like to send one to her aunt who teaches at Duke. Let me know.
Thanks. Patricia.

It was fun to see these messages. I printed out several to share with my students as I distributed anthologies to them. They too were thrilled with the final product.

I should also mention that largely because of the success of *Designs of the Mind and Heart*, I was able to put together a computer lab in my classroom. Apple Computers and my school district curriculum department worked together to bring to our little network a total of eleven computers, a new laser printer, a scanner, a CD-ROM drive, software, and a telecommunications hook-up. With so many different groups vying for scarce technology dollars, this finished anthology was the deciding factor in allocating funds to my program.

Although at times I was certain that I had bitten off a good deal more than I could chew, it was a terrific feeling to see the project completed. Also, I think it's important to mention that despite some difficulties with telecommunications, it would have been impossible even to consider a project of this scope through the U.S. mail and the telephone. There is simply no way that this amount of communication could have occurred in such a short time. One of the best features of the BreadNet network is the dynamic and rich diversity of voices and cultures from around the country. *Designs of the Mind and Heart* reflects this diversity.

The following poem, by Shania Gamble, Kayenta, Arizona, can speak better than this article for why this type of project should happen:

I Remember

I sat watching the glittering sky,
Darkness covered the windows,
And the moon hung like a lantern in the sky.
Grandma sat near the fire shaping freshly mixed clay;
I was young and the sudden beauty of the potteries on the shelf caught my
    unawareness.
Are you making another pottery, Grandma?
Yes, this one is special, she said. This one tells the stories.
This one speaks. This one is about tradition.

I remember the smell of raw clay baking over the fire that night;
I remember Grandma telling her stories;
I remember the people, the cows, the sheep, and the children that she painted
    on the pottery.
She made them come to life. They were the stories and traditions

Grandma told me about.

Years later I took the pottery from the shelf.
I slid my fingers over its smooth surface; the beautiful designs and patterns lit
    my eyes.
I gently wiped away the dust, and beautiful colors appeared, colors as beau-
    tiful as the land.
I heard the stories from the pottery; they told what Grandma used to tell.
I found what was forgotten over the years;
The pottery spoke to me and I remembered
What Grandma told me about.

Carefully as I began to put the pottery back in its place,
It fell through my hands,
At the slip of my fingers came
The slip of the traditions and the stories I was told.
Lost sheep, lost cows, and forgotten stories
Lay scattered on the dirt floor.

Grandma walked in and ever so sadly she picked up the broken pieces.
Tears rolled down her face.
Tears that all the potteries in the world couldn't hold.
Where are the sheep, are they still here?
Where are the cows, are they still around?
Are the stories still being told?
And what about the children, what are they becoming?
They're still here, Grandma. I can put the pieces back together, I said,
As I took the pieces in my hand.
I can bring them back.
I can make my own pottery to tell the stories and the traditions
You used to tell.

She wasn't crying over the broken pieces.
She was crying over the broken people.

Douglas E. Wood and Kurt Caswell

Making Connections

The USjApanLINK Project

How It Began (Kurt Caswell)

I was beginning my second year as an English teacher in Chitose, Hokkaido, Japan, but I was back in America for the summer. I had enrolled in a graduate program at the Bread Loaf School of English at Middlebury College in Vermont. It was there that I met Douglas E. Wood.

I remember Doug as a lithe, focused figure hunched over his laptop computer on the New England front porch of our dormitory. He was a genteel history and geography teacher from Columbia, South Carolina, and I was a transplanted Idahoan. We had little in common. I had heard English spoken with a foreign accent every day for the past twelve months, but this was the first time I'd heard English spoken in person by a Southerner.

One day, Doug sat with me at lunch. He had some questions, he said, because he had heard I lived in Japan. Ask away, I said. He did, and then went on about how we might conduct an on-line electronic mail exchange between his middle school students in South Carolina and my Japanese students in Chitose. Oh, you mean like a pen-pal thing, I said. But he didn't just mean a pen-pal thing. Doug wanted our students not only to correspond via e-mail, but to exchange personal narratives, opinions on literature, and cross-cultural observations and nuances, to explore ways we might foster a stronger relationship between the two countries.

I didn't know Doug, and he didn't know me, but I liked his ambition. He had a good idea of what he wanted to do. And I was pretty much in the dark. So I followed his lead, and we wrote a small teacher research grant entitled "Advocacy and Action for Cross-Cultural Understanding" to help pay our on-line phone bills, and a ten-month, week-by-week timeline detailing the exchange. The other thing I learned about Doug during that summer was that he can sing—really sing.

At the end of the summer, we returned to our respective schools and went to work.

Setting Up the Classroom (Douglas E. Wood)

When I returned to South Carolina, I created a special exploratory class at my school (Summit Parkway Middle School) designed to focus on what we were calling the USjApanLINK Project. The seventh graders who participated in the project were recommended by their teachers. I also invited a number of eighth graders, based on previous academic merit, to take on the project as an extracurricular course, and they agreed to meet with me twice a week after school.

The course gave me the opportunity to design innovative methods of instruction not usually offered in the traditional middle school curriculum. Although writing was central to the project, I used many other resources to supplement the discourse on-line. The students read books, articles, and documents about Japanese history and culture. They studied *kanji* through the delicate art of calligraphy. (*Kanji* are the Chinese characters from which written Japanese is derived.) I invited specialists from the University of South Carolina and the greater Columbia community to present their insights on Japan. In addition, the students studied Japanese language for sixteen weeks with one of our parents, Mrs. Lin.

Our classroom was equipped with eight computers. We used two to send writing to the students in Japan. Three of the computers were laptops that the students could take home to work on assignments. The students had to complete the writing assignments both in their journals and on computer disk. Some actually preferred to compose on the computer first and later transfer the writing to their journals. When the students completed their assignments, they edited their work. One designated student uploaded the writing to BreadNet, the telecommunications network of the Bread Loaf School of English. (Although one student was charged with this task, I made sure each student got some experience with uploading and downloading.) By uploading all the students' work at one time, we avoided heavy long-distance costs. This method of uploading text is efficient and cost-saving not only for the sender, but also for the receiver. In Japan, Kurt was able to download all the writing in one or two files, thus avoiding the tedious task of downloading numerous individual files, and spending long periods of time on-line. The whole process was often completed in under one minute.

(Kurt Caswell)

ACS Gakuin in Chitose is a private English academy where students from four years old through adult come to study spoken English. At the time of the USjApanLINK Project, I had four high school English classes, each meeting once a week. These students came to ACS after their regular day at a public school, where they studied mostly grammar. They came to ACS to use the language. The USjApanLINK Project was perfect for meeting this goal.

We had been working for several months in a conversation textbook, but all of the students agreed that the project would be a much more engaging way to study the language. They would be able to use their English to communicate with real people their own age, and they would make many new friends. I opened the exchange to my middle school classes as well. However, many of the middle school students found the level of English proficiency too demanding, and thus participated sporadically. Because ACS is a private school, I was able to implement this new curriculum right away. In a Japanese public school, rigorous examination schedules and curricula would have made the project difficult.

In contrast to Doug's classroom at Summit Parkway, ACS did not have even a single computer. At that time, I had little knowledge of networks or e-mail. Doug taught me the basics of BreadNet before we left Bread Loaf, and I bought a modem on my way back to Japan. My notebook computer was all we had on my end.

Thus, I collected my students' writing and entered everything at home. When I collected a good number of documents, I logged onto the network and uploaded everything at once. The whole process took less than one minute. As I had to call directly from Japan to Vermont, it was of great importance to keep long-distance costs low. To download, I simply copied files into my word processing software, then logged off BreadNet. This process also took less than a minute. I could then read and format the documents for my students off-line. This meant I often had to disentangle files with messages for many different students, and format, print, copy each message separately and for the appropriate student. Comparatively, uploading and downloading were a snap. It was not unusual to spend three hours formatting and printing documents from one download.

Another drawback of having only one computer was that my students did not have much opportunity to learn to use e-mail. Surprisingly, Japanese public schools are years behind American schools in educational technology. I occasionally brought my computer to school and encouraged my students to enter or dictate their next correspondence as a break from writing longhand. I demonstrated uploading and downloading, and even browsed through other conferences on BreadNet with them. But with so little hands-on training, the students did not fully experience the real power of electronic mail and networking. Still, it was not the technology that made the project exciting for the students. It was the direct link to an American classroom, and the friendships they built through the use of their English.

Writing a Curriculum (Douglas E. Wood)

When I give presentations on telecommunications to other teachers in my state, many ask me the simple question: "Why do you feel a need to do on-line exchanges?" I tell them I started doing telecommunications with my students in response to the curriculum that already existed in my classroom: a special seventh grade social studies program centered around the theory of "less is more." Instead of teaching about every country in the world, we focus on three thematic units: Competition for Resources; Charting the Global Connections; and War: A Severing of Connections. The students focus on a single question with each unit, respectively: How are the peoples of the world dependent upon one another for their existence? How do conflicts arise as peoples throughout the world try to balance traditional ways of living with new ideas and technologies? How can conflicts between peoples of the world be resolved peacefully? (At that time, I had no idea that what we were doing was supported by many researchers in the educational reform movement.)

The summer before I conducted my first on-line exchange, I wanted to do something to boost the first unit, Competition for Resources. This particular unit dealt with the environment. I decided that along with other activities covering these issues, my students needed an on-line exchange with a classroom in another country. Why? Because greater meaning can be derived through true communication. Learning about a country in a textbook is one thing, communicating with individuals who actually live in that country is quite another. The best way for my students to see how the peoples of the world were interdependent was to get to know and understand another culture. The environment is one topic where individuals can clearly see how the environmental policies of one country inevitably affect others.

I always try to make clear to other teachers—and my students—that the idea is not to replace a given curriculum with an on-line exchange, but to supplement it. The curriculum should drive the technology, not the other way around. Technology should not be used for the sake of technology. Technology should be carefully constructed from the curriculum, so that students can clearly see the value and reason for its use.

I had learned much about this from the on-line exchange I conducted concerning environmental issues. The exchange began when I wrote a paragraph outlining my ideas and posted an "all-call" on the Internet. At the time, I was using a program called Kidlink, which linked teachers and students from all over the world. In my "all-call," I asked for any teacher outside the United States to participate in the environmental issues project with me. I also described clearly what I wanted from the exchange, proposing a two-classroom exchange. I did this in the very beginning of the year, because I did not know how long it would take for someone to respond. After a couple of weeks, a teacher responded from Dublin, Ireland. We had a marvelous time talking back and forth using electronic mail. I explained to him that I wanted more than just the run-of-the-mill pen-pal exchange. The phrase "pen-pal" connotes a certain superficiality. Many pen-pal exchanges never get beyond the basic exchange of hellos. This can also be true of unplanned, sporadic, electronic mail exchanges with no "reason" for in-depth, meaningful communication. Therefore, it is imperative for teachers to design a curriculum that goes well beyond pen-pal issues, and offers the deeper, more aesthetic realm of connecting with another human being.

In such a project, it is important to limit the number of students involved, choose a distinct timeframe, and decide on a common reading text. My Irish colleague and I planned a month-long exchange with one class each out of all the classes we taught. (Although this was unfortunate, it was necessary. In a previous mini-exchange with a local school, I tried to spread the exchange among all of my classes. It was a miserable failure due to the difficulty of keeping up with so many individual exchanges.) The four weeks we chose for the exchange coincided with the time both of our classes would be studying environmental issues. The common reading for the exchange was *Earth in the Balance* by Vice President Al Gore. The students started to make connections with their own communities, and share thoughts about improving the global environment. The reading of a common text really contributed to making the exchange more meaningful for the students.

The Irish exchange is an example of two teachers meeting each other, pre-planning, and implementing an exchange, completely through the Internet. If you take this route, please keep in mind that you must be diligent and patient. I sent out several requests and it took a while before someone eventually responded. You must also make sure that the letter of invitation you post on the Internet contains clear objectives and goals. Then, when you find a partner, you must somehow engage the individual so that you can get to know him or her better, and you must make certain that the individual will complete the long journey with you.

The lessons that I learned in the Irish exchange, particularly from a pedagogical standpoint, helped me a great deal in designing the curriculum for the exchange with Kurt and his Japanese students during the next school year. The Japanese exchange grew out of my need to improve our third thematic unit: War: A Severing of Connections. Throughout this unit, we studied the causes, devastation and the results of World War Two. The central question of this unit (How can conflicts between peoples of the world be resolved peacefully?) was the one I really wanted my students to grapple with. I wanted them to go beyond textbooks, films, newspapers, and the plethora of other materials on the subject of World War Two. I wanted my students to think for themselves and to develop cogent arguments. In my opinion, understanding between cultures is a beginning to preventing conflicts. For the students to see this, another dimension of inquiry was needed, and the opportunity to start an exchange with Kurt's Japanese students was exactly what I was looking for.

Although my curriculum ideas rested on this third thematic unit, Kurt and I had to design an exchange that would be both flexible and solid enough to last an entire school year. Over the summer, at Bread Loaf, we planned our project and wrote a proposal for a teacher research grant to support the telephone costs involved. (Writing a grant not only gives you the opportunity to possibly have additional funds for classroom use, but the process of writing gives a teacher the added opportunity of reflecting upon practice.) To begin the project, we decided to provide background information about the United States and Japan, as well as about our two schools, to our respective classes. The students would then write autobiographical narratives—about themselves, their families and their communities. Kurt and I would also write narratives. Although we had planned to evaluate the narratives and carefully "match" students with partners of similar interests, the students took this task upon themselves. This spontaneous turn gave them a greater degree of ownership in the project, and enlivened their attitudes toward their partners. The classes also exchanged packages of pictures, maps, and small knickknacks from their communities via conventional mail. After that, one of the most fabulous and successful components of the exchange occurred: Eight Days. For eight days, the students chronicled their lives in journals and shared all of the pieces with their partners and the other students. This gave them the chance to peer into the windows of each other's lives. It added a dimension to the exchange that moved the two classes beyond being merely pen-pals. Next, the students exchanged their favorite poems and gift boxes. Finally, the students read a common text: John Elder's *Following the Brush*, which chronicles the year-long stay of an American family in Japan.

In our original grant proposal, we planned many other activities. However, as all good projects do, the USjApanLINK exchange took on a life of its own. During the project, two major earthquakes hit Japan and, of course, the students exchanged their concerns about these terrible calamities. I looked for a balance between planning and flexibility.

What the Students Said (Kurt Caswell)

Doug and I forged our friendship on-line rapidly, out of necessity. We simply had to foster a good working relationship for the sake of our students. I remember reading the first few excited messages from Doug when he and his class were featured on the PBS television program "The Merrow Report":

> Kurt,
> I want to commend you and your students for a terrific, wonderful job!!!!!!!!!!! The session was great!!! The autobiographical narratives were absolutely stupendous!!!!!!!!!!!! I appreciate all of your hard work . . . we barely made it. I checked the folder at 9:30 and I did not see anything and I almost had a heart attack. They were all up there at 9:45 . . . 5 minutes before the cameras were rolling. THANK YOU!!!!!!!!!!!!!!!!!!!!!!!
> Doug

By contrast, the student's first exchanges tended to be reserved, if not a little formal:

> (*Note: In the following on-line excerpts, grammar mistakes have been retained.*)

> My name is Kotono Togashi. I'm sixteen years old. My birthday is February 18th. My blood type is O. There are six members in my family. I have three young sisters. They are 14, 12, 10 years old. Only my sister who is the youngest sister keeps her goldfish. We never keep another animal. I'm a student. I go to Kitahiroshima High School in Hiroshima. But I live in Chitose. It takes about one hour to go to school. I like when I go home from school with my friends. Because it is enjoyable to talk with them. So, I enjoy to talking for an hour walking, in the train, and in the bus. I was belong to badminton club when I was a junior high school student. It is very interesting sports. But now I belong to flower arrangement club. I arrange flowers once a week at school. After I go home, I arrange flowers again, and it is decorated at the front entrance. I have taken an electric organ lesson for twelve years. I played electric organ on the stage at Sapporo Snow Festival. I have two questions.

1. Japanese are learn English at junior high school, high school, and university. How many people learn Japanese in America?

2. I like bread better than rice. But, Japanese live on rice. How many times do you eat rice in a week or month?

My name is Mary Hays Huguley. I am eleven years old and I'm in the seventh grade at Summit Parkway Middle School. I live with my parents, my nine year old brother, Mark, four cats, Simon, Sebastian, Onyx, and Anna, a newt, Sir Isaac Newton, a frog, Squirt, three hermit crabs, Fuddy, Duddy, and Curious, and one nameless snail. My birthday is on Sept. 9, 1982. My favorite subject is social studies. I like to read, write, draw, ice skate, and play basketball. My favorite food is oysters with melted cheese, onions, mushrooms, and bacon on top. I have blue eyes, brownish blond hair, and I'm 59 inches tall. My mother teaches the first grade at Pontiac Elementary School. My father is an Inspector at SLED. SLED stands for state law enforcement division. I live 25 minutes away from my school. I have nice neighbors and there are lots of kids in my neighborhood. That includes one of my best friends, Lauran Riser. Summit Parkway Middle School is very big and overcrowded. There are about 1,237 kids at this school, but my classes are pretty small. Everything looks the same and it's easy to get lost here. It's a pretty good school though and I like most of my classes.

The students became acquainted with each other through autobiographical narratives and responses. Choosing their own partners helped, because it showed them that they had a lot in common from the start. What really catalyzed the process, however, was the "Eight Days" journal exchange. The students lived with their journals for eight days, carrying them everywhere they went: around school, at home, out shopping, to the movies. This exchange got the dialogue going, and kept it going throughout the year. Even when we shifted our focus to other topics, the students continued to write about what they had shared in Eight Days.

The students worked hard. Although each student had a partner with whom they corresponded throughout the exchange, we encouraged everyone to respond to other students, even to the group as a whole.

Then came the two exchanges of packages—the exchange of maps, pictures, and knickknacks from Chitose and Columbia in the fall, and the exchange of gifts at Christmas:

Thank you for sending us the introductory gift box. It is soooooo cool! I like the paper doll the best. But I also like the pictures, poster, & the pizza advertisement. Do y'all really eat squid & manaise on your pizza. I could never do that. I eat pizza with just cheese nothing else. I liked looking through the brochures. Japan is really beautiful. Thank you again. Ours is on the way.
Sincerely,
Liza Lewellen

Dear Mary
Thank you for your present. I received it last week. I put on the wall Indian Dream Catcher, and hang the keyholder on my desk light. I saw Dream Catcher for the first time. I thought it is interesting. Did Indian people make and use it years ago? Could they catch the dream? I want to catch my dreams.

I wish you catch your dream, too. I saw designs of American paper money except one design for the first time. I have only one cent real money. I got it three years ago. English teacher who is Canadian gave me for a prize in my English class. I became happy when I received your presents. Thank you. I use these carefully.

From Kotono

The excitement of opening these packages piqued the students' interest in their cultural differences still more, and strengthened developing friendships. This was evidenced by the evolution in the students' writing from a formal style to a more relaxed vernacular.

Next, we exchanged favorite books, poems, and songs. This allowed the American students to read some Japanese literature and lyrics, and the Japanese students were able to read American literature and music lyrics. This exchange was somewhat troubling for the Japanese students. Understanding poetry and lyrics in English—particularly metaphor—was difficult for them. Moreover, metaphor is often weakened, or even lost, in translation. The Japanese students worried that the Americans would not fully understand their favorite books, poems, and lyrics. Still, what is important is that the students made great efforts to broaden their understanding of each other's cultures. They were challenged to think about ideas that they had never encountered before.

The following are a few excerpts from this exchange:

Hello Mary. How are you?
I'm sorry. I haven't a favorite book. So I write about the book which I read recently.

Its title is "Vulgar Japanese." It was written by a Korean woman name Yu Jensun. She has been living in Japan 8 years with her husband, and her son. She writes bad things about Japanese people.

She says, "Japan is really special, strange country. The more I live, the more I realize this thought become strong. Japanese is not individualistic. The trustworthy thing is not Japanese, but only goods which made in Japan. When Japanese evaluate something, they follow the opinion which is said by the first person."

I thought she says the truth in many parts. We must review our life, thoughts, culture, and so on.

And she write many other things. For example, the affair of cut China Chagori (it is Korean cloth) by Japanese, the disturbance of rice, the craze of washing off the dirt in Korean style, Japanese house like a rabbit hutch, the cemetery in town, shop, and so on.

    Kotono

Dear Kotono,
Here is a poem I like because it's about my country.

On an Invitation to the United States

I

My ardours for an emprize nigh lost
Since Life has bared its bones to me,
I shrink to seek a modern coast
Whose riper times have yet to be;
Where the new regions claim them free
From that long drip of human tears
Which peoples old in tragedy
Have left upon the centuried years.

II

For, wonning in these ancient lands,
Enchased and lettered as a tomb,
And scored with prints of perished hands,
And chronicled with dates of doom,
Though my own Being bear no bloom
I trace the lives such scenes enshrine,
Give past exemplars present room,
And their experience count as mine.

    —Thomas Hardy

Bryan Romig

A Rose
by Tomihiro Hoshino
(1978)

The flower of a light color is a mother's color.
It is a warm mother's color that weakness and sadness mixed.

Hoshino is a well-known poet in Japan. He writes poems and paints pictures with a pen in his mouth because he is physically handicapped. But his pictures are very beautiful. My mother and I like his poems and pictures.

Tomoko Kondo

Throughout the year, the students were encouraged to send e-mail to their partners—or to any student on the other end—outside the formal exchange. Doug and I felt that this freedom would not only improve the exchange, but also allow friendships to develop naturally. And it did. Several students wrote to each other consistently throughout the year. Doug and I were surprised by the strong friendships that developed between our students. But it wasn't until I saw Doug again that I realized we too had become good friends. Perhaps it was because we were so focused on our students that we didn't think about ourselves as being much more than facilitators. This note should have clued me in:

> Kurt,
> I have to admit that I am excited about the idea that you will be returning to the U.S. I know that it was a difficult decision for you. I wish you the best of luck and I look forward to seeing you on campus this summer as well.
>
> P.S. I appreciate the Trek words. Here is one of my favorite lines: There are always possibilities. . . .
>
> Doug

The Trip (Kurt Caswell)

The USjApanLINK Project culminated with Doug and his Summit Parkway students traveling to Chitose. Obviously, a trip like this is by no means essential to a successful exchange. In fact, there were times Doug and I felt that planning for the trip had taken too much control over the exchange, and that we would be better off giving it up. The trip was almost a completely separate event, and it was as if we had conducted two exchanges, one electronic and one physical. The trip required the work of over 100 parents and volunteers. We were successful only because all of us wanted to make it happen. The last words I had said to Doug before leaving Bread Loaf to start the project were, "See you in Japan." But it wasn't until all twenty-two students and ten chaperones from South Carolina walked through the arrival gate at New Chitose International Airport that we knew we had done it.

*   *   *   *

Masao Saito, the founder and director of ACS, who would be retiring with this final project, leaned over the table and offered Doug another uni. "Most Americans don't like this kind of stuff," he said. But Doug is not like most Americans. He accepted, and placed the orange, sweetishly-soft, raw sea urchin roe on his plate. He paused, sized up his foe, dipped the uni in soy sauce, and ate it with an expression of joy.

After dinner, Mr. Saito went home, and the rest of the small dinner party went on to a local seafood and sake shop called Yumeya. Here, under the influence of the dimmed lights, and the Japanese night, Doug expressed his true feelings about uni. "Well," he said, "I wasn't going to let that uni beat me."

It was Doug's moxie that made the trip to Japan possible. He had been instrumental in raising funds for the trip. In early December, we formed committees and drafted the itinerary. We wanted to expose the students to as much of Japanese life as possible, so we planned a variety of activities. The final itinerary looked like this:

June 6	Arrival
June 7	Public school visit
	Tea ceremony
	Kendo demonstration
	Chitose salmon museum
	Barbecue
June 8	Jidaimura (Edo Period theme park)
	Shiraoi (Ainu Village)
June 9	Mt. Tarumae climb (cinder cone volcano)
	Overnight at Lake Shikotsu Kenshu Center
	Mimi Nashi Hoichi (dramatic performance of a Japanese ghost story by Kurt Caswell, Sven Hindman, and Kishida Norihiro)
June 10	Hike to Lake Shikotsu village
	Welcome to Chitose! (community party)
June 11	Host family day
June 12	Sapporo by train
June 13	Departure

On the first day, we visited four different public middle schools in four small groups. At Chitose Jr. High School, the American students were greeted with a banner across the entrance, "Welcome to our School." They were the center of attention in every class they attended. They were greeted with vigorous handshaking and bombarded with questions about themselves and their hometown. Before lunch, we drank green tea with the principal. He gave each student a gift, and sang a traditional Japanese song about cherry trees blossoming in the spring. The American students had learned the song during their language lessons with Mrs. Lin, and were able to sing with him. He smiled, surprised and pleased. When we left the school, all the windows on all three floors were filled with waving hands.

On the morning of June 9, we drove west from Chitose into the Shikotsu-Toya National Park to climb Mount Tarumae. As are most mountains in Japan, Tarumae is an active volcano. We ate bento (boxed lunch) prepared by the students' host families, and posed for photographs next to one of the most effusive vents rolling gas into the sky. From the summit, we could see Lake Shikotsu at the mountain's base (the second deepest lake in Japan), the Chitose River Valley and the Pacific Ocean, laden with clouds.

That night, we stayed at the Lake Shikotsu Kenshu Center. We invited the Japanese students involved in the project—and anyone else who wanted to come—to join us for a party. It was here that many of the online partners met for the first time. There was the brief hesitation that comes with any first meeting, but then, as if realizing that they knew each other already, everyone began talking and playing ping pong, badminton, and softball. It was also here that Doug gave his first vocal performance in Japan. Sven Hindman (another English teacher from Idaho) and I performed a dramatic Americanized rendition of an old Japanese ghost story called "Mimi Nashi Hoichi." Afterward, our narrator, Kishida Norihiro, asked if he couldn't read a story for which he had composed music. Then, another friend played a traditional Japanese song on her clarinet. After these two spontaneous performances, it was only natural to have a contribution from the visiting Americans. Doug's students called him before the audience, and he sang "Summertime." For me, Doug's performance was one of the highlights of the entire exchange. As he sang, I looked out into the crowded room and realized that here was a group of people who had thrown away cultural biases and allowed friendships to blossom.

Reflections (Douglas E. Wood)

I must admit that I feel a sense of post-exchange blues. Both Kurt and I were immersed in the project for a full year; it was certainly the center of our lives. Writing this chapter with Kurt has brought back many memories of hard work and difficult times.

For me as a teacher, this project was liberating. I was free to design curricula and put my plans into action. My administrators gave me free reign and supported me every step of the way. When I first gave my principal, Mrs. Jo Hecker, details of my plan, she said, "What can I do to help?" I also had the support of my coordinator, Dr. Julie Long, at the district office. Her philosophy on good teachers is very simple: "I support them and get out of the way." This freedom allowed me to pursue my own classroom inquiry. Reading the hundreds of pages of transcripts and journal entries throughout this exchange helped me to learn much about my own classroom practices and to look at them with a critical eye. I could go on and on about what the project meant to me, but I would like to bring in another voice that is too often excluded from educational research: that of the student. Two months after we returned from Japan, during their summer vacation, my students got together and wrote about their experiences. They then put together a book of pictures and letters, and presented it to me. Here are a few excerpts:

> Braden Core: Maybe someday when I am old, gray, overweight, and much wiser I will be able to completely grasp what I have experienced, but certainly not until then. Although this visualization may not occur for a while, that does not mean that I can't apply this to every aspect of my being!!!

> Kathy Lin: Thanks for giving me the chance of learning about another culture. It was fun, educational, and entertaining all at the same time. Not to mention all the e-mail to send, fundraisers to organize, brownies to bake, after-school meetings to attend, and lectures to endure.... All I can say is the ever simple but meaningful . . . thanks.

> Kalenia Franklin: Thank you for selecting me to be a part of the class of a lifetime!!!

> Chris Lin: All it took to make the Japan experience possible was a lot of cases of writer's cramp on the part of the students (all of us) and extremely hard work and tolerance on you and Kurt's part.

The exchange was a great success. But it could have been even better. Certain things, if we had them to do over again, we would have done differently. One such area was reading the common text. Kurt and I should have spent more time developing a pace for the reading of John Elder's *Following the Brush*; our classes were not synchronized. One reason for this was that the Japanese students were reading and writing English as a second language. For them to read an entire book in English was extremely difficult, and they could read only short selections at a time. Elder's book offers many insights into both Japanese and American classrooms—and ways of thinking. The students might have been able to match many of the observations in the book with the writings from their partners had we coordinated this part of the exchange better. We could have provided more prompts and time for discussion.

To understand the power of communication through e-mail, it is necessary to use it. Students learn a great deal and get more excited about on-line exchanges when they have direct access to technology in the classroom. But as with Kurt, many teachers have only their own home computers. This does not mean an exchange with limited technological resources cannot be successful. But it does require a great deal of dedication on the part of the teacher. In any event, the technology itself should never be the focus of an on-line exchange. The people on the other end are what makes an exchange successful.

Recommendations

Here are some recommendations for conducting your own on-line exchange:

1) The tighter the focus, the more successful the exchange.

2) Consistent dialogue between the two (or more) classrooms in completing assignments is essential for success. Students want responses to their work from their partners in the exchange. Teachers are responsible for assuring that this happens, otherwise students may become disillusioned about their work.

3) Teachers should be aware that when it comes to technology, students learn fast, often rapidly exceeding their teacher. Teachers should not be afraid to learn from their students, and should provide opportunities for them to explore, and expand their knowledge of the technology. Many times over, the students in the USjApanLINK Project proved that students can be the best advocates of technology in the classroom.

4) Flexibility is important, but it must be balanced with a well-planned curriculum that drives the technology.

5) Participating teachers should meet face to face if they desire a physical exchange between their classes. Posting a general invitation on a commercial network can be successful. However, we would not recommend planning a physical exchange until you verify the other teacher's integrity and commitment through a personal meeting.

If you follow these basic recommendations, you will have a successful and enjoyable experience, maybe even a great one.

Vicki Hunt

The Raptor Project

I BELIEVE IN the use of computers for writing and in telecommunications for transmitting that writing, because I have seen students who had previously written little or not at all, who, when set in front of the computer, produced pages and pages of manuscripts. There is something about writing for the unseen audience out there at the other end of the line that inspires students not only to write more but to produce better writing. I also believe connecting kids with other kids around the country through an electronic network helps break down cultural, ethnic, and economic barriers.

Last year my students were invited, through the Bread Loaf Rural Teacher Network, to take part in an on-line conference for the study and exchange of writing about birds of prey, or raptors. Because I team-teach in an American Studies class, I asked my colleague Dwight Rawlings, a biology teacher, to team-teach with me. He agreed, and he and I both attended a weekend retreat at which we received training in raptor identification and habits from members of Hawk Watch International and from the Tucson Wildlife Rehabilitation Center. Dwight and I returned to school full of enthusiasm, ready to begin.

The location of our school, as well as our diverse ethnic population, made for an interesting exchange. Peoria High School, located about twenty miles west of Phoenix, Arizona, is still mostly surrounded by alfalfa and cotton fields, with the beautiful White Tank mountains visible from our campus, about ten miles to the west. We knew that the open fields, with an abundance of field mice, provided a suitable habitat for hawks and other birds of prey. We also knew we could incorporate raptor stories from classical as well as Southwestern myth and legend into our study, as well as environmental issues. There was much to be excited about.

Dwight and I brainstormed some informal objectives for the project, but agreed we would play each day as it came and do a lot of monitoring and adjusting. We hoped that our students would:

1) gain a scientific understanding of raptors (identification, habitats, food, etc.);

2) gain an appreciation of raptors' precarious position as an endangered species;

3) learn about raptors' place in classical and Southwestern mythology and folklore; and

4) improve their reading and writing skills and learn how to use computers.

While four teachers in New Mexico and Arizona took part in the project, I arranged to trade writing on-line primarily with one other teacher: Phil Sittnick, in Laguna Pueblo, New Mexico. He and I engaged in early planning on-line. We had different hardware and software, but the common link was BreadNet, the telecommunications system of the Bread Loaf School of English. When a group of teachers is ready to begin a conference on BreadNet, Rocky Gooch, the telecommunications director, opens a file specifically for that exchange. Ours, called "Raptors," was an open file, meaning that any of the several hundred people connected to BreadNet could read and respond to anything in the folder. Phil and I also communicated through e-mail.

It is easy to make beautiful plans for our students, but when they show up, that's when the fun begins! The twenty students in Dwight's ESL biology class ranged from grades 10 through 12, and in age from fifteen to twenty-one. Eighteen were from Mexico, one was from Vietnam, and one was from Korea. Three had spent most of their school years in Peoria, but several others were experiencing their first year in an American school. They represented all levels of ability and language proficiency. Many of the Latinos did not read or write Spanish well, and so had even more trouble with English. Several had attendance problems, and many arrived sleepy or late (this class began at 7:20 in the morning). However, the one common denominator was their courtesy and willingness to try what was asked of them.

Dwight had begun to tell his students about the project a week or so before I joined his class. Their curiosity piqued, they had lots of questions the morning I arrived. "Miss, what is a raptor?" "Miss, do we get to go on a field trip?" Their chatter conveyed their energy and enthusiasm.

Before the on-line exchange began, Dwight and I began studying raptors with his students. (Phil was simultaneously presenting essentially the same information to his students in Laguna.) Dwight began with a biology lesson on raptor identification. A dynamic CD-ROM showing a hawk diving into the water and coming up with a fish in its talons captured the students' attention right away. Dwight also provided a glossary of terms such as birds of prey, carrion, decay, endangered, habitat, incubate, plumage, predator, prey, roost, scavenger, soar, species, talons, thermal. We encouraged the students to use these words when speaking and writing. Another early lesson included slides of eagles, hawks, falcons, vultures, ospreys, and kestrels for identification purposes, focusing on differences in beaks, wings, and talons, as well as variations in colors and eating habits. Dwight then asked students to identify hawks and vultures, both common to our area.

A major focus of the biology portion of the study dealt with raptors as an endangered species. Students were quite fascinated by them, and several told stories about relatives who had captured eagles and kept them in cages for long periods of time. We talked about the fact that many hawks are becoming "city dwellers" due to the encroachment of cities onto the desert or farmlands. (Teachers can acquire this information from Hawk Watch International, as well as from many handbooks on raptors such as *Amazing Birds of Prey Eyewitness Juniors Series, The Encyclopedia of Birds, The Birder's Handbook,* and *Audubon's Birds.*)

After we felt that the students had a basic knowledge of the differences between raptors and other types of birds, I began to discuss their place in mythology and folklore, with an emphasis on the Southwest. Phil had a long list of myths and legends from which I selected a few I thought the kids would find interesting. Given the many Hispanic students in the class, I began with the legend of the Mexican flag—how the early Aztecs had built their capital, now Mexico City, on the spot where they saw an eagle sitting on a cactus growing out of the middle of a lake in the desert. As with most legends that are passed down orally, the students discovered that there were many variations of the same story.

After more discussion of folklore, particularly "origins stories," I read aloud two Zuni legends, "The Youth and His Eagle" and "Eagle Boy," and the students compared the two stories. Next I read "The Eagle's Nest," a Navajo legend, and "The Moqui Boy and the Eagle," a Tewa legend, which we compared to the Zuni stories. One more prewriting activity followed: Dwight and I divided students into groups of three and gave each group a story to read. Then one student from each retold the story (in the storyteller tradition) to the class. This called upon their reading skills as well as their speaking skills.

Finally, about two weeks into the four-week project, it was time to get the kids on-line. I hadn't really tested their writing skills yet, but

Dwight warned me that they were varied and limited. My March 27 note to BreadNet reads:

> Well, Phil, Dwight and I jumped (flew) into the raptor thing with his ESL class today and we're all having a great time. These are the sweetest kids I've ever taught. Tomorrow they go on their "field trip" down the road to a cotton field. We're equipped w/ binoculars and cameras—so that almost guarantees that no hawks will show up. Phil, how about sending right away those personal introductions that your kids wrote—and anything else they may have written on disk for this project. I think the first actual writing I'll have these guys do is the introductions, and if they had some idea whom they were writing to it might be easier. I'm going to take them to the writing lab, even though many say they've never typed—should be fun!!! . . . If you have pictures of your students, please send them, too. We'll do the same. Please keep telling me anything that's working.

Phil wrote back:

> Vicki, I've got this great file of writing my kids have done, but I'm having problems uploading it—I can't as of yet, but will keep trying, and will send it to you ASAP. Great to hear you're having fun!

Peoria High School's computer writing lab is comprised of twenty-eight Mac Classics equipped with Microsoft Works and two ImageWriter printers. There is nothing fancy about these computers, which the Language Arts department received from the business department when they upgraded, but they are so much better than the old Apple IIEs that we had. Because few English teachers in my school feel comfortable taking classes to the lab, and because most of their classes are larger than twenty-eight students, the lab was available for us to use whenever we wanted over the four weeks. Only three of the girls in the class had had some formal computer training, but that was all it took for us to have the peer helpers we needed to make the lab time a success. While several of the others could type, most confessed to never having used a computer at all, so we placed the three girls around the lab to train the others. We gave each student his or her own disk so each could learn how to name and save files. (The program At Ease prevents students from saving to the hard drive on these computers.) We also asked everyone to use twelve-point Courier type, as this converts well on-line, and keeps students from getting sidetracked with exotic fonts and sizes.

Phil finally successfully uploaded twelve pages of student writing from his Laguna Pueblo middle schoolers, which I separated, printed, and passed out to our students. I explained how the writings had come through phone lines to my home computer the previous night. I have never heard a class so quiet as they read the letters from the New Mexico students. We had them pass a few on to someone else, so that each student got to read several letters. Then we asked them to read aloud a few they liked. They were impressed that some of these kids had even written poetry about raptors. Not one student complained that these letters were from middle schoolers—the age difference seemed to get lost somewhere in cyberspace.

Using one of the letters as a model, we then asked our students to introduce themselves to the Laguna Pueblo students. After a few moans and groans about not knowing how to type, or not knowing what to say, the students began writing about a subject each was familiar with—himself or herself. Again, silence reigned as students, deep in thought, composed their lives on the screen. Even though Dwight and I told them not to be concerned at this point with grammar, punctuation, or spelling, some of them asked for help finding the correct English word. Dwight was good at finding cognates, and sometimes asked the class to guess the mystery word. In this way it became a warm, supportive, interactive activity.

These first introductions were the hardest for our kids; they wanted to do a good job for their faceless audience in New Mexico. Students learned to use the spell-check, and we encouraged them to print out hard copy, which would then be peer-edited so they could make corrections. Dwight and I acted as cheerleaders, challenging them to keep going, to push for more, to think of livelier words. And they rose to the challenge. Dwight, who had seen their short answers to test questions all year, admitted that this experience raised his expectations of these students. He was, in fact, amazed at the work they were producing.

Return e-mail from the New Mexico students told us that most of them are Native American, and they like hunting, fishing, bull riding, and horseback riding, as well as basketball, soccer, and football. Many of them are in large families, just like the Peoria students. They take mostly the same classes, but their school has only around 200 students, whereas Peoria is a giant at 1,700. Many of the Laguna students are natives of the area, while all of the Peoria kids had immigrated from another country, mostly Mexico. The common link was the study of raptors. The Laguna students were studying them in biology class, and listening to the same myths and legends in English class.

We received the following poems from them:

Zapptor Raptor

Eagles soaring high
above the sky
Whooping eagle heading for its meal
Eagle prayers swelling through the thermals
Eagles up high sailing toward the hot sun
Hawks hanging in the trees.

Hawk talons digging into its prey
They have keen sight viewing the town
Mighty hawks fighting for

survival in the forest
Brave eagle soaring with pride.

—*Monica Bowman*

Pride

The hawks hang around in the dark.
As for the eagles they soar high through the wind
And they talk with the gods above.
No other is stronger than the eagles.
He has a special touch of talent.

—*Cheryl Silva*

In the first exchange, some students at both sites asked questions. "Do you believe in shooting raptors or saving them?" "Do you think raptors can see in color?" "Have you ever had a cache of eagle or any kind of bird feathers?" Most of our students simply introduced themselves:

Hi my name is Edgar E. Esparza and I'm an 11th grader at Peoria High School. I'm from Monterrey, Nuevo Leon, Mexico. I have lived in United States of America for 4 years in Peoria, Arizona. Today 3/31/95 is my birthday.

Hi, my name is Joo Park and I'm a 10th grader at Peoria High School. I'm from Pusan, Korea. I have been here 1 year and half. I live with my sister. And I have a brother. He is in college. My parents live in Korea. They visit us three times in a year. I come here abroad for study. I will go back my country after college. I miss my friends but I have fun here too.

I believe the magic ingredient for this project was the computers. It allowed the kids to get their thoughts down more quickly, with a finished product that looked professional when they had finished. Most of our students tried to allot time at the end of each period to print out a hard copy to take home with them. They seemed proud of what they had written. In an on-line correspondence with another Bread Loaf teacher in Arizona, I wrote:

> How is your raptor project coming? Mine is very "different." I've never taught ESL and admit I'm not "equipped" to deal w/ students at this level. If it were just lack of English language it would be one thing, but, of course, as with Anglo students, abilities vary greatly. Some didn't read or write well in Spanish, so of course they don't do well in English. We even have one 21-year-old girl and here we are communicating w/ Phil's 8th graders. The kids are certainly not complaining—they love the access to the computer writing lab, as no one has ever taken them there before. Many of them use the one finger approach to keyboarding, but they do get a little bit on disk during the period. They were pretty comfortable w/ introducing themselves, but today we started the "responding" part, and they were a little more reluctant. It's really cute—I found several of them working back in their introduction folder from Friday—"just adding a little more to my introduction." Dwight says it's the best writing they've done all year—and the most honest.

Our students had no trouble, once they got started, communicating with the Laguna students. They wrote in an informal manner as if writing to old friends. The plan we used was that each student chose one of the original Laguna introductions and corresponded individually with that student. Again, I took the disks home and uploaded the files to BreadNet. I did not change or correct any of the students' writing. The following are a few excerpts from the letters:

> Dear Monica. How are you? I hope, that you are doing fine, Now do you want to know, what is my favorite raptor. Well, my favorite raptor is the Eagle, you know why? because besides being pretty is the symbol of my country, in Mexico City. There are raptors that live in my city. I didn't know that the baby Eagles, called Eaglets, thank you for letting me know. Well it is a pleasure knowing you, I would like to know you in person, for talking about of the raptors. Bye, girl take care. Irene Armendariz

> My name is Ausencia Vazquez I'm 16 years old. I read your poem about raptors. The name of the poem is pride. I really like is real interesting poem. I'm not real good writing poems or reading poems but I really like yours. . . . I hope some day to get to learn about all kinds of birds that there is in the world. That's to much to ask but I hope to learn to recognize a raptor from a long distance. I hope some day we get to meet each other in person or that you can write to me in my home.

By this time, about three and a half weeks into the writing portion of the project, the students were ready to try their hand at some stories and poems. Students were reporting to the writing lab each day, finding their disks, and getting started without prompts from Dwight or me. Their motivation was high. Our purpose with the imaginative writing was to help students synthesize their knowledge of raptors and folklore, as well as to use their imaginations to create a piece to go out on-line. This would combine all of the objectives we had established in the beginning.

Again Dwight and I became cheerleaders, coaxing them on, applauding small achievements, supplying missing words, as the students worked and worked and worked. For a full week they worked, some with language dictionaries in hand, to complete their stories. Since our guidelines had been purposely vague so as not to limit the kids, we received a variety of stories. Since neither Dwight nor I had ever engaged in a project like this, neither of us had any idea what to expect. What we received pleased me and astonished and elated Dwight, who had been working with these kids all year. Again I loaded all their stories onto a master disk, without correcting errors, and uploaded them onto BreadNet. The following are excerpts from a few, selected for variety. Aucensia Vasquez's introduction spoke of the diversity of the oral tradition:

> The legend from the Mexican flag. What's the meaning of the eagle in the Mexican flag? There are so many different legends that people tell to their kids and the legends keep on going in different ways and different tales. The one that I know you are going to know it from my point and the one that my parents have told me. The one that my teachers told me when I was in the elementary school in Mexico. The legend has been change so many different ways.

Park Joo's story resonated with Korean folklore:

> A long time ago there is a small town. The town was so beautiful and clean. The village people was really poor but, they have good mentality. People and eagle was very good friends. That time eagles can talk with people. One day one old lady come to the town. She was so ugly and looks like monster. But people were nice to her however she was so mean and strange. After she came to the town some weird thing occurred in the village. A lot of trees dead and a lot of animals dead. . . .

The rest of Park's story abounded with monsters, magic eagles, and sticks changed to stones.

Husef set his story in the south of Africa where, he said, "there were no food for a Harpy Eagle's talon. There were no rabbits, no mice, and no frogs. . . ." Another student recounted an old family version of the story of the founding of Mexico City. Angel Vasquez set his story in the jungle of South America, but modernized it by making his protagonists a group of students who were trying to learn about the life of animals in the jungle.

The students showed great imagination in the formation of their stories, and were conscientious in their attempt to conform to standard English. (Many stories contained a wonderful musicality from interjected words in Spanish.) After reading the kids' stories, I wanted to publish them in an anthology, but we didn't have time. However, Peoria's ESL language teacher has agreed to begin her year helping the kids revise their stories for publication.

In a telecommunications conference there are always surprises. One week before school was out, we received responses to our stories from another New Mexico classroom. My students were surprised and delighted. Victoria Gonzalez, a student in Roseanne Lara's class in Anthony, New Mexico, wrote: "Dear Angel Vasquez, I really liked your story. It was short, but nice. I've never heard a story like this one. I really wouldn't like to be the student the man killed." Another, Nathaniel Acosta, wrote, "Dear Angel, I like your story because it talks about our culture and tells things that I have never heard. Those are nice things that people tell another person about something that they don't know about." Andy Pavia wrote, "I liked your story. Grandparents are cool. I read your story five times and made a copy and hung it in my room. P.S. write me back." Iris Rojas wrote, "Dear Eric Toras, I like this story. It's all about our culture. My *abuela* told me that story about how we got the eagle with the snake. But I guess I never really believed it."

These responses reveal the connections made between students hundreds of miles apart, students who will never meet face to face, but who have formed a bond through their writing. For many of our Peoria students, the move to the U.S. had been a huge step in broadening their world. The step they took through cyberspace also broadened their world. Letters came in from New Mexico long after this project ended, and, as I delivered them to Dwight's classroom, I found myself wishing we had extended the project a little longer—that we had honed some of those writing skills begun in the writing lab.

Dwight, however, continued to take this ESL class to the lab for the remainder of the year. They wrote a mini-research paper and answered all test essay questions on the computers. Using computers not only helped the students get their ideas into writing, it gave them the confidence that they had something worth saying.

This year, my American Studies classes have been involved in many on-line exchanges, and I have found that the same common ingredients help students' writing to improve. First and foremost is the interest (curiosity) created by writing to an invisible audience, whether it is in Vermont,

Mississippi, or Alaska. One of my classes is corresponding via Internet with a class in London. The other thing that piques students' interest and improves their writing is the fact that someone besides the teacher is writing back to them. This makes the critiquing of their poetry, for example, more conversational and less authoritarian. With each major writing project my students complete, I try to find an audience to exchange with. We also enter an exchange with every novel we read and with many poems.

As Dixie Goswami, director of Clemson Writing in the Schools, notes, "When the communication is really working, the technology is invisible." I believe this to be true as I watch students who have little or no keyboarding experience, working in a decrepit computer lab with no direct telecommunications link in that lab. I watch them lay all that aside to create imaginative stories, honest reactions, and links to a world outside their own.

Carol Stumbo

Changing a State

IT IS FOUR in the morning. There is no sound in the summer darkness. I sit on the edge of my bed, holding a cup of hot coffee, staring at my clock-radio, waiting for the alarm to go off. Today I will drive from the mountains of eastern Kentucky to the flatlands of the Bluegrass for meetings at the Kentucky Department of Education. These monthly trips are part of my job as the director of a regional service center.

Our center, one of eight across the state, serves 131 schools in fifteen school districts. The centers were established to decentralize the Department. Six to nine consultants at each center, usually teachers, provide information, assistance, and resources to approximately 3,000 educators—a responsibility that is, at times, overwhelming. Sometimes, I am so tired that I do not always know where I am on the parkway or interstate, but I have never hesitated to make the drive. As a public school teacher, I have waited too long for this opportunity.

As Kentucky begins another pivotal year in a state reform that educational experts have called the most ambitious one ever attempted, concern is rising for the future of the Kentucky Educational Reform Act (KERA). Many of the legislators who supported KERA are no longer in the legislature. Some have left willingly. Others have been voted out, often citing their support of KERA as one of the reasons. Will the new leaders stay the course? Or will they begin to dismantle the reform?

The political winds are volatile. Education is being debated in Kentucky as it has never been before. We ride a roller coaster driven by emotions and opposing attitudes and viewpoints. One of the most heated debates in the early stages of the implementation of KERA concerned the role that technology would play. Believing technology to be an important tool for improving our schools, powerful Kentucky legislators fought for quicker implementation of the Kentucky Educational Technology System (KETS).

KETS is an ambitious program that in time will link all schools to the Kentucky Department of Education and provide an on-ramp for schools to one another and the Internet. When fully implemented, KETS will involve 150,000 student workstations, 35,000 teacher stations,

1,400 school management systems, and 176 district administrative systems. The projections have fluctuated as the costs and the length of implementation time have increased. Districts must match funding from the department to pay for the new technology.

With the completion of the District Administrative System (DAS), the first phase of KETS, much of the debate regarding technology seems to be fading in Kentucky. DAS allows district offices to communicate directly with the Kentucky Department of Education, and provides several important services. District offices will be able to report data on budgets and operations directly to Frankfort, the state capitol; to acquire information quickly from Department staff; and to communicate with other districts. But probably the most important service that DAS will provide is that of creating a kind of gateway for schools—to regional hubs, and then on to Frankfort, and finally to the Internet. Once this second phase, currently in progress, is completed, students and teachers statewide will be able to use the Internet for as long as they wish at no expense. University campuses will also be part of this state system. The technology experts at the Department have created a system that teachers can learn to use in a few minutes, with none of the usual frustration and anxiety associated with getting on-line.

While it is too early to say what the full impact of KETS will be, especially at the classroom level, some changes are already evident. For years, the tall building in Frankfort that houses the Kentucky Department of Education has been referred to as the "Tower" by both Department and district employees. To KDE employees, the name simply denotes a large structure that dominates the Frankfort skyline; but to local school districts, it symbolizes an organization that is removed from the daily realities of schools. Now, though, daily access through telecommunications is beginning to change the image and relationship between the Department and school districts. Through e-mail, school officials at the local level have equal access to associate and deputy commissioners, division directors, consultants, and secretaries. Interestingly, this tends to flatten the traditional hierarchy. Everyone involved is on a first-name basis. Knowledge seems as important as position.

The Department itself is undergoing internal changes as a result of the technology. To a large extent, e-mail has replaced the telephone. For people who are constantly on the road or in meetings, e-mail ensures that your message reaches the individual that you are trying to contact and is suitable in form. In some curious way, the changes are tied to the medium itself. One of the technology consultants recently told us about an employee who was unhappy with a decision that had been made by his supervisor. The employee composed a note protesting the decision, but instead of posting it simply to his superior, he copied it to several others—people in higher positions. If it had been a letter, the consultant argued, the employee would never have distributed it that widely. Something about e-mail—perhaps its ease and informality—had dissolved the boundaries.

The Department has also established a Web site that provides information and resources to districts, teachers, schools, parents, and students, all of whom can access it electronically in a matter of moments, at no expense. Educators can download content guidelines and key chapters in the state's curriculum frameworks. In turn, district Web pages can be accessed through the central KDE site.

Administrators and teachers now go directly to the Internet to do research. The implications for professional development are great. Traditionally, educators in our region have been unable to keep up with the most recent developments in education because of our distance from universities and professional development centers. Now, through the Internet, they have easy access to databases such as ERIC and ASCD; they can examine lesson plans created by professional organizations across the country, or browse in the libraries at Princeton or Stanford University. This ability to acquire information may be less important to teachers in urban areas, but to teachers in rural areas, where library facilities are limited and where bookstores are few or non-existent, these new resources are liberating and intoxicating.

Districts are also becoming resources for one another. Wolfe County, a small rural district located at the foothills of the Appalachian mountains about a two-hour drive from our center, has established its own "home page" for teachers in the district. All fifteen school districts in our region will be able to access the information posted there. And by working with local companies to open up the Web sites to the community as well as to the schools, Wolfe County has taken a lead in establishing a bridge between homes and schools using telecommunications.

Some important collaborations are also beginning to develop among districts separated by hundreds of miles. Pike County, our largest school district, has applied for and received a federal grant to implement a project known as R.U.N. This project will link students in rural Pike County with students in Louisville, which is Kentucky's largest city.

Using a combination of telecommunications and teleconferencing, students who have never seen a live ballet or heard a mountain dulcimer will have the opportunity to do both through this connection. Students from Pike County will be able to see and talk to staff from Louisville's Kentucky Arts Center and Speed Museum. Louisville students can be exposed to eastern Kentucky writers and music. Small rural schools that cannot afford the staff necessary to teach specialized courses (in foreign languages, for example) are enriching curricula by computer hook-ups with master teachers in urban areas.

While some teachers have already taken the initiative and jumped in with their students, the challenge of KETS and telecommunications still lies ahead for most Kentucky teachers. The teachers who seem to be adapting share some common characteristics. They are reflective, familiar with teacher research, able to collaborate with others, and willing to share responsibility for learning with their students. Those teachers who have been trained in the Foxfire process and teacher research or have taken part in on-line networks are handling the demands of KERA with more ease.

It was, in fact, an electronic network that had sustained me as a teacher by allowing me to be part of an on-line community. For several years before the passage of KERA, I belonged to BreadNet, a network of teachers who had attended the Bread Loaf School of English in Middlebury, Vermont. Bread Loaf had a special program for rural teachers, and the school in some cases loaned teachers computers during the school year so they could work together via telecommunications. Bill Wright, BreadNet's director, taught us rural teachers to do what he called "guerilla telecommunications"—getting on- and off-line quickly to keep expenses down. Bill and some other staff helped us solve our problems with technology.

Before Bread Loaf, I had not worked in any significant way with computers because I saw no need to: the result of ignorance and isolation. After witnessing how Bread Loaf teacher Dixie Goswami used the technology, I returned home and asked my principal to let me use the Apple lab when it was empty. There wasn't a long line of people waiting to use the lab. I began to use it for writing and telecommunications and brought most of my classes into the conferences on BreadNet.

On BreadNet, teachers from all across the country came together to share ideas, philosophies, and practices. Most of us had never met face to face. What we knew about one another, we learned at the other end of a computer and modem. We maintained the community through the events in our own lives: the war in the Persian Gulf; the Challenger explosion;

Hurricane Hugo; and the World Trade Center bombing. The on-line community survived departures and personal tragedies, applauded job promotions, and celebrated weddings. It was a wonderful experience, and one that contradicted the notion that a pre-existing community is necessary for successful telecommunications.

But while personal contact is not necessary, certain things have to be present. There has to be a tolerance and appreciation of diversity and a willingness to share and learn—to collaborate. Some of the most important professional development experiences I have ever had came from my association with the Bread Loaf teachers, and they were continuous. They connected to the work in my classroom. I would learn about some resource or article that I had never heard of and the reference would send me to a bookstore or library. Teachers on the network would describe their current teaching practices and discuss trends in their particular states. One of the conferences was called "Assessment." Vermont was just beginning to use writing portfolios, and a Vermont teacher, Tish McGonegal, taught us all a great deal. What I learned from Tish was especially useful to me when Kentucky later began to develop portfolios. The diversity of the community itself was appealing: Lucy Wollin taught at the School of Performing Arts in New York; Ike Coleman in South Carolina; John Forsyth at a small school in Wilsall, Montana; Joe Bradfield in rural Iowa; Susan Wood in Estill County, Kentucky; and Lucy Maddox at Georgetown University in Washington, D.C. It was unlikely in a rural school of eighteen teachers that I would have had access to such diversity.

The right connections through technology allow teachers to learn about new ideas and practices. It is understandable that collaboration between teachers at a given school is often difficult. High school teachers often seem to work in more isolation than other teachers—perhaps in part because we have been trained to be content specialists. The cultures of most schools do little to support the exchange of ideas; for many teachers, it is actually easier to begin collaborating with people that they do not see on a daily basis. It has taken most of my professional life to reach the point where I really collaborate with other teachers. At my school, the sharing that did occur was was often superficial. We loaned each other materials, but it was almost as if we were afraid that we would hurt each others' feelings if we went further and shared our ideas and knowledge or suggestions for improvement. Our conversations in the teachers' lounge usually revolved around our personal lives and the day-to-day business of school. On BreadNet, I was always challenged, a little fearful at times, but there was never any doubt in my mind that I was growing.

My experience with BreadNet prepared me to some degree for my work at the Department of Education and for KERA, by encouraging me to collaborate with other teachers. Even after I left the classroom, telecommunications continued to play an important role in my learning. Notes such as the one below, by Emmy Krempasky, an elementary teacher from Paducah in western Kentucky, helped me understand what we were failing to do as we implemented reform. Although Emmy and I knew one another, we were not close friends or colleagues. But our relationship developed through a small computer network of Kentucky teachers called the Kentucky Telecommunications Writing Project, or KTWP.

Like many Kentucky teachers, Emmy was confused by some portions of KERA. Initially, I wanted to believe that this was the result of the fact that she lived in the far western part of the state, which like eastern Kentucky had in the past been historically left out of the state's communication loop. But it soon became clear that Emmy's problem was not due to a lack of information, but rather that a barrage of information was coming at her from different sources. Like most learners, Emmy needed clear information and time to process the information. Despite publications, broadcasts, meetings, and workshops, three years into the reform Emmy still had many questions about KERA:

> Carol,
> Thanks for your quick response. I really appreciated your willingness to help me understand what is happening. It just seems that we hear so much. I just try to make sense of all the different things that I'm hearing. People are interpreting things their way. Then things change so quickly. When I mentioned to my friends what you said about an average of two years (in terms of compiling the assessment results), they thought I was crazy. I just want to know what is going on and what it all means to my students and myself.
>
> I guess my first misunderstanding was thinking that assessment was to assess (that's a funny-looking word) individual student growth. So you are telling me that the purpose of assessment is to determine a school's program and its effectiveness. Where have I been? Don't answer that. I didn't know that we were allowed to see the tests. Help me with terminology please. What do you mean by "core concepts"?
>
> Why aren't other grade levels getting the information that the testing grades are getting? The only reason I know anything is that my best friend used to teach 4th grade. Should the schools be taking on that responsibility and developing our own guidelines for portfolios? I'm having my students keep portfolios, but I don't think they follow the state guidelines, because I haven't seen the guidelines. We've been asking for copies for some time. The special ed. teacher that also has fourth grade students still hasn't received her

math portfolio information. She is still sharing her copy. I've looked at copies, but those teachers are very hesitant about letting them out of their hands. Do you have thoughts on these situations?

I'm just wanting to be a better teacher. I want to do what I can. I just want to know what I can do. I'm going to keep asking questions until I have a better understanding.

Still foggy and confused,

Emmy

I realized from Emmy's note ("I just want to know what [reform] means to me and to my students") that most teachers, like other learners, want the information about KERA in a very personal, practical manner. Understandably, Emmy wanted to know how the changes related to her role in the classroom, and she wanted access to the information she needed. The note also helped me to understand that the communication that we at the Department of Education had just assumed was taking place was getting blocked somewhere.

The following year, Emmy was assigned to teach fourth grade, one of the three grade levels (along with eighth and twelfth) at which student math and writing portfolios had to be completed and assessed. Emmy was terrified, but she had an on-line community who supported her as well as we could. We couldn't help laughing as she wrote note after note beginning with, "I can't believe I am teaching the fourth grade!" It was almost as if she somehow thought that if she said it often enough, her predicament would become easier to deal with. I hope that we helped her.

Oddly enough, it was not through the normal channels of assistance in the Kentucky Department of Education that Emmy received help when she was reassigned. One of the other teachers from the Kentucky Telecommunications Network conducted a staff development session at her school. (Emmy would later tell him that another teacher at her school had attributed her entire understanding of KERA to his visit.)

Emmy went on to become one of the teachers selected in Kentucky to participate as a technology specialist in the state math and science program. Last year, she traveled to eastern Kentucky to do a session for teachers enrolled in a summer writing institute sponsored by our service center. Emmy came to introduce teachers to networking, but as we discovered, many of these teachers were just learning word processing for the first time, an indication of how much work there is still to be done.

Although more collaboration has begun to take place under KERA, many teachers are still working alone in their classrooms. They have not changed. Those teachers are important if we are really serious about wanting to improve schools. They are not only in the best position to make those improvements; they are the only ones who can. As James Britton has said, "What is not done by the classroom teacher can not be done by anyone else." No reform effort can succeed without them, but in order to help bring about those changes, teachers must be willing to be learners again, to reflect on their own practices, to collaborate, to take on new roles.

Were legislators correct in their belief that the technology should have been in place sooner? Could technology have eased some of the growing pains caused by reform? Most of us have learned in Kentucky not to engage in second-guessing. We know that we have made and will continue to make mistakes. Looking at the past is productive only if we learn from it. Certainly, telecommunications could have intensified the potential for networking and communication among teachers, but there are still some serious questions about what conditions are necessary before teachers can and will even use telecommunications. To ensure that technology is used wisely, Kentucky is investing not only millions of dollars in technology, but an equal amount in staff development—in collaboration and teamwork; the writing process; core concepts in math, science, social studies, language arts; and different learning and teaching styles. Workshops in technology have focused on technical training, but more importantly, they have also emphasized the integration of technology and curriculum.

I do not know what the fate of reform in Kentucky will be, but I do know that the growth that has taken place in the state has been remarkable. Seventy percent of the schools have met their improvement goals on KIRIS, the state assessment. Colleges are reporting that students are entering their doors as better writers. While poor districts have not closed the gap in student performance between themselves and the more affluent districts, they are growing at the same rate. It is the first time that they have ever experienced this growth. As educators, we have come so far.

There is more work to be done and more tools to be made available to teachers. But technology is only a tool, one that can reflect only what is in our minds and hearts. Reform will not happen teacher by teacher, nor can it happen from the centralized efforts of a state department of education. Reform will not happen from either a bottom-up or top-down approach, but will from a carefully orchestrated combination of both. What we must change is not just a state department of education, but how we see ourselves and our students. I believe that teachers have the courage to make those changes. Just recently, I opened my e-mail to find a first note from Emmy. On her own, she has found her way into the new system. I take her arrival as a good omen.

Emmy Krempasky

Hurricane KERA

Weathering Educational Reform with Telecommunications

PADUCAH IS A CITY on the banks of the Ohio River in the far western corner of Kentucky—an area saturated with rivers, lakes, and high humidity. Recently, students at Dove Anna McNabb Elementary in Paducah became weather watchers. As part of a telecommunications project, my students researched, observed, recorded, and predicted the weather. During the study, we watched the Weather Channel as a hurricane made its way up the Gulf Coast, and I remembered when another hurricane had caused havoc as far inland as Paducah. I looked out my window, ran downstairs, and turned on the local news. The rest of the community was waking to a similar scene. Streets were flooded. Cars were stalled. Neighbors were rescuing friends from the high water. None of us was prepared for the intensity of that storm.

In a climate of educational reform, the Kentucky Educational Reform Act (KERA) hit much like a hurricane. In 1990, amid concerns of parents, teachers, and administrators, the Kentucky Supreme Court declared the state's educational system unconstitutional. Although political debate and mandates of massive change swirled around me, I ignored the warnings. Little did I understand how KERA would affect every area of education—and my classroom.

As a teacher who recognizes the important role of assessment, I welcomed the establishment of statewide academic standards. Under KERA, the Kentucky Instructional Results Information System (KIRIS) and performance-based assessment were designed to promote high-quality instruction and increased expectations for all learners. An assessment system was established to hold schools and school districts responsible for improved student performance. Students in grades four, eight, and twelve would be assessed annually, using portfolios in writing and math, open-ended questions in content areas, and a group performance event.*

---

* An assessment task that requires students to apply what they've learned in a group setting, and then individually to answer follow-up questions.

Agreeing with the new forms of assessment and academic standards was easy for me. I taught fifth grade. I could continue to do my job and go home with just the usual pressures and paperwork of teaching. Imagine my surprise and dismay when my principal informed me I would now be teaching fourth grade. Keeping teachers in fourth grade had become a struggle statewide. Because of the pressure KIRIS testing placed on them, many found other positions. Consequently, I was being moved to the fourth grade. I felt stranded, the water rising all around me. How would I address the issues of the statewide assessment in my instruction? What really bothered me was that I felt totally unprepared.

Fortunately, I had an advantage. As a member of the Kentucky Tele-communications Writing Project (KTWP), I had the resources of a group of seasoned professionals at the end of my keyboard. I shared the news with my fellow KTWP teachers:

322 (of 325) EKREMPASKY Aug. 9, 1993 at 23:08 (854 characters)
NEWS FLASH!!!!!

I'm a fourth grade teacher! I'm a fourth grade teacher! This is a note that can't translate the doom and despair that I feel. I'm a fourth grade teacher! You might think that with the ! mark that I'm exclaiming excitement, thrill, delight, or even pleasure. I'm a fourth grade teacher! I'm not excited or thrilled or delighted or even pleased with the announcement. I'm a fourth grade teacher! What am I to do? I'm a fourth grade teacher! I'm a fourth grade teacher! I'm deeply concerned about the age of the students. I'm a fourth grade teacher! Will they be able to communicate with the older students on the KTWP network? I'm a fourth grade teacher! Will this change in my teaching assignment blow my participation in KTWP? I'm a fourth grade teacher. HELP!
　　Any thoughts or whatever will be greatly received!
　　Emmy
　　I'm a fourth grade teacher!

My KTWP friends and neighbors began to rally around me. They threw floatation devices. They weren't going to let me drown. Quickly, they supported me by welcoming my fourth graders:

Dear Emmy and friends,
I've been thinking about your dilemma (fourth graders) and I'm sure your new students will greatly benefit from having an enthusiastic teacher. How did you wind up with 4th grade? Obviously, it sounds like you were not expecting it. I used to be a 1st grade teacher and when I was hired for 8th, I told everyone from my principal to my husband to friends to anyone who would listen that I COULD NOT do it. I was scared to death, but now I love it. I'm sure KTWP will be able to embrace 4th graders. It will add another

challenge and dimension to this already challenging and ever-changing project.

The books you mentioned for the reading conference sound fine. *Sounder* really is not lower level, more 7th or 8th grade. We can leave it as a choice in case students at that level want to read it. I had students who read *Tales of a Fourth Grade Nothing* and loved it. Have you ever read *The Not Just Anybody Family* by Betsy Byars?

Bev

After other encouraging notes from teachers in KTWP, I began to calm down. I was going to be able to keep my classroom. That was good. The only problem was that I would be isolated from the other fourth grade classrooms and teachers. Many days passed when I didn't see the other fourth grade teachers, except at lunch.

I started with the "easy stuff" first. I reviewed the district curriculum, the state academic expectations, the Kentucky Curriculum Frameworks, KIRIS assessment practices, and the tentative plans we had made in KTWP earlier in the summer. As I made plans for the year, I sought to combine the fourth grade curriculum with the writing skills they would need for the open-ended response questions on the spring tests. What things would I need to change in my teaching strategies? What materials would I be able to keep? What materials would I need? I gathered materials appropriate for fourth grade students and prepared myself for that first day.

I was ready. The students came in. I was nervous, more like my very first teaching day. But right away I introduced the students to telecommunications and explained how they would use computers to write to students across the state. They were eager to begin right away. I wasn't ready. The students wrote short notes introducing themselves and describing their school. Oh my! Their writing was choppy and undeveloped. My doubts increased. How were we ever going to be able to communicate with the older students, much less meet the KERA academic standards? I would have to teach new skills.

After some mini-lessons on basic editing and revision, we began what became the most gruesome part of the experience: typing the student work on computer. The first couple of students took most of the morning to type their short pieces. I had only two computers in my room and our school didn't have a computer lab. I could tell this was going to be a long year. I had students use an old Tandy computer to practice keyboarding skills. They chose to do this on their own time. In fact, they quickly devised a competition among themselves: each wanted to be the fastest typist.

Improving their typing skills eventually allowed the students to spend more time editing and revising their work. Surprisingly, students grasped the basic ideas of revising and editing fairly quickly. They realized how the computer made it easier for them both to write and rewrite. Computers also allowed them to turn their messy handwriting into legible, appealing pieces. Students found how to give their work a more polished look by changing fonts and sizes. Triple-spacing and enlarging the type made peer editing and revising hard copy more convenient. They worked in groups to edit and revise, with many mini-lessons on group revision and editing. Most of the fourth grade writing was carefully considered and reworked before being placed on the network for others, not just me, to read.

The different conferences on KTWP created a variety of occasions for writing and reading. For instance, my students wrote collaboratively, in small groups, working their individual pieces into one. The conferences also allowed the students to have a variety of good models to read. The older students' writing particularly gave my students ideas and strategies for their own writing. One good example was the Endangered Species Project—a science project involving bird watching and observation of patterns that required sharing data and descriptions of Paducah with other classes on the network. We had already received introductions from two of the other schools, but I didn't show those to the students until they had each drafted an individual piece. As Mallory, Jessica, Amy, and Antonio discussed what should and shouldn't be in their combined introduction, word choice became very important. They scribbled, erased, scribbled, erased, and discussed until, with cooperation, communication, and the models from the other schools, their writing became something they were proud to send:

Note 3? by EKREMPASKY on Feb. 22, 1994
To: Science Talk
From: Mallory, Antonio, Amy, and Jessica

Dear KTWP,
Paducah is located in the northern part of the Jackson Purchase. Our school is on Park Ave., which is a very busy street. Because it is on a very busy street it might frighten the birds so they won't eat out of our feeder.
 Our birdfeeder is in the middle of the front part of the schoolyard. We are going to fax you this letter. We mostly see blackbirds at our feeder. Our birdfeeder is made out of a plastic gallon milk carton. Half of the side is cut out to put our seeds in. Our birdfeeder is hanging on a very minor tree. The tree has no leaves on it. We put it in the middle of the schoolyard so we can

watch birds out of the hallway windows. We all think that was an interesting idea.

We check and refill the feeder every day. We also watch the birds eat out of the birdfeeder every day. We think most of the birds will eat off the ground. We enjoy watching the birds eat the birdseed.

We have many books in our classroom so that we can study birds. We are even making birds and hanging them up in the classroom. We have also drawn birds and hung them up in the hall. Mallory and Jessica are making a papier-mâché flamingo. The flamingo is rather large. They used balloons for the body and head. They also used rolled-up newspaper for the legs and neck. Amy rolled up newspaper and made it bend for the beak. She also did this for the neck, Mallory, Jessica, and Amy made a hummingbird. They used two ziploc bags to make the hummingbird's wings. The reason they made the wings out of ziploc bags is because hummingbirds fly so fast you can hardly see their wings when they fly. Everybody in the classroom thought our bird was very interesting. They had lots of fun making it.

Mallory McNeely
Jessica Smith
Amy Carr
Antonio Williams

Like others, this particular writing assignment met several of the KERA mandates. One is that students must learn to write and write to learn. The quality of fourth grade writing is evaluated by a portfolio assessment, according to established criteria. The Kentucky Holistic Scoring Guide identifies six categories: establishing and maintaining a purpose and communicating with an audience; idea development and support of details; organization; sentence structure; effective language; and lack of mechanical errors. In scoring student work, the first three categories are more important.

In the piece above, the fourth graders were aware of their purpose and audience. Their idea development and supporting details were limited, but they had been a bit overwhelmed by the newness of the project. Their sense of organization was weak. They did fine with the final three criteria.

Statewide portfolio requirements are also mandated. At the fourth grade level, each writing portfolio must contain a personal narrative; a piece whose purpose is either to present or support a position, idea, or opinion, or to tell about a problem and its solution, or to inform; a story, poem, or playscript; a piece from a curriculum area other than language arts; a personal selection; and a letter to the portfolio reviewer. As we planned the work on the KTWP project, we kept in mind these areas of writing. Students writing to KTWP did each of these things.

In addition, KTWP gave my students a real audience to read their pieces, and gave them some freedom in their writing. For instance, certain of my students loved writing about themselves, yet found it difficult when their only audience was me. Knowing that other students on KTWP would read their work challenged my students to write better, and offered them something of a "comfort zone."

> Hi! My name is Daniel Fukuhara, I am nine years old and live in Paducah, Kentucky. I am going to tell you a story that happened to me when I was young.
>
> When I was five years old I used to love going to Noble Park pool. I went there every summer and loved it until my cousin Collin Roof dared me to jump off the high diving board. I can't believe he dared me to do that. I was only five years old. I guess I was the one that was stupid because the next thing I knew I was climbing up the ladder, so I knew there was no turning back. But was I really going to do it. That's the question that would soon be answered.
>
> I decided I was going to hurry up and get it over with. I could feel my hands trembling with fear. My hands were dripping with sweat as if they were turned over buckets of water. The bars on the ladder felt as if my hands and feet were on a hot skillet. I was holding onto the bars so tight that it felt like the bars were melting in my hands.
>
> I finally got to the top. It felt like I was standing in the solar system I was so high. Then when I looked down I saw my two cousins laughing at me as if they were hyenas. Then I saw a little rock on the edge so I went to go pick it up, and when I did I accidentally fell over the edge. I felt the wind pull my hair back like a girl was pulling it. Then I hit the water. When I hit the water I felt a sharp sting hit my stomach. I sank into the water like the wreck of the Titanic.
>
> When I came out of the water I saw a red mark on my stomach. Then I went over to my cousins and said " . . . Looks like I did it!"

Other conferences encouraged students to write fiction or poetry. Some conferences published final drafts only, while others were designed to elicit critical responses. Using such suggestions took some work for my fourth graders. Often the feedback responses from older students on KTWP gave my students new ideas and insights.

As the year progressed and the students participated in more conferences, my own confusion and stress faded, and I began to see that the integration of what I was doing on-line and what I was doing in the classroom had a positive effect on the students. I also saw strengths and weaknesses in my own teaching, but generally I felt as if I had weathered the hurricane.

Usually, after a major storm, officials come to assess the damage. Unlike homeowners who wait patiently for insurance money and governmental aid. I found myself too anxious. Yes, I was waiting for the "official" scores, but in the interim, I went back through my students' portfolios and I looked at those from other classes at McNabb. Overall, the students were very weak in writing for a purpose and for an audience. My students seemed to do better with this area than other classes, but there was room for improvement from them in this area. We began addressing this issue schoolwide through many writing and reading activities, so that students could better understand the purpose of their writing and their audiences.

I also wanted to find ways to address the matter of organization. The students' writing didn't seem to flow very well. I targeted organization as an area of focus for my teaching and began to examine strategies to help students write with clarity, conciseness, and fluidity.

In my second and third years teaching fourth grade, I incorporated many lessons from my first year. The final results of the portfolios reflected this:

My first year
Novice: 10 (43%)
Apprentice: 9 (37%)
Proficient : 4 (20%)

My second year
Novice : 3 (21%)
Apprentice: 6 (42%)
Proficient: 3 (21%)
Distinguished: 1 (7%)

My third year
Novice : 7 (29%)
Apprentice: 7 (29%)
Proficient: 6 (25%)
Distinguished: 4 (16%)

So what have I learned in this short time of having access to telecommunications and integrating it into my classroom curriculum?

• Younger students can benefit from technology. They aren't intimidated by it. They learn quickly and efficiently.

• Students can revise and edit without complaining. Learning to type is a great asset. Having to write and rewrite in your own handwriting can discourage any young writer.

• Having a "real" audience and purpose for writing *will* improve student writing.

• Telecommunications is a cost-effective way to open up your classroom. Even students communicating within the same district can improve their writing by using it.

• Technology is stressful. Remember that when you become dependent on a machine, it won't work the time that you need it most. A notebook computer is very helpful to tired teachers. By taking the work home, you can avoid staying late at school to send and receive notes.

• Student research as well as teachers' professional development can take advantage of on-line projects and discussions. Some of the best professional development sessions that I have taken part in have been on-line, with teachers statewide and nationally.

• Caution is a must when your students are communicating on-line. Even if you think you know the recipients and senders, read what is sent over the lines.

• Change is good! Well, change is good when it is over. Change can be stressful, yet it challenges the best of us to make the best of the situation.

• Hurricanes don't last forever. While the Kentucky Department of Education and other state education departments realign themselves, correct problems, and address concerns, we teachers need to inform ourselves as much as possible. Reflection into our own teaching practices will benefit us and our students. As teachers weathering the same storm, we must be willing to be "real," sharing our failures as well as our success stories.

Susan Nelson Wood

Electronic Networks

Students and Teachers Creating a Common Place

WHAT OPPORTUNITIES does telecommunications hold for us as educators and learners? Zelda Fitzgerald said, "Nobody has ever measured, even poets, how much the heart can hold," and the same could be said about telecommunications. More than mere lights and wires, an electronic network is a human place, a place where conditions are prime for readers and writers to connect in new ways. As Howard Rheingold writes in *The Virtual Community*, "Something big is afoot, and the final shape has not been determined."[1] Curriculum—how best to use telecommunications—remains a great unknown. Who other than teachers and students is best equipped to decide?

In a way, the simplicity of network technology offers the ultimate hands-on experience. Buy a modem, join a network (any network), turn on the computer, and that's it. The tools are there, but how will we use them? Rather than attend another in-service workshop, rather than subscribe to a packaged program, rather than purchase memberships in preexisting networks and wait for someone else's curriculum, we can create our own.

I am very much an advocate of homegrown, grassroots networks. The key is to use telecommunications to suit your particular situation by considering imaginative ways to integrate it with what you are *already doing* in the classroom—the antithesis of electronic worksheets. For example, networks can serve as forums where teachers meet to exchange ideas. As Emmy Krempasky, a teacher involved in telecomputing, notes, "We have to make sure we don't get so comfortable in our own little world, the one we've created, that we forget to make it better by looking outside and seeing what others are doing." In this essay, I offer a few examples of small-scale telecommunications projects that might serve, in a general way, as models for other projects.

A few years ago, a group of Kentucky teachers and their students branched off from a larger network and started their own network (a network within a network, so to speak). I was one of those teachers.

"New Ground" became a private on-line community, a place to talk among ourselves about common concerns, issues close to home: Kentucky schools and reform, Vietnam veterans, illegal environmental dumping. My colleagues and I felt bold enough to take technological risks: instead of limiting ourselves to e-mail or exchanging files of student work, we opened a number of conferences—in essence, public forums for students and teachers to discuss any number of issues. We used the larger network to open private conferences with closed or limited membership, naming and defining topics, adding and inviting participants. Then together we created and shared curricula on our little network.

In our smallness, we found success. Many conferences thrived while others died, but anything seemed possible. We conducted literature groups, exchanged formal writing assignments, and enjoyed on-line discussion groups with teachers and students at other sites. Some conferences served a variety of purposes. Some were structured, others were quite informal. "Writing Workshop" was a place to talk about writing, to publish finished pieces, or to request responses on writing in various genres, at any stage of the writing process. "Book Talk" was an electronic dialogue covering books of all kinds and related topics, including censorship. "Math" was a collaboration between high school students and seventh graders exploring issues of academic difficulty and connecting mathematical abstractions to everyday life.

The teachers involved in our network believed in a student-centered curriculum. Much like Eliot Wigginton's Foxfire methodology,[2] our goal was to develop self-sufficiency in our students. Instead of serving as a filter through which all classroom reality must pass, we tried to get out of the students' way. The technology enabled us to stand back encouragingly, as students moved about the network—their network—picking and choosing from the conferences offered, reading and responding (mostly) freely.

We learned to value student-directed conferences. A good example is the conference three twelve-year-old boys in my eastern Kentucky reading classroom initiated to talk about their favorite author. Called "Mr. Macabre," the boys' conference was "a discussion on the author of such books as *The Stand*, *It*, and *Misery* . . . Stephen King." Their first note invited others to share their interest:

> Estill County Middle School welcomes you to take part in a discussion on Stephen King. We will discuss his books, his personality, and what people think about him.

Stephen King is a very controversial writer. Some people think his stories are good to teach and read, but others wouldn't dream of turning to the first page of his mildest stories. That's why we're starting this conference.

If you have an opinion, positive or negative, about Mr. King or his books, send it to us.

Thank you,
Mike Snowden
Joe West
Kevin Birchfield

That same day a teacher replied from across the state:

You have just found my genre. Is this open to teachers as well as students???

The next day, ranks swelling, the boys responded:

Teachers are involved in the discussion also. Do you like King? Our teacher doesn't. If you do like him, what is your favorite book? If not, what book do you despise the most? Hope to hear from you by Wednesday.

Thank you,
Mike Snowden
Joe West
Kevin Birchfield
Dustin Newlin

Soon, students and teachers from around Kentucky became involved. Distance was erased by modem, and all realized that on-line, everyone's equal, at least on *this* network. Teacher and student voices blended into one discussion, roles were reversed and merged ("Hope to hear from you by Wednesday"). The exchange of opinions and expertise was enthusiastic and gratifying because the interest was real. It had nothing to do with satisfying classroom requirements, but it had a lot to do with learning.

In many ways, "Mr. Macabre" was not a big deal. It didn't produce a world map stuck full of colored push pins, but it did flourish for many months, during which time its ranks of readers, writers, and fans grew. For the students and teachers, the conference was akin to what Harvey Daniels and Steven Zemelman describe in *A Community of Writers*: "a supportive group in which risks could be taken, real ideas and criticisms shared, and writing thus learned effectively."[3] At the end of the year, my students collected "their" conference notes and published a book about Stephen King for the school library. The skeleton on their book's cover wore a crown and a somewhat cocky grin.

*   *   *   *

Conferences can be exciting places for teachers to learn as well. According to Seymour Sarason, "It is virtually impossible to create and sustain over time conditions for productive learning for students when they do not exist for teachers."[4] Just as research tells us that a dissemination model is not an effective way to teach students, we know that traditional in-service and staff development methods sometimes fail for teachers. Teachers who discover the personal and professional virtues of an electronic discourse community firsthand develop the knowledge and skills they can use in their teaching.

Telecommunicating *can* become extremely time-consuming, and becoming knowledgeable about new things is never easy, but the rewards are lifelong. BreadNet, a national network of teachers who have attended Bread Loaf School of English, was my first experience with professional on-line conferencing. On BreadNet, I was able to discuss alternative assessment, books I was reading, and issues in student writing with other teachers. Very quickly, I became eager to involve students in the conversations, to elicit *their* perspectives as well.

I also wanted more teachers in my own state to benefit from telecommunications. Forming an electronic community of like-minded people is something like pioneering new territory, and pioneering women have long been a Kentucky tradition. A few years after the small network I mentioned earlier (New Ground) closed down, a few Kentucky teachers banded together to meet the demands of the 1990 Kentucky Educational Reform Act (KERA). Among the many KERA mandates was the stipulation that technology and writing be integrated into the entire curriculum. This led to the birth of the Kentucky Telecommunications Writing Project (KTWP), a network connecting just five classrooms from all over the state: fourth graders in Paducah; Chapter 1 eighth graders in Covington; high school students at the Brown School in Louisville; sixth and seventh graders at Saints Peter and Paul in Lexington; and high school students in rural Hi Hat.

Students in the Kentucky Telecommunications Writing Project wrote to each other in a variety of conferences, where they worked together on collaborative projects; their teachers wrote to "KTWP Journal," something like a virtual teacher's lounge or an old-time sewing circle. What was the pattern in the fabric of this private discourse community? It reminded me of a quilt. Just as in the quilting bee of Colonial times the needles would fly and so did the talk—news and gossip of friends and families as well as the swapping of tricks of the trade. As with quilting, the writing on "KTWP Journal" was created through the mutual reach of the teachers who participated.

Quilts represent place and time—particular patterns are regional, and quilts from different eras are distinctly different. The KTWP teachers represented place and time too, and the notes from "KTWP Journal" revealed their commonalities and differences, and told their stories. Unlike one-to-one correspondence by mail, notes posted to a conference are public. Notes may be addressed to an individual colleague, but it is always understood that the entire group will read each note. Like old-fashioned letters sent east by great-grandmothers, notes on "KTWP Journal" usually opened with some type of greeting. Most often, the notes followed a standard form. Likewise, notes typically closed with affirmations, words intended to leave the readers feeling good. Writers varied the form to suit their moods, revealing their individuality. (As in a quilt, each message told us "something of the memories, aspirations, small triumphs and defeats of its maker. It tells us much about her aesthetic sensibility, her skill, care, and imagination."[5])

The KTWP teachers shared ideas and asked questions about their profession. Much of what was mandated for students was also mandated for teachers. KERA asked students, as readers, to be able to make connections between a specific book and a broader theme. The KTWP teachers did the same thing. On-line, they often discussed what they were reading. They faxed each other articles and shared resources, and they also discussed what they read for pleasure. At other times the talk focused on what the students were reading. A major task for the KTWP teachers was to redefine the way writing was taught in their classrooms. By writing on "KTWP Journal," the teachers were defining writing for themselves. They came to talk about their own writing processes ("I wish I could learn to put more voice in my writing"); they discussed writing theory ("I'm wondering what we mean by 'writing' when we talk about improving it via telecommunications. Since 'writing' is a process, which part of the process do we hope to improve?"). "Questioning each other," one teacher wrote, "makes all of us think more. I just wish we could see students doing that on-line more."

The teachers wondered: "How can we get students talking more to each other, weighing what has been said, learning how to read and respond to one another?" They learned that there are no easy answers: "Why shouldn't the same thing be happening with teachers? If it isn't, then are we continuing to learn? Do we really want to produce graduates who can only deal with things if they remain fixed and constant—abide by the 'right' answer?"

Part of the answer for these teachers lay in building a community. In "KTWP Journal," sharing the personal as well as the professional created a sense of family and place. The KTWP teachers talked of relatives, relationships, recipes for soft pretzels, dog stories, family customs, friends, and family trips. Naturally enough, this spilled over into other kinds of personal talk: bitter cold, flash floods, snow days, burst pipes, problem pets, road conditions, personal injuries, dinner plans gone awry, frustrations, illness, student fights, paperwork, blizzards, car problems, furnace problems, flu, positive mammograms, car wrecks, broken bones, leaking roofs, pulled muscles, root canals, sleep deprivation, dogs dying, bills, children marrying, arthritis . . . anything can happen, and it did.

Technical problems, such as busy phone lines, running out of on-line time on individual accounts, computers down, line noise, uploading, classroom management and scheduling, sending laptops home with students, and implementing school technology plans were also part of life on "KTWP Journal." Perhaps it's the nature of the teaching profession to share war stories; perhaps like the great-grandmothers, these teachers quilted for a contented heart, stitching and talking and inclined to admit, "When we're together we don't even realize we're working."

The ability to make the best of adverse conditions was alive and well on "KTWP Journal." In fact, the network served as something of a lifeline in times of crisis; as one teacher noted: "I just thought it was interesting that although the vehicular highways were down, the information highway continued to roll." When a severe blizzard swept through Kentucky one winter, a blizzard of notes appeared on-line. As teachers had time to write and read and think, humor was another strategy for dealing with cabin fever and dangerous weather: "If we don't get back to school, we are all going to die of eyestrain."

The teachers also discussed the reform effort in Kentucky, its implications for change, and the status of the changes at the local level of each site, as well as the resulting stress. Suddenly faced with a barrage of curriculum standards, portfolio assessment, school-based management, and professional accountability, the teachers used each other to clarify and define the issues for themselves. Together, they sought practical solutions for the KERA mandates. Mired in the language of reform, they struggled to make the "big words plainer":[6]

My assistant principal is more worried about what is written in [my planbook] than what I'm doing in the classroom. He wants me to make sure that I'm teaching a "learning outcome," or is that "learner standard"? (What are they being called at this point?) This is the frustrating part to teachers. UGHUGHUGHUGHUGHUGHUGH!

While KERA touched all areas of the educational system and stepped on every toe, many of its changes were positive and exciting for the Kentucky teachers. The reform issues most discussed included how technology could be integrated into the curriculum—not just be an add-on—and alternative assessment, namely portfolios. Portfolio assessment in writing and math was mandated in every fourth grade classroom. Emmy Krempasky, the fourth grade teacher in the project, often wrote to "KTWP Journal" about the stress she was under: "I feel the weight of the whole school on my shoulders and I just feel like collapsing." Another teacher reported, "I've been running running running. Exhaustion is close at hand. The preassessment jitters are driving even the calm into turmoil." Time after time, the KTWP teachers helped each other overcome the pressures. One teacher admitted, "I know I wouldn't have ever made it back to school after Christmas if you hadn't given me support." The teachers helped each other simply by listening.

As well as a place to discuss issues and overcome stress, the KTWP teachers also used the "Journal" conference to make travel plans for face-to-face meetings, ride-sharing, reserving rooms, finding equipment, etc., and to negotiate more subtle problems related to group decision-making. They also used the wires for delegating tasks ("We haven't heard from you all yet about your slides for the presentation"); asking questions ("How many packets do you think we should prepare?"); making requests ("Let me know what I need to do"); and volunteering ("I would be willing to facilitate the next large-group meeting if no one else has offered"). As one of them explained, "The challenge for us adults, and ultimately the students, too, is to figure out how to find compromises and solutions that satisfy everybody's needs."

Another pattern appeared regularly throughout the notes. The teachers apologized to each other often. Most frequently, the apology was connected to how often they wrote—sometimes too much ("Forgive the length of my notes"); other times not enough ("Sorry I have not been writing at least once a week like I promised"). The teachers also apologized for the quality of their writing ("I hope it isn't seen as rambling"). They apologized for digressing, disagreeing, or talking behind someone's back, which revealed how important it seemed to them to maintain that sense of community support and to avoid a critical tone. And often the teachers also apologized for problems beyond their control: how text appeared on-line or student work that didn't get done as promised. Glitches, they learned, are a part of telecommunications, and so are mistakes. One morning Emmy, the fourth grade teacher, accidentally sent a piece of student writing to "Journal": "Ooops! Sorry about that. So much for putting on pantyhose while trying to send notes so early in the morning!" Often lines would be missing from the notes, or strange extra characters would appear, the product of mysterious forces beyond the sender's control.

The apologies, however, were far outweighed by the positive responses the teachers gave one another, words of encouragement, validation, and affirmation. Requests for help were usually answered. Reciprocity, tolerance, trust, and a willingness to participate are old-fashioned values and skills necessary for any successful community, whether at a quilting bee or in cyberspace. Almost all notes used the word "thanks."

*   *   *   *

Many professional networks exist. Teachers talk with teachers on commercial networks, such as America Online and Prodigy. Many state networks, like the Florida Information Resources Network (FIRN), link educators at no cost. The problem with large-scale networks, I would argue, is one of ownership and purpose. If what you seek is information, then visiting a Web site may suffice. If all you have is an ax to grind and you don't care who feels the sharpness of your wit, then posting to an educational bulletin board somewhere gives you an audience. The kind of professional collegiality I am advocating is hard to find on pre-existing services amid large numbers of participants. The challenge and the value comes from creating our own smaller networks, within a larger host network.

Telecommunications can be more than pen-pal letters, file transfers, one-sided publishing on the World Wide Web, or a strict point-and-click environment. Instead of visualizing a massive network of sites to "hit," it behooves us to consider small spaces, human places—common places fostering the "uncommon" kind of citizens that John Mayher had in mind when he noted that "autonomous professional teachers will not fit neatly into the pigeonholes of packagers and testers, but they are essential to the education of children."[7] Telecommunications, like teaching, is mostly about community, about quilting. Every quilt reflects the theme of self-sufficiency; the quilter, whatever her station, whatever her design, combines her own materials, skills, and plan to create a useful object where there was none before. Quilting continues in a "grassroots continuity that responds to fads by absorbing and refining them."[8] In the end, telecommunications isn't really about technology; it is about people connecting to people, absorbing and refining. New Ground, BreadNet, KTWP, and other small-scale electronic networks—as well as conferences like "Mr. Macabre" and "KTWP Journal"—are steps in this direction.

Notes

1. Rheingold, Howard. *The Virtual Community: Homesteading on the Electronic Frontier* (Reading, Mass.: Addison-Wesley, 1993), p. 11.

2. Wigginton, Eliot. *Sometimes a Shining Moment: The Foxfire Experience* (Garden City, N.Y.: Anchor Books, 1986).

3. Zemelman, Steven, and Daniels, Harvey. *A Community of Writers: Teaching Writing in the Junior and Senior High School* (Portsmouth, N.H.: Heinemann, 1988), p. 59.

4. In Larry E. Frase and Sharon C. Conley's *Creating Learning Places for Teachers, Too* (Thousand Oaks, Calif.: Corwin Press, 1994), p. xi.

5. Clarke, M. W. *Kentucky Quilts and Their Makers* (Lexington: University Press of Kentucky, 1976), p. viii.

6 . Ibid., p. 7.

7. Mayher, John S. *Uncommon Sense: Theoretical Practice in Language Education* (Portsmouth, N.H.: Heinemann, 1990), p. 286.

8. Ibid., p. 111.

Chris Benson

Computer Conferencing and the Changing Nature of Schoolwork

Computer Conferencing and Classroom Writing

Many good teachers with a passion for their subject are guilty of over-looking how that subject can be a source of confusion and frustration for their students. When a student enters into the study of an unfamiliar topic, he or she often feels like a stranger in a strange land. I certainly felt this way as a student. For instance, I remember chemistry in eleventh grade as a no-man's land, through which I moved quietly like a solitary refugee. I carried this feeling all through school, and I know many uncertain learners feel similarly isolated. This sense of isolation is especially acute in writing assignments.

As an administrator of a writing-across-the-curriculum program at the college level, I have helped many teachers design writing assignments for their students. Some teachers are not keenly aware of the social nature of writing, that sometimes the best writing is fermented in a social stew, and these teachers' assumptions about the role of writing in the classroom can actually impede students' development as writers. The most counterproductive of these preconceptions is that requiring *more* writing in a course—for example, by including more essay exams—is the same as *teaching* writing.

Many writing teachers are quick to point out that practice makes perfect. This may be true, but we must also ask what exactly students are practicing. Teachers who use writing solely as a means for testing are not helping the students to become better writers. In testing situations, students write in isolation, only to demonstrate what they know. In the real world, employers rarely ask their employees to write in isolation, just to see what they know. Writing serves far more complex purposes: to provoke action, to move others, to persuade, to inform, and simply to communicate. If we want students to master these skills, we must give students practice in them while they are in school.

With the growing ease of computer conferencing, teachers are now able to create social contexts for writing that approximate a real marketplace of ideas. My own introduction to computer conferencing came in a graduate course on epistemology and rhetoric, in which the class discussion took place entirely on-line. We read some difficult texts, and I often felt like a novice grad student, a freshman, and a first grader all rolled into one. Yet the opportunity to discuss those difficult ideas—in writing, with my peers, who were also struggling with them—helped me not only to master the material but also to extend my writing abilities.

In this way, computer conferencing offers students the kind of thinking and problem-solving we say we want them to engage in; it provides them with an all-important audience on which to practice and hone a variety of writing skills. In computer conferencing, writing is not a solitary endeavor, but a collaborative process in which individuals work through issues together, asking questions, making and testing hypotheses, and creating theories. Conferencing with peers also reverses the "unnatural" rhetorical situation that students usually find themselves in: in a traditional classroom, the student (a novice with respect to the subject under study) writes to the teacher (the expert) to demonstrate what he or she knows. I call this student-to-teacher relationship "unnatural" because in the real world the novice seldom writes to the expert this way. Computer conferencing creates a far more natural rhetorical situation—that is, peer-to-peer.

Computer conferencing also takes the focus off grading, another characteristic that makes it more like the workplace. Employers don't often have the time, or find it relevant, to "grade" their employees' writing. They do, however, make distinctions between good ideas and bad ideas. By doing this, they respond to the content of the writing with meaningful criticism, which to a writer is far more valuable than a simple grade. Conferencing encourages peers to respond to content—questioning, clarifying, criticizing, and extending the conversation toward the refinement of ideas.

When I think of the volumes of text that my graduate epistemology class composed in one semester, I can't imagine any teacher, even the most avid and conscientious grader of papers, scaling that mountain and reaching the summit. In fact, in active conferences most teachers find it necessary to allow the students to assume the primary role of responding. This changes the nature of what we all do in school. Students learn with greater autonomy, and the teacher is no longer the sole arbiter of knowledge in the classroom. The same goes for textbooks. Computer conferencing projects foster a sense of collaborative inquiry in which the students' ideas can actually supersede textbook knowledge.

I don't recommend that teachers attempt to grade their students' writing that comes out of a computer conference. Conferencing is ultimately a collaborative endeavor. This is not to say that the teacher should not be involved—far from it. I advise teachers to encourage individual students to write more or write more thoughtfully, using Socratic dialogue. Response from a peer audience will motivate students to write far more effectively than a single teacher can hope to do.

As conferencing software becomes more and more user-friendly, students at all levels can benefit from it. In fact, I've observed that today's students, born into the digital age, are far more adaptable to the technology than their teachers. Robert A. Hayden's "geek code," cited in Susan Leigh Star's book *The Cultures of Computing*,[1] posits a range of possible student attitudes toward computing (the "C" with its accompanying symbols is part of an intricate shorthand that "cybernauts" use to give themselves personalized signatures):

C Computers are a tool, nothing more. I use them when it serves my purpose.

C+ Computers are fun and I enjoy using them. I play a mean game of Wing Commander and can use a word processor without resorting to the manual too often. I know that a 3.5 disk is not a hard disk. I also know that when it says "press any key to continue," I don't have to look for a key labeled "ANY."

C++ Computers are a large part of my existence. When I get up in the morning, the first thing I do is log myself in. I mud [play multi-user dungeons (MUDs), interactive fantasy games, that can go on for days], but still manage to stay off academic probation.

C+++ You mean there is life outside of Internet? You're shittin' me! I live for MUDs. I haven't dragged myself to class in weeks.

C++++ I'll be the first to get the new cybernetic interface installed into my skull.

C- Anything more complicated than my calculator and I'm screwed.

C-- Where's the on switch?

C--- If you even mention computers, I will rip your head off!

Most K–12 students or recent high school graduates would probably locate themselves in the C through C++++ range, and virtually no youngster would be in the C- through C--- range. Today, virtually every student is curious enough to ask, "Where's the on switch?" and to proceed toward computer literacy.

One conferencing project I participated in recently linked five public school classes that were studying poetry. Junior high, high school, and a small group of college students selected poems to read and then wrote about them on-line. As in good conversation, the "rules" were few: each class got to pick some of the poems and each student was expected to contribute to the discussion. Students had no trouble responding to the poems, using stories and anecdotes from their own lives. One of the highlights was inviting a poet, Claire Bateman, to join the conference. Claire was so interested by the collaborative nature of the project that she posted two of her own poems for discussion. For students, the experience was more than a five-week unit on the study of poetry; it made poetry a real-world activity. All the participating teachers agreed that the student writing, focused on meaning rather than on a grade, was superior. A pleasantly surprising turn of events was that several students and teachers, following Claire's lead, began posting their own poems for response.

The cross-age aspect of our poetry conference was a matter of expediency rather than design. Finding a group of interested teachers hadn't been easy, so we chose not to limit the pool. In practice, the different grade levels of the students only enhanced the conversation. The high school students knew when they were writing to junior high students and vice versa, and adjusted their diction accordingly. Likewise, students have a tendency to look up to their "elders": for example, the junior high students conscientiously posted their best writing for their high school and college readers.

Another exciting aspect of computer conferencing is the connection of remote classrooms. Linking a class of Native Alaskan students with a class of urban kids in South Carolina creates, in and of itself, a strong impetus for the students to write. Such students are naturally curious about each other. But this doesn't mean that teachers need to set up conferences with far-off states, or even the next school district, to have a successful one. I have set up a successful conference in one section of an introductory college writing class. I required students to log into the conference to respond to the class readings. While I intended this conference to be an extension of class discussion, I found that certain students who were reticent in class were far more engaged in the cyber-classroom. Apparently, the act of writing gives some students the extra time they need to participate in a discussion.

Computer Conferencing and the Professional Development of Teachers

Just as computer conferences give students a rewarding environment for improving their writing and thinking, they are also highly valuable to teachers as a tool for professional networking. In my current work with the Bread Loaf Rural Teacher Network (BLRTN), I "talk up" ideas with teachers on the network and help them distill these ideas into articles for our semi-annual newsletter. The majority of BLRTN teachers are interested in professional development, educational reform, and student-centered learning. The computer conferencing system we use, called BreadNet, is like a convention center with many discussion sessions going on simultaneously. Some of the rooms are devoted to "conversation" about literature, others to school reform, nature writing, cultural traditions, current events, etc. I use the word *conversation* because the discussions unfold naturally, just as good conversation meanders down its own path. The range of topics is unlimited. If one thinks of the Internet as a global web of information superhighways where thirty million people commute daily, BreadNet is more like a small town, a matrix of lively interconnected streets.

The late language theorist and rhetorician Kenneth Burke used a now-famous metaphor, likening a discourse community to a parlor where a party rages.[2] There is a great fire in the hearth, which represents the "center" of the discussion, the place where the main voices rise above the rest. Other conversations happen on the periphery, but everyone in the parlor is vying for a place closer to the hearth, to be heard and to be warm. Burke's parlor, therefore, is a competitive place. This image has become known widely as the "Burkean Parlor." Academic discourse often takes form as a Burkean Parlor. Most academic journals, for example, require their submissions to go through a process that is so competitive it must be refereed, presumably to ensure fair competition between ideas.

Though the conferences I've discussed in this essay have taken place in an academic context, I would not describe any of them as a Burkean Parlor, but rather as communities of individuals sharing ideas and forming new ones. Good conversation requires give and take, a willingness to speak and listen, and the ability to know when to do which. Therefore, I think a teacher's role in computer conferencing should be to encourage collaborative and cooperative conversation and discourage one-upsmanship. In the best conferences, as in conversation, there is no need for a referee.

Any editor will tell you how e-mail and the Internet have transformed his or her job. It is now possible for me to make suggestions to a writer on Tuesday and to receive the revised essay on Wednesday. Yet as an editor of teachers, I have seen how electronic conversation has had even greater impact. The teachers I work with don't work in isolation—or even one-on-one with me—to generate drafts. Ideas are generated on-line through conversation with peers. Of all the computer networks and conferences and bulletin boards I've encountered, none has been as collaborative in nature as BreadNet.

I can't emphasize this model of collaboration enough. There are plenty of teacher conferences on the Internet, but what makes BreadNet special is that all the participants feel a shared investment. I encourage teachers who want to use computer conferencing with their students to provide some experiences beforehand that create this shared investment. For example, before starting a student conference, a group of South Carolina teachers held a weekend retreat to discuss the project. At that meeting, the teachers discovered that they were all interested in environmental issues and nature writing. After consulting with a professor of forestry, the group decided to focus on wetlands (see Linda Hardin's essay in this book). The weekend retreat to some extent ensured the teachers' future commitment to the project. Likewise, the students' initial field trips to observe wetlands helped to invest them in the project when it went on-line.

Of course, computer conferencing isn't the be-all and end-all to writing in school. There will always be a place for writing as a means of testing students' knowledge, and there will always be a place for teaching grammar and spelling and essay writing. But as I've noted, my opinion is that far too much writing in school is devoted to testing and far too little time—especially outside of English classes—to writing as a means to speculate, persuade, inform, and communicate. For this reason, I believe, teachers should work toward acquiring computing systems for their schools and toward involving students in conferencing.

President Clinton's vow to have all the classrooms in the United States linked electronically by the year 2000 is a huge promise, given all the impediments: the expense of conferencing systems discourages schools; the technology rapidly outstrips schools' ability to pay for it; maintaining and upgrading network access requires additional funds; wiring in old school buildings is usually inadequate.

Yet despite these obstacles, the technology will eventually arrive. Whether it arrives in a package that students and teachers can use is not clear. School districts strapped for money may be tempted to buy programs that produce "mass learning"—for example, "canned" lectures that homogenize learning, effectively diminishing the individual teacher's role. Administrators in state capitals don't always know what's best for individual classrooms, especially where technology is concerned. For this reason, teachers should be collectively advocating at the district and state level for technology that suits their own needs, fostering small-scale, collaborative conferencing projects based on their own curricula.

As classrooms become networked, I like to imagine that teachers will become more independent of their state departments. Giving teachers and students the ability to link up in collaborative projects on-line will result in an explosion of curricula at the grassroots. Textbooks, formerly written by outsiders and handed down through levels of administration to teachers and students, might become secondary to accessing the Internet. Learning will require accessing information, perhaps from remote sources, as well as constructing knowledge, and students will need to be adept in inquiry and collaboration, such as the type that computer conferencing fosters.

Notes

1. Star, Susan Leigh, ed. *The Cultures of Computing* (Oxford and Cambridge, Mass: Blackwell, 1995).

2. Burke, Kenneth. *Philosophy of Literary Form* (Berkeley: Univ. of California Press, 1973), pp. 110–111.

Select Bibliography

Barron, A. E. and G. W. Orwig. *New Technologies for Education: A Beginner's Guide.* Englewood, Colorado: Libraries Unlimited, 1993. A nuts-and-bolts introduction to teleconferencing and other technologies.

Beckner, W. and B. O. Barker. *Technology in Rural Education.* Bloomington, Indiana: Phi Delta Kappa, 1994. Makes the case for technology (especially telecommunications) as a tool for overcoming geographic isolation.

Birkerts, S. *The Gutenberg Elegies: The Fate of Reading in an Electronic Age.* New York: Fawcett Columbine, 1994. Takes a stand against the impact of electronic technology.

Bruce, B. C., J. K. Peyton, and T. Baston. *Network-based Classrooms: Promises and Realities* (Cambridge and New York: Cambridge University Press, 1993). Covers writing and computer networking.

Cochran-Smith, M., C. L. Paris, and J. L. Kahn. *Learning to Write Differently: Beginning Writers and Word Processing.* Norwood, N.J.: Ablex, 1991. Includes a thorough review of the research on using computers to teach writing in elementary schools.

Educational Media and Technology Yearbook. Englewood, Colorado: Libraries Unlimited. A resource of current developments, published annually.

Elder, J., B. Bowen, D. Goswami, and J. Schwartz. *Word Processing in a Community of Writers.* New York and London: Garland Publishing, 1989. A collection of practical writing ideas to use with computers.

Handa, C. *Computers and Community: Teaching Composition in the Twenty-first Century.* Portsmouth, N.H.: Boynton/Cook, 1990. Examines the social and political ramifications of electronic classrooms.

Harasim, L. M., ed. *Online Education: Perspectives on a New Environment.* New York: Praeger, 1990. Provides a range of perspectives for understanding the educational applications of computer networks and e-mail.

Hawisher, G. E., and P. LeBlanc. *Reimagining Computers and Composition Studies: Teaching and Research in the Virtual Age.* Portsmouth, N.H.: Boynton/Cook, 1992. Focuses on English/language arts.

Hiltz, S. R. *The Virtual Classroom: Learning without Limits via Computer Networks.* Norwood, N.J.: Ablex, 1994. Describes an on-line mathematics course.

Kurshaw, C., and M. Harrinton. *Creating Communities: An Educator's Guide to Electronic Networks.* Washington, D. C.: National Science Foundation, 1991. Somewhat dated, but still serves as a good introduction.

Matorella, P. H., ed. *Interactive Technologies and the Social Studies.* Albany, N.Y.: State University of New York Press, 1996. A current analysis of issues, especially regarding the Internet.

Means, B. *Technology and Education Reform: The Reality Behind the Promise.* San Francisco: Jossey-Bass Publishers, 1994. Takes an international perspective on innovations and educational change.

Monroe, R. *Writing and Thinking with Computers: A Practical and Progressive Approach.* Urbana, Ill.: National Council of Teachers of English, 1993. Offers examples and advice for teaching English with computers.

Myers, L., ed. *Approaches to Computer Writing Classrooms: Learning from Practical Experience.* Albany: State University of New York Press, 1993. Practical applications and specifics of computer composition classrooms.

Papert, S. *The Children's Machine: Rethinking School in the Age of the Computer.* New York: BasicBooks, 1993. Presents notions of educational change in a clear, readable style.

Perelman, L. J. *School's Out.* New York: William Morrow, 1992. Predicts the demise of schooling as we know it.

Raizen, S. A., P. Sellwood, R. D. Todd, and M. Vickers. *Technology Education in the Classroom: Understanding the Designed World.* San Francisco: Jossey-Bass, 1995. Examines curriculum standards and supports educational reform efforts.

Reagan, S. B., T. Fox, and D. Bleich. *Writing With: Toward New Identities for Students and Teachers.* New York: Longmans, 1994. Explores collaboration and the social constuctions of discourse.

Rheingold, H. *The Virtual Community: Homesteading on the Electronic Frontier.* New York: Addison-Wesley, 1993. A book about the human potential of life on-line.

Roberts, N., G. Blakeslee, M. Brown, and C. Lenk. *Integrating Telecommunications into Education.* Englewood Cliffs, N.J.: Prentice Hall, 1990. A somewhat dated but useful resource for creating "global" classrooms in different disciplines.

Selfe, C. L., and S. Hilligoss, eds. *Literacy and Computers: The Complications of Teaching and Learning with Technology.* New York: Modern Language Association, 1994. Explores issues of literacy and issues of technology, using clear examples.

Turkle, S. *The Second Self: Computers and the Human Spirit.* New York: Simon & Schuster, 1990. Considers the psychological aspects of the computer age.

Tuman, M. C.. *Word Perfect: Literacy in the Computer Age.* London: Falmer Press, 1992. Defines "literacy" as it is being shaped by hypertext and telecommunications.

————, ed. *Literacy Online: The Promise (and Peril) of Reading and Writing with Computers.* Pittsburgh and London: Univ. of Pittsburgh Press, 1992. A collection of stimulating essays on computers, literature, hypertext, multimedia, and the future.

List of On-line Resources

The following World Wide Web resources were compiled by Bram Moreines and John Ruttner of the Institute for Learning Technologies, Columbia University, and Jordan Davis of Teachers & Writers Collaborative. A word of warning: because of the changing nature of the Web, the addresses of these sites may not be current. For a continually updated version of these resources, we suggest that you link to them through the following homepages:

http://www.twc.org/tmhot.html

or

http://www.ilt.columbia.edu/K12/livetext/index.html
http://www.ilt.columbia.edu/K12/livetext/resources.html
http://www.ilt.columbia.edu/K12/livetext/english.html
http://www.ilt.columbia.edu/K12/livetext/poetry.html

(*Note: names in parentheses indicate the Web site author or host.*)

English Language Curricula & Resources

Language Arts Curricula & Pedagogy

Humanities in Cyberspace
http://www.teleport.com/~cdeemer/humanities.html
(Deemer) A hypertext discourse on the Internet's role in changing the teaching and scholarship, by a playwright and hypertext author.

Teachers & Writers Collaborative
http://www.twc.org/tmmain.htm
(Teachers & Writers Collaborative) Keep your eye on this beautifully designed site for resources on teaching writing and ways to connect to T&W projects.

Writers In Electronic Residence
http://www.wier.yorku.ca/WIERhome
(York) Homebase for Canada's Writers In Electronic Residence Program.

On-line Writing Lab
http://owl.english.purdue.edu/
(Purdue) Lots of information that'll help you with your writing: how to avoid sexist language, fix run-on sentences, put together a good résumé,

or follow MLA (or APA) format for citing your sources. The site also offers listings of writing materials and Writing Labs on the Internet.

The Global Campfire Home Page
http://www.indiana.edu/~eric_rec/fl/pcto/campfire.html
(Indiana) "Since the dawn of time, humans have entertained themselves and each other telling and retelling stories. You are invited to take part in this ritual that is as old as humanity itself. Read one of the stories that interests you, add the next part, and check back later."

Kairos: A Journal for Teachers of Writing in Web Environments
http://english.ttu.edu/kairos/1.1/index.html
(Education Dept., Texas Tech) Lots of interesting articles and features.

Monster Exchange Program
http://www.intac.com/~brunner/monster.html
(Brian Maguire's fourth grade class, Heritage Heights Elementary, Amherst, N.Y., and Sherry Devlin's fifth grade class, Brunner Elementary, Scotch Plains, N.J.) An example of how the Internet can help engage children in activities designed to develop basic skills through inter-classroom projects.

The Technical Writing Hub
http://www.europa.com/~ace/resource.html
(Ace Communications, Inc.) A well-organized and annotated index page to information and resources on technical writing and electronic publishing.

Writing Tools

The Virtual Reference Desk
http://thorplus.lib.purdue.edu/reference/index.html
(Purdue University Libraries) The most thorough indexed listing we've seen of on-line reference sites, from dictionaries and maps to periodic tables.

Hypertext Webster's Dictionary
http://c.gp.cs.cmu.edu:5103/prog/webster
(CMU) Submit a word you want defined, and all the words in the returned definition are hyperlinked to their respective definitions.

The Elements of Style
http://www.cc.columbia.edu/acis/bartleby/strunk/
(Strunk, William, Columbia) The 1918 version from Project Bartleby.

Inkspot: Resources for Young Writers
http://www.inkspot.com/~ohi/inkspot/young.html
(Debbie Ridpath Ohi, inkspot.com) Extensive primer, contest guide, and index "for writers, especially those who write for children."

Fun Writing Tools

Addventure!
http://www.addventure.com/addventure/
(addventure.com) Write your own adventure, or add to collaboratively written adventures in progress.

Anagram Insanity
http://infobahn.com:80/pages/anagram.html
(infobahn.com) Actually creates anagrams from entered phrases. Amazing!

Casey's Snow Day Reverse Dictionary (and Guru)
http://www.c3.lanl.gov:8075/cgi/casey/revdict
(Los Alamos National Labs) "Finally, the remedy for that tip-of-the-tongue feeling! You type in a definition, and Casey's dictionary will tell you which word you are trying to think of!" (Well, sometimes . . . but it's fun trying.)

CRAYON: Create Your Own Newspaper
http://sun.bucknell.edu/~boulter/crayon/
(Bucknell) This site gives the user an opportunity to design his or her own on-line newspaper, and add "syndicated columns."

Shakespearean Insult Page
http://alpha.acast.nova.edu/cgi-bin/bard.pl
(Nova Southeastern) A delightful pastime: reloading this page gives the user a fresh new incomprehensible Shakespearean insult.

HAL
http://ciips.ee.uwa.edu.au/~hutch/Hal.html
(Jason Hutch, CIIPS) While the conversations won't be nearly as coherent as in *2001*, dialogue with an AI program is something everyone should try at least once.

World Writing Center
http://wwwbir.bham.wednet.edu/wws\wws.htm
(Wednet) Birchwood school's interactive story-building Web page, by and for students.

On-line Libraries

Alex (Gopher)
gopher://rsl.ox.ac.uk:70/11/lib-corn/hunter
(Oxford) Alex allows users to find and retrieve the full text of documents on the Internet. It currently indexes over 700 books and shorter texts by author and title, incorporating texts from Project Gutenberg, Wiretap, the On-line Book Initiative, the Eris system at Virginia Tech, the English Server at Carnegie-Mellon University, and the on-line portion of the Oxford Text Archive.

Anamnesis
http://www.jhu.edu/~english/anamnesis/
(Johns Hopkins) This interface provides access to over 300 authors and over 3000 of their novels, essays, poems, and treatises, located in various archives all over the Internet.

Bartleby (Project)
http://www.cc.columbia.edu/~svl2/
(Columbia) Academically scrutinized editions of classic works for readers and scholars.

Children's Literature Web Guide
http://www.ucalgary.ca/~dkbrown/index.html
(Calgary) An astoundingly complete reference, with links to all kinds of resources.

Bibliomania
http://www.bibliomania.com
(Datatext) On-line library of out-of-copyright classic fiction.

Gutenberg (Project)
http://jg.cso.uiuc.edu/pg_home.html
(Boston University) An effort to create a hypertext catalogue of all books stored as electronic text on the Internet.

The Modern English Collection
http://etext.lib.virginia.edu/modeng.browse.html
(Virginia) A long list of locally digitized electronic texts, annotated and with illustrations.

On-line Books
http://www.cs.cmu.edu:8001/Web/books.html
(Carnegie-Mellon) A state-of-the-art electronic text finder and language
resource meta-list.

Other On-line Collections by Subject/Type

WWW-VL: Writers' Resources On The Web
http://www.interlog.com/~ohi/www/writesource.html
(W3 Virtual Library, interlog.com) Subject categories include: Children's,
Horror, SF/Fantasy, Mystery, Poetry, Romance, Screen/Playwriting, Journalism, Tech/Scientific, Business Writing, Travel Writing.

Banned Books On-line
http://www.cs.cmu.edu/Web/People/spok/banned-books.html
(Carnegie-Mellon) A special exhibit of books that have been censored or
the objects of censorship attempts. The books featured here, ranging from
Ulysses to *Little Red Riding Hood*, have been selected from the indexes
on the On-line Books Page.

Canadian Writing
gopher://access.mbnet.mb.ca:70/11/member-services/cdn-writing
(MBNET) A place to read literature originating from all parts of Canada,
and in all genres.

Greek Mythology
http://www.intergate.net/uhtml/.jhunt/greek_myth/greek_myth.html
(J. M. Hunt, intergate.net) An introduction to Ancient Greek mythology,
combing information from a number of sources. Includes: The Gods, He-
roes, Creatures, Stories, Family Trees, Greek vs. Roman Mythology, etc.

LaughWEB
http://www.misty.com/laughweb/index.html
(Misty.com) A subject guide to the current humor circulating the Net. See
also The Mother of all Humor Archives (Cornell), a student homepage.

Sean's One-Stop Philosophy Shop
http://www.rpi.edu/~cearls/phil.html
(RPI) "What I'm trying to do with this page is create the ultimate philosophy link list. By that I mean the list of all links to all servers in the known
cyberworld."

Religious Text On-line Search
gopher://ccat.sas.upenn.edu:70/11/Archive/Religion
(Pennsylvania) Gopher-based search engine.

Women Homepage
http://www.mit.edu:8001/people/sorokin/women/index.html
(MIT) A collection of women's resources, from many disciplines and political orientations. See also TAP: The Ada Project (Yale), a page dedicated to the role of women in computing.

Language Arts Index Sites

The English Server
http://english-server.hss.cmu.edu/
(Carnegie Mellon) Carnegie-Mellon's student-administered server to English literature and language arts. A top-flight resource.

English-Language Arts
gopher://unix5.nysed.gov/11/K-12%20Resources/English-Language%20Arts
(New York·State Dept. of Education) An extensive K–12 resource list from the New York State Department of Education.

Language Arts
gopher://psupena.psu.edu/1$k%20LANGUAGE-ARTS
(Penn State) A gopher list of language arts projects and articles.

The Written Word
http://www-hpcc.astro.washington.edu/scied/word.html
(Washington) An on-line English server.

LiveText Poetry Page
http://www.ilt.columbia.edu/
(ILT/Columbia) A simple list, for quick perusal of classic and current poetry on the Web.

Teachers & Writers Collaborative's On-line Residency
http://pindar.ilt.columbia.edu/twc/
(ILT/Columbia) In collaboration with a T&W poet, poetry students from New York's School for the Physical City are creating multimedia exhibitions of their work. Visit the SPC Poetry Page showcasing student performances using RealAudio software and digitized video clips.

Poets
http://www.yahoo.com/Arts/Humanities/Literature/Genres/Poetry/Poets/
(Yahoo Index) Poetry listed by author.

Electronic Poetry Center Author Home Page Library
http://wings.buffalo.edu/epc/authors/
(SUNY Buffalo) Poetry listed by author.

Poetry
http://www.yahoo.com/Arts/Humanities/Literature/Genres/Poetry/
(Yahoo Index) Poetry listed by poem title.

Poetry
http://english-server.hss.cmu.edu/poetry.html
(Carnegie-Mellon) Listing of poems and authors.

The T. S. Eliot Page
http://www.next.com/~bong/eliot/index.html
(telospub.com) One of the greats.

The Joseph Ceravolo Page
http://www.csam.montclair.edu/~ceravolo
(Montclair State) Another one of the greats.

School Resources Group Sections

Technology Planning Guides

Creating Learning Communities
http://www.cosn.org/EPIE.html
(P. Kenneth Komoski, EPIE, and Curtiss Priest, CITS) "A useful tool for those school and community decisionmakers who may agree with the goal of networking, but who are concerned about the practicality of achieving it for their schools and communities."

National Center for Technology Planning
http://www2.msstate.edu/~lsa1/nctp/
(Larry Anderson, Mississippi State) Research articles about technology planning plus a sampling of state, district, business, and higher education plans and planning guides, from a K–12 networking expert.

Reinventing Schools: The Technology Is Now!
http://xerxes.nas.edu/nap/on-line/techgap/
(National Academy of Sciences) A beautiful hypertext record of a conference entitled "Reinventing Schools: The Technology Is Now," held May 10–12, 1993, which presented "a plausible future for the use of technology in education."

Challenges and Strategies in Using Technology to Promote Education Reform
http://www.ed.gov/pubs/EdReformStudies/EdTech/approaches.html
(OERI, US DOE) A comprehensive, readable essay published by the Office of Educational Research and Improvement.

Guidelines for Designing Effective and Healthy Learning Environments for Interactive Technologies
http://wwwetb.nlm.nih.gov/monograp/ergo/index.html
(Michael Weisberg, National Library of Medicine) This paper briefly reviews ergonomics research on visual display workstations, and presents guidelines on how to design an ergonomically correct workstation.

School Network Development: Publications
http://info.ckp.edu/publications/publications.html
(Common Knowledge: Pittsburgh) Articles, proposals, and reports from a Pittsburgh Public Schools project "seeking to develop new environments for teaching and learning using the technology of wide-area computer networks."

Technical Guidelines For Schools
http://www.svi.org/guidelines.html
(SVI.org) As clear and technologically savvy a primer and guide as you're likely to find. Highly recommended.

Technology Planning Guide
http://nwoaux.nwoca.ohio.gov/Plan/Plan-Home.html
(Ohio) A well-designed and indexed guide for technology planners with a bureaucratic bent, with links to worksheets and activities.

Quality Education Data
http://www.infomall.org:80/Showcase/QED/
(infomall.org) QED has tracked technology deployment and in public schools since 1981. Here are results of annual surveys of virtually all public schools in the U.S. (more than 80 percent) for technology usage.

U.S. Department of Education
http://www.ed.gov/index.html
An extensive site, including Hypertext Publications (http://www.ed.gov/
pubs/index.html), a gopher server of on-line documents (gopher://gopher.
ed.gov/), and WAIS searching of Eric Digests (gopher://inet.ed.gov:12002/
7waissrc%3a/EricDigests).

Nationally Recognized Technology Plan Examples

Baseline Survey of Testbed-Participating Schools
http://copernicus.bbn.com/testbed2/TBdocs/surveys/
Baseline_report_8_31.html#RTFToC1
(BBN) Results of an extensive survey providing a statistical portrait of
the charter group of school members of the National School Network
Testbed, Phase 2. A unique hypertext format allows users to post comments to issues raised by each section.

Technology Challenge Grants
http://www.ed.gov/Technology/Challenge/ProjectDesc/index.html
(U.S DOE) The U.S. Department of Education is awarding $9.5 million
in Challenge Grants for technology in education to nineteen school districts to fund community initiatives using information technologies and
the Internet to "transform their factory-era schools into information-age
learning centers." Includes initial abstracts from the nineteen local school
districts.

Acceptable Use, Censorship, and Copyright

The Internet Advocate
http://silver.ucs.indiana.edu/~lchampel/netadv.htm
(Indiana) Helps users to to: 1) respond to inaccurate perceptions of porn
on the Net; 2) promote positive examples of youth Internet use; 3) develop an "Acceptable Use Policy" (AUP) and provide examples of AUPs
from schools and libraries; 4) consider software to block Internet sites;
and 5) network with organizations committed to electronic freedom of
information.

Acceptable Use Policies
gopher://riceinfo.rice.edu:1170/11/More/Acceptable
(Rice) Gopher of guidelines for—and examples of—Acceptable Use Policies from various universities.

Censorship on the Internet
http://www2.magmacom.com/~djakob/censor/
(David Jakob, magmacom.com) A comprehensive exegesis on the issue, with extensive links to everywhere.

The Copyright Website
http://www.benedict.com/
(benedict.com) An excellent, thorough, yet readable primer to copyright issues. "Real world, practical and relevant copyright information of interest to infonauts, netsurfers, webspinners, content providers, musicians, appropriationists, activists, infringers, outlaws, and law abiding citizens."

Internet Education Issues
gopher://gopher.oise.on.ca:70/11/resources/IRes4Ed/issues
(Ontario Institute for Studies in Education) A gopher of graduate level materials on important global, local and technical issues, from censorship to ethical use.

Technology Funding, and Purchasing

Apple, Inc. Web
http://www.apple.com
(Apple.com) See also: Apple Gopher for products, pricing, and downloads.

Yahoo–Education: Grants
http://www.yahoo.com/Education/Grants/

K–12 Grant and Funding
http://unicron.unomaha.edu/dept/econ/funding.htm
(Omaha) On-line funding guides and information, including: Grant-getter's Guide, Internet Resources for Non-Profit Organizations, US DOE Discretionary Grants, Fellowships in Educational Research.

Money Matters
http://www.ed.gov:80/money.html
(US DOE) An on-line guide to student financial assistance, grants and contracts for K–12 schools from the Department of Education, as well as other funding opportunities.

Technology Planning Index Sites

Educational Technology
http://tecfa.unige.ch/info-edu-comp.html
(CERN, Geneva) An immense World Wide Web Virtual Library index site.

Reform and Technology (Gopher)
gopher://nysernet.org:3000/11/
School%20Reform%20and%20Technology%20Planning%20Center
(Nysernet) K–12 gophers from the School Reform and Technology Planning Center. If you haven't found it yet, you'll probably find it here.

Notes on Contributors

NANCY STOUT BELL is a middle school language arts and math teacher at Saints Peter and Paul School in Lexington, Kentucky. She and her husband, John, have three children, Quin, Rhodes, and Laura.

BILL BERNHARDT is the author of *Just Writing* (T&W), and has written articles on many aspects of writing and literacy. He teaches at The College of Staten Island-CUNY and conducts hands-on workshops for teachers in the U.S. and abroad.

CLAIRE BATEMAN taught at Clemson University and has worked extensively for the South Carolina Governor's School for the Arts. Her first collection of poetry, *The Bicycle Slow Race,* was published by Wesleyan University Press. A second collection, *Friction,* is forthcoming from Pecan Grove Press. She lives in Chattanooga, Tennessee.

CHRIS BENSON is publications coordinator and editor for the Bread Loaf Rural Teacher Network. He has taught literature and advanced writing at Clemson University, and is an associate of Write to Change, a nonprofit sponsor of literacy and social action projects.

R. W. BURNISKE, whose on-line projects have been honored by the International Society for Technology in Education and International Schools Services, has taught in Egypt, Ecuador, Malaysia, and the U.S. He is currently a research fellow in the Computers and English Studies program at the University of Texas. He lives in Austin with his wife, Jackie, and their two sons, Justin and Christopher.

KURT CASWELL lived and taught in Chitose, Hokkaido, Japan for two and a half years. He has published articles, essays, and stories in numerous newspapers, magazines, and journals. He lives and teaches in Idaho.

SCOTT CHRISTIAN is a teacher at Nikiski Middle School in Nikiski, Alaska. He is currently on a year's leave of absence in Juneau, Alaska, where he is pursuing various writing and research projects. His book *Exchanging Lives: The Emergence of a New Literacy* will be published by NCTE next year.

JENNY DAVIS lives in Lexington, Kentucky, with her husband and four children. She teaches fifth grade and is the author of three novels, *Goodbye and Keep Cold,* *Sex Education,* and *Checking on the Moon.*

KAREN FERRELL taught math and computer literacy for eleven years in the Northwest Independent School District in Fort Worth, Texas, before becoming the district's Instructional Technology Coordinator. She has published in *Annie's Attic, Workbasket, Telecommunications in Education News,* and *R & E Journal.*

BETTE FORD was a high school English teacher in the Mississippi public schools for twenty-four years. She currently teaches composition and literature at Jones Jr. College in Ellisville, Mississippi. She has published articles in several educational periodicals.

PHYLLIS GEREN is chairperson of the Technology in Education Department at National Louis University. She has worked with teachers over the last twenty-five years to effectively integrate technology into the classroom.

ROCKY GOOCH is Telecommunications Director of the Rural Teacher Network of the Bread Loaf School of English, Middlebury College. He works with schools and individual teachers on electronic networking and multi-media authoring projects.

DIXIE GOSWAMI is a member of the faculty of the Bread Loaf School of English and coordinator of the Bread Loaf Rural Teacher Network. She directs Write to Change, a not-for-profit organization that promotes action research and community writing partnerships.

LINDA FRIDDLE HARDIN is a lifelong resident of Greenville, South Carolina. She is a graduate of Furman University, University of Missouri, and the University of Georgia. She has studied in the People's Republic of China through a Fulbright, and at Oxford through an English-Speaking Union Fellowship. She is married to Eugene R. Hardin III and has a son, Ramsey, age five.

THARON W. HOWARD is associate professor in Masters of Art and Professional Communication at Clemson University, where he directs the document design lab, the multimedia authoring classroom, and the usability testing facility. His book *A Rheoteric of Electronic Communities* will be published by Ablex in fall, 1996.

VICKI HUNT is an American Studies teacher at Peoria High School in Peoria, Arizona. Married, with three adult children, she received a Masters in Curriculum and Instruction from Chapman University and is now studying at the Bread Loaf School of English. She was named Cuthburt-Douglas Scholar by the English-Speaking Union in 1990.

EMMY KREMPASKY is a fourth grade teacher at McNabb Elementary in Paducah, Kentucky, where she chairs committees on writing instruction and technology. She serves on several district and statewide technology and assessment committees.

ROBIN LAMBERT is Assistant Director of the Program for Rural Services and Research at the University of Alabama, where she works with the PACERS Cooperative of Small Schools. She coordinated the Kentucky Telecommunications Writing Project in 1994–95 while living in eastern Kentucky.

TREVOR OWEN is Program Director of Writers In Electronic Residence and is on the faculty of education at York University. He is co-author of *The Learning Highway: A Student's Guide to Using the Internet in High School and College* (Key Porter Books) and editor of *Telecommunications in Education News*. He serves on the NCTE's Instructional Technology Committee.

BEVERLY PAETH began teaching in 1970, at the Paderewski School in Chicago. After sixteen years away from teaching, she became an eighth grade Chapter 1 reading teacher at Holmes Jr. High in Covington, Kentucky. She is currently a Title I elementary teacher in the Covington ISD.

GREG SIERING is a doctoral student in composition at Ball State University. He is a member of the Alliance for Computers and Writing, a coordinator of the MUD-based Netoric Project, and the Links Editor of the on-line hypertext journal *Kairos*. He can be reached at 00gjsiering@bsuvc.bsu.edu.

JANICE M. STUHLMANN is on the reading faculty in the Department of Curriculum and Instruction at Louisiana State University. She is interested in the ways technology can enhance low-achieving elementary students' reading and writing abilities. E-mail: janice@asterix.ednet.lsu.edu.

CAROL STUMBO is director of Region 8 Service Center for the Kentucky Dept. of Education. Her work has appeared in *Students Teaching, Teachers Learning* (Boynton Cook/Heinemann) and the *Harvard Educational Review.*

DOUGLAS E. WOOD was a seventh grade social studies teacher at Summit Parkway Middle School in Columbia, South Carolina. He was selected as the 1994 South Carolina Technology Educator of the Year. Currently, he is pursuing a master's degree at the Bread Loaf School of English and a doctorate at Harvard University Graduate School of Education.

SUSAN NELSON WOOD is assistant professor of elementary education at Western Oregon State College. After attending Bread Loaf, she participated in on-line reading projects with her middle school students in Estill County, Kentucky. Her dissertation, from the University of Florida, is a three-year study of teachers in the Kentucky Telecommunications Writing Project.

OTHER T&W PUBLICATIONS YOU MIGHT ENJOY

The Teachers & Writers Handbook of Poetic Forms, edited by Ron Padgett. This T&W bestseller includes 74 entries on traditional and modern poetic forms by 19 poet-teachers. "A treasure"—*Kliatt*. "The definitions not only inform, they often provoke and inspire. A small wonder!"—*Poetry Project Newsletter*. "An entertaining reference work"—*Teaching English in the Two-Year College*. "A solid beginning reference source"—*Choice*.

Personal Fiction Writing by Meredith Sue Willis. A complete and practical guide for teachers of writing from elementary through college level. Contains more than 340 writing ideas. "A terrific resource for the classroom teacher as well as the novice writer"—*Harvard Educational Review*.

Deep Revision: A Guide for Teachers, Students, and Other Writers by Meredith Sue Willis. Filled with practical and interesting ways to revise both fiction and nonfiction. "An outstanding book"—*The Writing Notebook*.

Educating the Imagination, Vols. 1 & 2, edited by Christopher Edgar and Ron Padgett. A big selection of the best articles from 17 years of *Teachers & Writers* magazine, with ideas and assignments for writing poetry, fiction, plays, history, folklore, parodies, and much more.

The Story in History: Writing Your Way into the American Experience by Margot Fortunato Galt. Combines imaginative writing and American history. "One of the best idea books for teachers I have ever read"—*Kliatt*.

Poetry Everywhere: Teaching Poetry Writing in School and in the Community by Jack Collom & Sheryl Noethe. This big and "tremendously valuable resource work for teachers" (*Kliatt*) at all levels contains 60 writing exercises, extensive commentary, and 450 example poems.

The Writing Workshop, Vols. 1 & 2 by Alan Ziegler. A perfect combination of theory, practice, and specific assignments. "Invaluable to the writing teacher"—*Contemporary Education*. "Indispensable"—Herbert R. Kohl.

Old Faithful: 18 Writers Present Their Favorite Writing Assignments edited by Christopher Edgar and Ron Padgett. "Highly recommended"—*Kliatt*. "A lively anthology"—*College Composition & Communication*.

•

For a complete free catalogue of T&W books, magazines, audiotapes, videotapes, and computer writing games, contact Teachers & Writers Collaborative, 5 Union Square West, New York, NY 10003–3306, (212) 691-6590. The T&W catalogue is also available at our Web site: http://www.twc.org